European Social Problems

European Social Problems is the first book to examine social issues in Europe from the perspective of the social sciences. It considers many of these social problems following the UK's 'leave' vote. Key topics examined here include:

- immigration;
- multiculturalism and religion;
- health;
- inequalities;
- education;
- riots and protest;
- drugs and crime;
- sexuality.

These core issues run as a thread through Europe and are experienced by Europeans themselves as social problems. As such, this text facilitates students' direct engagement with some of these problematic constituents in their own lives. This text is suitable for those studying social policy, sociology, politics, international relations, criminology and education studies. In this way it functions as an accessible 'reader' for final year undergraduates as well as postgraduate students.

Stuart Isaacs is a Senior Lecturer in Social Policy and Sociology at London Metropolitan University. He is the co-author of *Contemporary Political Theorists in Context* (2009) and *Political Theorists in Context* (2004), as well as the sole author of *The Politics and Philosophy of Michael Oakeshott* (2006), all published by Routledge. His research interests are in political and social theory. He has recently been made a University Teaching Fellow in recognition of his outstanding contribution to teaching and learning.

European Social Problems

Edited by Stuart Isaacs

LONDON AND NEW YORK

First published 2017
by Routledge
2 Park Square, Milton Park, Abingdon, Oxon OX14 4RN

and by Routledge
711 Third Avenue, New York, NY 10017

Routledge is an imprint of the Taylor & Francis Group, an informa business

British Library Cataloguing in Publication Data
A catalogue record for this book is available from the British Library

Library of Congress Cataloging in Publication Data
Names: Isaacs, Stuart.
Title: European social problems/edited by Stuart Isaacs.
Description: 1 Edition. | New York : Routledge, 2017.
Identifiers: LCCN 2016055548| ISBN 9781138919938 (hardback) |
ISBN 9781138919945 (pbk.) | ISBN 9781315687513 (ebook)
Subjects: LCSH: Europe–Social policy–21st century. |
Multiculturalism–Europe. | Social integration–Europe. |
Unemployment–Europe. | Social values–Europe. | Riots–Europe. |
Education–Europe.
Classification: LCC HN373.5 .E976 2017 | DDC 306.094–dc23
LC record available at https://lccn.loc.gov/2016055548

ISBN: 978-1-138-91993-8 (hbk)
ISBN: 978-1-138-91994-5 (pbk)
ISBN: 978-1-315-68751-3 (ebk)

Typeset in Bembo
by Sunrise Setting Ltd., Brixham, UK
Printed and bound by CPI Group (UK) Ltd, Croydon, CR0 4YY

Contents

Contributors

Sandra Abegglen is a Senior Lecturer in Education Studies and Course Leader of the BA Hons Education Studies at London Metropolitan University. Her research interests are in the areas of education, peer-to-peer learning, mentoring, identity, visual narratives and qualitative research methods.

David Blundell leads the Education Subject Group at London Metropolitan University and has previously worked as a primary school teacher, FE lecturer, community sport worker and academic at London South Bank University. David teaches, writes and publishes on histories of childhood, and children's spaces and places in education and schooling.

Jessie Bustillos is a Senior Lecturer in Education studies at London Metropolitan University. Her research interests include exploring the potential of intersectionality in education and gender studies, the influence of digitised networks in education, online ethnographies and visual methodologies, post-humanism and new materialisms in education.

Peter Cunningham is a Senior Lecturer in Education Studies at London Metropolitan University. He coordinates CiCe (Children's Identity and Citizenship in Europe), a large multi-disciplinary, pan-European academic network supported by the European Commission, concerned with what and how young people learn about their participative citizenship.

Wendy Fitzgibbon is Reader in Criminology at the University of Leicester. She is the author of *Pre-emptive Criminalisation: Risk Control and Alternative Futures* (2004) and *Probation and Social Work on Trial: Violent Offenders and Child Abusers* (2011). She has published widely on risk, probation and privatisation.

Norman Ginsburg has been Professor of Social Policy at London Metropolitan University since 1996. He has researched and published across a range of topics, including housing, urban regeneration, racism, migration, globalisation, political economy of welfare and cross-national social policy analysis. He has been a member of the Editorial Collective of the journal *Critical Social Policy* since it started in 1980.

Jeffrey Haynes is Professor of Politics in the School of Social Sciences and Director of the Centre for the Study of Religion, Conflict and Cooperation, London Metropolitan University. He is the author, co-author, editor or co-editor of more than 40 books. During 2015–17, he is undertaking research into the United Nations entity 'Alliance of Civilizations' as part of a large research initiative funded by the USA-based John Templeton Foundation.

Stuart Isaacs is a Senior Lecturer in Social Policy and Sociology at London Metropolitan University. He is the co-author of *Contemporary Political Theorists in Context* (2009) and *Political Theorists in Context* (2004), as well as the sole author of *The Politics and Philosophy of Michael Oakeshott* (2006), all published by Routledge. His research interests are in political and social theory. He has recently been made a University Teaching Fellow in recognition of his outstanding contribution to teaching and learning.

Jane Lewis is a Senior Lecturer in Sociology at London Metropolitan University. She has wide expertise of conducting research and teaching in social and spatial divisions and inequalities especially in relation to cities; globalisation and global inequalities; and urban regeneration and housing policy.

María Encarnación López is a Senior Lecturer in Sociology at London Metropolitan University (LMU) and Associate Fellow of the Institute for Latin American Studies (University of London). Recent publications include academic articles on sexual freedom, gender, human rights and democracy in the Hispanic area. She is the author of *Homosexuality and Invisibility in Revolutionary Cuba* (Tamesis, 2015) and is currently writing *Hispanic Women Writers in the Twenty-First Century* (Tamesis, 2017).

Brian McDonough is a Senior Lecturer and Course Leader of Sociology and Co-Director of the International Centre for Community Development at London Metropolitan University. He teaches on a wide-range of programmes for sociology and social policy students. His research interests include work, expertise and the use of information and communication technologies in the workplace. He is a co-author of *Social Problems in the UK*.

James Morgan works as a Senior Lecturer of Criminology at London Metropolitan University. His research career began with a doctoral thesis concerning persistent heroin use, researched whilst volunteering as a harm reduction worker at a drugs service. He is also interested in many other aspects of illicit substance use and regulation.

Jennifer Newton has researched in mental health and social care, in voluntary sector project management roles and later as a university lecturer. Now a manager in the School of Social Sciences, her latest publication is *Preventing Mental Ill-health: Informing Public Health Planning and Mental Health Practice* (Routledge, 2013).

Matt Scott is a Lecturer at London Metropolitan University and Goldsmiths College and also works as a Policy Manager at London Voluntary Service Council. He is chair of the Community Development Journal and a joint author of *Access to Justice for Disadvantaged Communities* (Policy Press, 2015).

Daniel Silverstone is a Reader of Police Studies at Liverpool John Moores University. His primary interests are the incidence of organised crime and its policing. He is currently researching the links between organised crime and modern-day slavery as well as the issue of trafficking of people from Vietnam to the UK.

chapter 1

Introduction
What are European social problems?

Stuart Isaacs

1.1 Introduction

It is the morning of June 24th, 2016. The UK has just voted to leave the European Union. This is one of the most momentous historical events to occur in Europe since the end of the Second World War. It breaks a pattern of European integration that many hoped would ensure that conflict, bloody or otherwise, would disappear from the continent. For Britain, in particular, the consequences may radically change the direction of the policies that has shaped its institutions for decades. Furthermore, it could lead to the break-up of the United Kingdom (UK) and the possibility of an independent Scotland.

The last time that the UK suffered a crisis of global identity and insecurity was over sixty years ago. This followed the well-known withdrawal from Suez. The Suez crisis triggered an awareness that Britain's global power status was fading and with it control of the Empire. Churchill's famous 'three circle' strategy, denoting Britain's intention to maintain influence in the three spheres of Empire, Europe and the Atlantic alliance, suffered a terminal break-down. From this point onwards, reluctantly and dragging its feet, the UK recognised that Britain's primary economic and political interests resided with its European neighbours. As the Empire collapsed in the 1960s European integration grew as it moved from a European Coal and Steel Community (ECSC) to the European Economic Community (EEC). The UK was pragmatically drawn towards the EEC and yet remained politically sceptical of joining a pan-European organisation with the potential to override its own sovereignty.

There has always been a political and cultural ambiguity about the British relationship with Europe. Significant as the referendum decision of the British people (soon no longer to be citizens of Europe but solely subjects of the Crown) might well prove to be, the outcome should perhaps not be a surprise. Despite a shift towards the European 'circle' after 1956, Britain did not join the original ECSC and fudged membership of the EEC in 1961/2 and 1967/8. When they did finally join, in 1972, a referendum was soon called (by 1975) to see whether or not they ought to stay in the then renamed European Community (EC). On this occasion the vote was a resounding 'Remain'.

The history of the UK and it relationship with the various political institutions of Europe (which today, of course, we know as the European Union (EU)), has been a turbulent one. Most of the arguments that finally won over the British politicians and public to accept full membership of the EEC in the 1970s had been pragmatic. Being closer to Europe politically was a necessary evil in order to gain economically. This argument finally fell apart in 2016. Yet despite the UK apparently wrenching itself from the Common Market, as well as the political and legal framework of the EU, this historic change of direction has much less impact on *social* issues. The social problems which the whole of Europe still faces, 'Remain'. Despite the potential economic and political upheaval of 'Leave', the social issues which have emerged as pan-European since the Second World War will not change. They are not dependent upon the UK's membership of the EU or on the EU itself staying as it currently is. Whether it is Brexit or Nexit or any other change to the organisational structure of the EU, the construction of social problems as European problems is now sedimented. Organised crime, social protest, migration, religious tension, poverty, unemployment, homophobia, health and educational inequalities, and each of the many topics you will find in this text all have a European dimension to their character, proliferation and possible policy resolution that will not suddenly go away.

As we have argued in our first text, *Social Problems in the UK: An Introduction*, (Isaacs, 2015), social problems, while intertwined with economic and political problems, may be distinguished from them. This is because the types of issues discussed in this context require an understanding of their historical construction, policy development and sociological dimension. For (a simple) example, approaches to migration will differ according to the historical-cultural acceptance of 'Others', constructing a particular discourse around immigration. So it is that the language that surrounds debates about immigration needs analysis from a social science point of view. In the UK refugees have gradually come to be defined in predominantly negative/sceptical terms as 'asylum seekers'. The exception to this is when tragedy occurs. Then the term 'refugee' tends to be restored. In countries where there is a different social context a subtly different discourse emerges. So we find that in Ireland the more positive/accepting terms 'Asylum finders' and 'New Irish' are often deployed.

Discussions about the social construction of migrants or, indeed, any of the topics set out here, requires not just an economic or political analysis to understand them but one from the point of view of the social sciences too.

Stuart Isaacs

In this text, then, you will find an argument that European social problems are a distinctive set of issues, entangled with but relatively autonomous from economic and political debates. European social problems are also not defined here as issues that are only found within the EU's member states. In the chapters that follow it is maintained that European social problems may be separate from the policies or organisational concerns of the European Parliament, its courts, the European Commission, and so on. Just as in our previous text it was argued that UK social problems are not defined by what government prioritises or what might be newsworthy debates, so here European social problems are defined as a matter of social research concern, identified by the authors. To go further it may be added that while the idea of a 'social Europe' has been a much discussed issue in academic literature over the past twenty years or more, the reality is that the EU barely touches upon social issues except where they affect labour laws within its jurisdiction. Therefore, any meaningful discussions about European social problems must go well beyond the limited horizons of the EU. The understanding of 'Europe' used in this book is much broader and opaque than the boundaries provided by the EU, so much so that it could be argued that while this text is the first to examine European social problems from a social science point of view, it does so while arguing it is not possible to have a catch-all definition of 'Europe' at all.

1.2 Europe: a theory

There is no such thing as Europe. But there are European social problems. How can these two statements make logical sense? The premise of this text is that Europe is an unstable, contingent, shifting entity. A brief history of Europe, even over the last thirty years or so, would be enough to illustrate this. Nation-states come and go. Territorial boundaries change regularly. The volatile Balkans is often the most graphic example of this. This instability goes back over 500 years (Larrabee, 1992; Ascherson, 1995) and was accelerated after the end of the Cold War with a rebirth of nations and the break-up of Yugoslavia. But it is not merely geographical boundaries that alter with such changes. The constitutive and fluid dynamic of regions brings into question the integrity of the state. If the state cannot be relied upon to be a focus for continuity then a broader framework of analysis is needed to understand regional political and social issues. This has been recognised across the social sciences, even in the normally conservative and realist area of security studies (Buzan and Hansen, 2009).

The internal coherence of countries also resides on shifting sands. In the 1920s during the Weimar period, social theorists like Weber and Heller were desperate to establish liberal democracies in Europe as a way to avoid war and political extremism. Weber argued that only a limited ballot-box democracy – that allowed for the expression of a very narrow range of political views – could do this. Heller maintained that a basic social homogeneity was necessary in order to make the stability of modern democracies possible. Ultimately they both admitted that such a project was unlikely to succeed given the increasing heterogeneity of Europe. This can be illustrated today by the Scottish independence movement in the UK, Basque regionalism and the Catalan call for autonomy. The federalism of France and Germany are set up to try to negotiate this lack of social homogeneity. Elsewhere, in countries like Italy and Ireland the lack of state penetration builds in tensions between polities and 'clients'.

Institutional and cultural haziness are also characteristics of modern European states. The ability of state institutions to make unilateral decisions has been highly questioned in relation to globalisation and localised decision-makers. The implementation of state policy is similarly fragmented in practice. Cultural heterogeneity is an influence on the way that centralised state prescription fails to function universally. In some regions this may be partly due to the increase in multicultural and multi-faith identities, as well as changes to occupational roles and social class. The rise of a fragile sense of identity, as Guy Standing has noted in his work on the 'precariat', is prevalent among European populations.

To write of 'Europe', then, as simply and transparently synonymous with the EU would be a reduction of a complex truth. 'Europe' is a construct, a meaning for an empty vessel that is bounded only by a hazy regional boundary and abstracted only generally from the continents it does not geographically define. In this text the contestation is that any notion of Europe must be open to particular contextual understanding. Many European states are connected by formal, legal and institutional ties, not only through the EU. However, internal tensions within states at a political, institutional and cultural level means that these formalised arrangements are not sufficient to synthesise Europe into a single fixed object of study. It could not be otherwise, unless we were to ignore the heterogeneous make-up of Europe at multiple levels: local, national and regional.

For any thorough comparative analysis of European countries to take place different levels of analysis are needed. A monolithic notion of 'Europe' would be a very crude perspective indeed, one that does not mirror the diversity of experience of modern Europeans. Rather, at the very least a sense of the interrelatedness of local, national and regional analysis has to be part of any discussions around 'Europe' given that we can only speak of and analyse parts of what is associated with Europe in particular contexts.

This argument impacts upon social issues and social problems as it points us towards a position where the most pressing European social concerns can be said to be based around diversity and this fragile sense of definition and identity: issues of class, ethnicity, gender, sexuality, disability, poverty, wealth, health, housing and all the related social problems to be found in this book. All these social problems have at their heart the question of convergence and difference. In other words, it is the very lack of a homogeneous, single objectifiable Europe that makes an understanding of European social problems all the more urgent. A recognition of the diversity, heterogeneity and need for various levels of analysis is a necessary context for exploring social problems that appear common across Europe.

Many decades ago Michael Oakeshott, writing as a political philosopher, noted that the character of the European state, since its modern emergence in the sixteenth century, had never had a complete or fixed identity but was always,

Stuart Isaacs

'an association in the making' (1975: 196/7). By this he did not mean that Europe was still incomplete as a single political entity, or that it was on some kind of teleological journey to become whole. Rather, he was voicing the very same non-foundational point of view set out here: Europe will always be, 'in the making'. It can never be complete because politics is never complete. It resides, as Oakeshott famously stated, 'on a boundless and bottomless sea' (Oakeshott, 1991: 60).

Perhaps the most well-known thesis that best captures the sense of Europe that is being proposed here is in Benedict Anderson's notion of nation-states being 'imagined communities'. This classic argument maintains that nation-states are socially constructed entities based around the same core perception of a people, however different the nuances of their ideas about nationhood might be (Anderson, 1991). Without wishing to diverge into discussions about the theoretical premise and arguments of Anderson's work, of which there have been many, suffice to say that here the social construction of 'Europe' is taken as a matter of perception among individuals, social cleavages, political actors and the media in the same general manner that Anderson understands nation-states. These perceptions may differ and clash in many respects but these overriding arguments do not disrupt the underlying foundations upon which the debate engages. So, for example, for all the differing points of view about the EU from the 'Leave' and 'Remain' camps in the UK, both camps were able to converse because they shared a basic common ground regarding their construction of the role of the EU.

Philosophically, historically and conceptually it has been argued above that 'Europe' is a construct. Speaking more recently, with the voice of political practice, the great German sociologist Jurgen Habermas has similarly stated that nation-states in Europe are becoming more and more fragmented. This, he argues, also affects their capacity to act politically (IPPR, 2014). Since the periods when Oakeshott and Anderson were first setting out their arguments it has become more and more of a mainstream position in political theory and political science to assume that nation-states are not singular political actors. Rather, theories of governance have arisen that understand political and social change being enacted in terms of a network of policy-making institutions operating at various levels from local to global. Alongside this sit NGOs and informal networks of power, be they social movements or organised criminal gangs. This myriad and non-linear understanding of how policy and practice emerges can be said to be the broad working model of contemporary studies in European politics and society. It is into this body of literature that this text on European social problems fits.

It is, then, argued here that Europe ought to be understood as constructed and contextualised in particular debates. The discourses on European social problems can, it reasonably follows, include or exclude particular nation-states without setting limits or boundaries as to what constitutes 'Europe'. In this text you will find that countries including Kazakhstan and Turkey may be included in 'Europe', while at other times Europe appears as Western Europe or North, South, West but not Eastern Europe. Europe is throughout this text taken as a fluid, ambiguous construct of which, say, the EU is just one construct, a 'nodal point' (Laclau,1990) but not a foundational one. There is, in this sense, no such thing as Europe. What we take to be Europe (and what each author in this book means by Europe) is a matter of debate and contestation around particular sets of issues.

Such an understanding of Europe goes against realist, empiricist, legalistic and political constitutionalist views. It opens up a more creative debate for the range of social sciences that are presented in this text. It also paves the way for a discussion of social problems away from narrow economist terms and towards issues of social justice that dominate debates within the social sciences. In this way this text continues the perspective of our previous book on UK social problems and issues (Isaacs, 2015). The methodology of social construction that framed that text is still to be found here in the notion of Europe given above. However, the emphasis here is now much more on the problem-solving, policy dimension of social problems and the role of social science in analysing these (see section 1.3). Authors in this text diverge in terms of their explicit application of social construction as an overriding theory or methodology, although it is consistent in relation to the notion of 'Europe' that is articulated in each chapter.

1.3 Social problems

The approach to Europe as an 'imagined' fluid construct that arises out of the acknowledged heterogeneity of European actors, institutions and structures can also be associated with the societal failure of Europe in the twentieth century. This failure provoked two world wars. As mentioned above, the subsequent desire to aspire to an ideal of a stable integrated Europe where mutual interests and enterprise would mitigate armed conflict led eventually to the EU. However, this new Europe became an ideological battle-ground itself between politicians, polities and parties. Many saw the new post-war Europe as more or less able to solve a range of social issues around inequality, social justice and citizenship. This increasingly became the hope of many social policy commentators (Ginsburg, 1997). However, just as the idea of a 'social Europe' was emerging so too was the influence, first, of the New Right and then neo-liberalism which began to dominate the agendas of many European countries from the 1980s. As the contemporary European political and social debate grew on all ideological sides the discourse about social issues began to generate the problems it sought to fix. Issues of work, crime, poverty, health, immigration, education and so on were seen to have a core thread as common European experiences, as European institutions, research and communications spread. Whatever the varied political views that play out in today's European debates, sceptics and pro-Europeans, and all those between, all argue on the same grounds with the assumption that there are European social problems. As Brexit has revealed, across Europe there are those that seek to mitigate these European social problems by completely withdrawing from integrationalist agendas and rather seek to strengthen their own national laws and autonomy. And then there are other polities that seek to further European integration to remedy some of

Stuart Isaacs

these issues. In all the countries of Europe, though, this polarised debate exists in multiple forms between parties and people and the national media, creating a perennial tension about how to resolve European social problems.

The theoretical approach that informs what has been maintained regarding Europe and European social problems also defines what we mean here as a general social problem. A social problem in this text is taken by the authors as historically, culturally and contextually constructed. Social problems are not fixed or given and they change over time. Why we might choose to study or discuss one issue as a pressing problem is a matter for judgement and argument. Judgements tend to come from our ethical sensibilities. Arguments about social problems are, therefore, always politicised. Most often they are based upon our ideas about social justice. However, as social scientists we cannot make claims about the importance of a particular social problem without citing social research. This may be quantitative or qualitative but it is usually both. Quantitative evidence alone cannot justify the urgency of a social problem. We do not choose to focus on a particular social problem because of how many people it affects. If we did we would not look at issues that affect a minority of people but which we find needs discussion on the grounds of social justice.

Social problems emerge for a variety of immediate reasons. But underlying the concern is usually the perception of a threat to our social structures. This perception may come from politicians, the media or on-going public debate. Many social problems have existed for a great deal of time. Even if they are not at a current, particular moment of public debate, issues such as poverty, racism, organised crime, unemployment, old age, discrimination on grounds of disability, mental health, and so on are latent conflicts within European societies. So while social problems come and go as public discussion shifts many of the core problems of modern capitalist societies have persisted for decades. In this way some agreement about social problems is not too difficult to identify. It is how to go about resolving social problems that causes much more varied, politicised and passionate debate.

The social problems chosen by the authors in this book, as well as the sub-topics within these, are a matter of knowledge and judgement. In the social sciences there will, of course, always be disagreements about which concerns are the greatest. In so far as each of these authors are specialists in their field, the issues chosen sum up the current state of debate regarding some of the most pressing social problems that face Europeans today. A brief summary of the chapters is given below.

1.4 Chapter summary

In the UK a number of commentators observed that the referendum on European membership was fundamentally a vote about immigration. Immigration has, arguably, been the most dominant debate in Europe for nearly two decades and an ever-present social issue since the end of the Second World War. Given that immigration has been and continues to be such a dominant European social problem, Part I of this text groups together a number of chapters that discuss this and the related issue of multiculturalism.

Following the introductory first chapter, Ginsburg begins Chapter 2 by outlining the key features and controversies of immigration within Europe over recent years. In so doing he takes a case study and comparative approach looking at Germany, Sweden and Hungary, and then turns to the EU. In his analysis of European migration he points to both 'welcoming' and 'exclusionary' constructions of refugees/migrants in these instances and the social issues of Islamophobia and racism.

In the third chapter, Matt Scott looks at the way migrants have been socially constructed in Europe. He picks up on the themes set out by Ginsburg, most notably the way migration is organised around two foci: border issues, often referred to by the shorthand of 'Fortress Europe'; and integration issues, including more permeable notions of the EU as 'gatekeeper'. Scott argues that migrants have been constructed in various ways including as 'proto-terrorists' and as various 'health threats'. The policy solutions that have emerged to then quell these 'moral panics' have perpetuated the development of insular and xenophobic discourses of crisis, constructing a sharp polarity between 'us and them', which has led to a much contested politics of immigration control. The controversy pertaining to immigration within Europe is concluded by a reflection on issues of multiculturalism and multi-faith societies.

In Chapter 4, Haynes undertakes an investigation into how Islam in Europe has been reconstructed since the waves of Muslim migration in the 1970s and 1980s. After first considering Western Europe in general, the author undertakes particular studies of the UK and France. Haynes points to a remodelling and re-assumption of our understanding of the public roles of Islam and religion in Europe. And he examines this new dynamic relationship and looks at its impact on notions of European citizenship.

Overall the authors of these chapters argue that despite the divergent social contexts and policy directions discussed there is some convergence between previously differing societal responses to immigration that tends towards a greater degree of social tension and conflict.

The social issues that make up Part II of the book come under the broad heading of 'Inequalities'. Of course, almost all the social problems discussed here have some aspect of broad inequalities about them. However, the areas collected here all relate specifically to issues of wealth, income and class.

Chapter 5 opens by assessing the evidence that seems to indicate that inequalities are increasing in cities across Europe. Evidence from Stockholm to Paris, and London to Istanbul demonstrates the recent growth in socio-spatial inequalities and segregation. Lewis reviews debates concerning the growing social polarisation and the social class restructuring of European cities. A case study of growing poverty and inequality and the 'residualisation' of social housing in London is used to illustrate this. Debates concerning the ethnic segregation of cities are also examined.

This debate is continued in Chapter 6 where McDonough maintains that over the past two decades Europe has seen a tumultuous period of insecure employment. The expansion of the EU, the financial collapse and the emergence

Stuart Isaacs

of new forms of information and communication technologies have all made work 'precarious'. European business has also changed, now able to operate across different countries giving prevalence to a new 'shrinking' and arguably much 'smaller' Europe. This chapter discusses the impact of these recent shifts and looks at how they are fundamentally affecting what we understand as paid employment. It explores the social impact and the new social problems arising out of the changing relationship between work, employment, unemployment and mediating technologies.

Inequalities are approached from a slightly different perspective by Newton in Chapter 7. Here the author considers the four 'd's relating to health inequalities: diabetes, depression, dementia and death. In each case she points to the reason why these often individualised issues are, in fact, social problems. Moreover, the argument continues that there is a sociological character to these health concerns largely correlated with social class. As such, it is not only the stigmatised individual that ought to be targeted by health agencies, but government policies aimed at us all.

Part III of this text tackles education. This is not merely undertaken in terms of schooling but is associated with the broader social construction of childhood and learning through multiple agencies. The section begins with Chapter 8, which concerns a critical appraisal of the dynamic between early childhood and schooling by Blundell and Abegglen. They start from the findings of successive Unicef reports that present some striking contrasts in children's views on their well-being across the continent. The chapter critiques the assumption of a universal childhood as an 'ideal form' by examining the validity of the view that a single narrative for the condition of childhood can be sustained. Education and schooling provides a context for the examination of this encounter between 'ideal forms' and the diversity of childhood experiences. The chapter concludes by looking at the prospects for modern childhood under conditions of rapid technological and political change in Europe.

Chapter 9 broadens out the debate by enquiring into the relationship between digital technologies and education. This study is undertaken in the context of seeking to understand the issues involved in a Europe where the neo-liberal discourse dominates. Bustillos argues that this gives rise to a 'digital divide', which cross-cuts various social groups within Europe creating 'digital haves' and 'digital have nots'. Moreover, this divide is getting gradually more complex and differentiated. The author argues that only structured policy decisions, potentially led by the EU, can address some of these problems in European education.

The final chapter in this section focuses upon the role of formal education in relation to children and young peoples' identities as citizens of Europe. Blundell and Cunningham argue that educational policy formation at a European level, and its enactment within nations is premised on presumptions of 'shared values' and a democratic system that assumes pluralism and active participation in society. However, competing conceptions of Europe and what it means to be European give challenge to this education project. In light of this, the chapter explores multiple and nested identities, with concern for both majority and minority groups, and argues that education can promote the voice of the 'Other' through active citizenship. Nevertheless, the project is fragile because interpretations of what values are shared may lead to policy and practice that is both assimilationist and excluding.

The concluding Part IV of *European Social Problems* groups together a number of pressing social controversies. These last three chapters all concern social problems not yet raised but which have received a significant degree of heated debate over the last few years. First, in Chapter 11, Fitzgibbon notes that Europe has seen a number of direct action protest movements taking to the streets in recent years. These have been over diverse issues such as environmental concerns, perceptions of injustice in criminal justice, education changes and moves to criminalise squatters and travellers, to name but a few. These actions involve criminal trespass and violation of property, and engage young people drawn from the 'precariat': largely young people from deprived communities, either in and out of insecure, low wage, unskilled employment or facing the prospect of such a status when leaving secondary education. The author examines recent case examples across Europe to critically apply the concept of the 'precariat' to understand the social problems posed by these rioters engaged in protests.

Chapter 12 continues upon the general terrain of crime and deviance by exploring how the European drugs problem is changing. Morgan and Silverstone focus on the threats from synthetic drugs and the new availability via online sources. They map out the distinctive trends in consumption of older drugs such as cannabis and cocaine, then the chapter moves on to discuss how preferences for illegal drugs are shared across social economic and ethnic categories. Drug trafficking is looked at and whether or not organised crime groups are involved in this is discussed. Responses to drug trafficking show opposing paradigms of drug regulation across Europe. A comparative study of the UK and the Netherlands is undertaken to illustrate this. The advantages and disadvantages of both approaches are outlined and indications of where policy might be heading is set out.

The final chapter of the text centres on the controversy arising out of homophobia in Europe. According to López there is evidence of a social ambivalence in Europe regarding the issue of homosexuality. In spite of the fact that European states are in general tolerant towards homosexuality, to be homosexual in some places in Europe is still a social problem. The author argues that homophobia exists in Europe at different levels and causes a devastating impact on the lives of individuals. Interpersonal and cultural homophobia manifests itself in physical and verbal aggression and is especially dramatic in some East European countries where sexual discrimination is not penalised (i.e. Russia, Belarus and Ukraine). Furthermore, homophobia in Europe is often a social norm and behaviour codes that enhance sexual discrimination are developed by governments, as well as education or religious institutions. This indicates the importance of the role of social and political institutions for bringing about change.

Stuart Isaacs

Bibliography

Anderson, B. (1991) *Imagined Communities* (revised and extended), London: Verso.

Ascherson, N. (1995) *Black Sea*, London: Random House, p. 197.

Buzan, B. and Hansen, L. (2009) *The Evolution of International Security Studies*, Cambridge: CUP.

Dyzenhaus, D. (1999) *Legality and Legitimacy: Carl Schmitt, Hans Kelsen and Herman Heller in Weimar*, Oxford: OUP.

Ginsburg, N. (1997) 'Social Europe: a new model welfare?' *European Dossier Series 44*, London: UNL.

IPPR (2014) 'In favour of a strong Europe' Jurgen Habermas, www.ippr.org/juncture/in-favour-of-a-strong-europe-what-does-this-mean, last accessed 24 January 2017.

Isaacs, S. (2006) *The Politics and Philosophy of Michael Oakeshott*, Oxon: Routledge.

Isaacs, S. (2015) *Social Problems in the UK: An Introduction*, Oxon: Routledge.

Laclau, E. (1990) *New Reflections on the Revolution of Our Time*, London: Verso.

Larrabee, S. (1992) 'Instability and change in the Balkans', *Survival*, vol. 34, no. 2, Summer, pp. 31–49.

Oakeshott, M. (1975) *On Human Conduct*, Oxford: Clarendon Press.

Oakeshott, M. (1991) *Rationalism in Politics and Other Essays*, ed. T. Fuller, new and expanded edition, London: Liberty Press.

Sanders, D. (1990) *Losing an Empire, Finding a Role: British Foreign Policy since 1945*, Hampshire: Macmillan.

part I

Immigration and multiculturalism

chapter 2

Constructions of the 'migration crisis' in Europe

Norman Ginsburg

2.1 Introduction

This chapter discusses the many different constructions put on the phenomenon of immigration in Europe. It contrasts welcoming perspectives with exclusionary ones. The starting point is the migrant crisis of the mid 2010s, which has brought these different perspectives into sharp relief. The development and key elements of these constructions are considered in Germany, Sweden, Hungary and the European Union (EU) itself. There is convergence in terms of racist, Islamophobic and xenophobic constructions, promoted by the far right and penetrating deep into the political mainstream. But there is also a less histrionic convergence around more welcoming constructions, motivated by humanitarian and human-rights concerns, as well as the demand for migrant workers, particularly in North West Europe. Exclusionary constructions obviously open the way to the building of bigger walls, more incarceration and deportation, and more deaths and suffering among aspiring migrants. Welcoming constructions should necessitate a fair distribution of the burden across Europe as a whole, with supportive services to facilitate temporary or permanent settlement.

2.2 The refugee crisis

What is widely referred to as the European 'migrant crisis' emerged during 2015. It should be more accurately described as a 'refugee crisis', because the great majority of those involved were 'political migrants' taking refuge from conflict and violence in Syria, Afghanistan, Eritrea and many other places. In 2015 it became a 'crisis', rather than merely a socio-political problem or issue in Europe, simply because of the large numbers of people involved, and the numbers dying in the process; 3,772 died in 2015. At least one million asylum seekers, refugees and would-be economic migrants got to the border of the EU in 2015. There were many more aspiring to do so and held in refugee camps in Turkey (two million), Lebanon (1.3 million) and other states on the outer periphery of the EU.

Immigration, both 'economic' and 'political', has been a socio-political issue for West European nation states since the end of the Second World War (and much longer than that). From the 1980s the EU has sought an ever closer convergence of immigration policy. The scale of the 2015 crisis has exposed its fragility, as member states have retreated into national discourses and policy making.

The current crisis has served to illustrate the widely varying social constructions around the issue both *within* and *between* member states as well as at the EU level. These range on a continuum from exclusionary hostility to a cautious welcome. Despite Germany's recent 'welcome' for refugees (see section 2.3) there has been virtual silence from other Western leaders in support of Germany's efforts to provide progressive leadership through the crisis. Political leaders in Poland, Croatia and Hungary, as well as the Polish President of the European Council (the 'leader' of the EU), blamed Chancellor Merkel for 'inviting' refugees to come to Europe. European states have tried and failed to develop a collective strategy for distributing refugees across the 26 member states who are in the Schengen zone, the supposedly border-free area within the EU. There has been a marked absence of solidarity among EU states in response to the crisis. 'National regime dominance' has been the norm (see Bremmer 2015).

2.3 Germany

In the midst of the 2015 crisis, the German federal government led by Angela Merkel relaxed EU rules for the entry of refugees, forecasting that Germany was likely to receive 800,000 refugees in 2015 at a cost of £4.4 billion in 2016. Chancellor Merkel said: 'We can do it . . . the world sees Germany as a country of hope and opportunity'. The implication was that refugees from oppression and civil war were welcome; while she admitted that 'refugees will change Germany' (Huggler 2015), she hoped this would be in a positive sense, of course. Her other message was that the 28 nation states of the EU 'must share the responsibility for refugees seeking asylum . . . if Europe fails on the question of refugees, its close connection with universal civil rights will be destroyed' (ibid.).

The 'welcoming' construction of the immigration question has always had some resonance across Europe but it certainly came to the fore in Germany during this crisis, where it has a name – *Willkommenskultur*, meaning 'welcome culture'. It was originally coined by German regional politicians keen to attract foreign skilled workers to meet shortages in particular places. It was also intended to counter xenophobic and racist hostility to refugees in the early 1990s.

Norman Ginsburg

Today *Willkommenskultur* is supported by a broad coalition of leftists, liberals, churches, minority ethnic and refugee NGOs, and even some football fans. Merkel is pushed along by vibrant politics on the issue in Germany, both for and against refugees, though the momentum seemed to be moving against her by early 2016.

Germany's policies on asylum seekers and refugees originate with the establishment of the Federal Republic (FRG) in West Germany in 1949. As a measure of atonement for the fascist and anti-Semitic past, and to soften the emphasis on the FRG as the ethnic German homeland, the most liberal asylum legislation in Europe was included as Article 16 of the Basic Law. It gave any politically persecuted individual the right to apply for asylum and the right to remain in the country while the application was evaluated. Numbers were relatively small until the late 1970s, when the regime in Turkey adopted repressive measures against leftists and Kurdish nationalists, some of whom naturally sought refuge in the German Turkish communities. From the mid 1970s onward, the government introduced a series of increasingly severe measures to deter asylum seekers, and to accelerate the processing of applications and the removal of those whose applications had failed (Schuster 2003: 193–203).

Nevertheless, by the early 1990s Germany was allowing entry to many more asylum seekers than ever before and ten times more than any other European country. In 1992 while Germany accepted over 438,000 asylum applications, Britain and France each accepted only around 25,000. Of the people gaining entry to the EU(12) as refugees in 1992, 78 per cent went to Germany. Most of those entering came from former Yugoslavia, Romania and Bulgaria, but around 30 per cent came from Africa and Asia. The 'asylum crisis' of the early 1990s took place in the context of resettling large numbers of ethnic Germans from Central and Eastern Europe, but the government received little or no support from other EU members in coping with the unprecedented number of asylum seekers. Indeed, the other EU states with the exception of Belgium explicitly rejected Germany's proposals for sharing the burden at a summit meeting in 1991 (Bosswick 2000: 54).

The early 1990s asylum crisis was accompanied by a sharp rise in racist attacks on foreigners as a whole. Given the indifference of other EU states and the growing public hostility to refugees, Article 16 was severely amended in 1993, known as 'the asylum compromise'. Refugees staying or even in transit from allegedly safe third countries were now refused entry and their asylum applications considered while they remain outside Germany (Bosswick 2000: 49–53). Over 80 per cent of asylum seekers had travelled from such 'safe' countries, particularly the Czech Republic and Poland. As Gibney (2004: 103) says, 'by the late 1990s, Germany had constructed what amounted to a buffer zone of surrounding states that made overland movement in search of asylum in the FRG either impossible or illegal'. After 1993, the number of asylum applications fell immediately to less than 130,000 a year and by 2004 was down to less than 37,000. In a decade the asylum regime in Germany shifted from being the most liberal in Europe to being as illiberal as most other EU states, as they competed with each other to prevent refugees from arriving at their borders.

constructions of the 'migration crisis'

After years of debate, Germany's first Immigration Law came into effect in 2005 but the 'ban on recruiting foreign labour remained in effect for unskilled, semi-skilled and even skilled workers' with exceptions for 'certain jobs as long as no German . . . is available to fill the position' (BmI 2005: 31). The new legislation nevertheless opened the door for more officially sanctioned labour migration, and aspired to facilitate the settlement of migrants by simplifying the residence regulations and developing social integration measures.

From 2005 German law declared that 'in processing an application for a work permit (henceforth linked to a residency permit), consideration should be given to the labour-market situation, the fight against unemployment and the exigencies of securing national competitiveness' (Menz 2013: 111). However, businesses successfully lobbied for high skilled migrant workers to be allowed entry on a managed basis in view of labour shortages in a range of occupations including engineering, financial services and ICT. The 2005 Immigration Law certainly marked a decisive shift away from the 'not a country of immigration' discourse towards managed migration, something which is explicitly recognised as such by the federal government (BmI 2005: 6).

So what explains the emergence of the *Willkommenskultur* construction in contemporary Germany, embodied in Chancellor Merkel's stand? First, as suggested above, since the Second World War Germany has received millions of refugees from Central and Eastern Europe, including 'ethnic Germans', particularly in the immediate post-war decade but also after the fall of the Berlin Wall in 1989. So the arrival of 'political' migrants is a comparatively familiar process, which has been followed by some measure of successful integration into German society. Second, there are particular demographic features of contemporary Germany – a declining and ageing population, with labour shortages and insufficient people of working age to pay taxes and social insurance contributions to sustain pensions and social care services. New young and educated migrants are, it is argued, vital to long-term prosperity. Third, the crisis has also been seen as an opportunity to repair the political damage in Southern Europe, particularly in Greece, caused by the severe austerity measures imposed by the German-led financial authorities. It so happens that Greece has been under the most severe pressure from incoming refugees.

Opposing the *Willkommenskultur* are social constructions hostile to or at best sceptical about immigration to Germany, which are uncomfortable with the development of Germany as a multi-ethnic society. As elsewhere, much of this discourse emanates from the far right, which has a presence in local and regional government, but nothing to compare with their more prominent position in France, the Netherlands, Sweden and Denmark. The far-right Republican Party (REP), formed in 1984, advocates forced repatriation of foreigners and a unification within Germany's 1937 frontiers, including large tracts of Polish territory. The REP and other far-right parties have on occasion achieved as much as 14 per cent of the vote in regional state elections, but they are not represented in the national parliament. Neo-Nazis and skinheads have been a more immediate and violent threat to minorities on the streets.

Norman Ginsburg

In recent times, as elsewhere, the political and policy significance of Muslim identity has become an increasingly important element in public discourse in Germany, closely intertwined of course with the presence of people of Turkish origin, who make up the majority of the 3.5 million identified as Muslims. Foroutan (2013: 5–7) reviews considerable evidence of Islamophobia within public opinion in Germany, possibly stronger than other North West European countries. Patriotic Europeans Against the Islamization of the West or PEGIDA is an anti-immigration right-wing anti-Islamist political organisation founded in Dresden in October 2014. It has been organising weekly demonstrations against what it considers the Islamisation of the Western world, calling for more restrictive immigration restrictions, particularly for Muslims. Politicians, clergy and industry leaders have publicly condemned PEGIDA as xenophobic and Islamophobic.

Islamophobic and other racist constructions are not by any means confined to the far right. As elsewhere in Europe, they have some support within the 'mainstream'. This is exemplified by the popularity of a book by Thilo Sarrazin entitled *Germany Abolishes Itself*, published in 2010. It has sold over 1.5 million copies. Sarrazin is a member of the Social Democratic Party, as well as having served on the board of the German Central Bank. The book inaccurately alleges the failure of most Muslims to integrate into German society and that they are largely dependent on benefits. Sarrazin suggests that German national identity is threatened by the low fertility rate of 'autochthonous [ethnic] Germans' and the higher fertility rate of Muslims. There has been both approval and condemnation of Sarrazin's constructions. Examining media and political reaction to them, Piwoni (2015: 96) concludes that the political and media establishment 'managed to codify his thoughts according to their own consensual ideas about integration and immigration'. This consensus concedes that 'the success of integration is dependent on the individual migrant (and not the society)' while also upholding 'Germany's identity as a pluralist society that is open to immigrants who are ready to contribute to Germany's welfare' (ibid.: 96).

The passage of immigration legislation in the 2000s took place against an intense public debate about German culture and identity, formed around the concept of a German *Leitkultur*, the notion of a predominant, essential national culture, a particular version of Western Judaeo-Christian civilisation. Defining the key characteristics of a modern *Leitkultur* (a 'signature' culture) has understandably proved difficult and controversial, but it certainly goes well beyond the values of liberal democracy (Pautz 2005). The advocates of the *Leitkultur* insist that foreigners have to assimilate fully into it, and cannot retain or combine it with their own. Such a view continues to be quite widely held, possibly more so since 9/11. The *Leitkultur* discourse is perhaps a coded message with a Catch 22 attached – immigrants must assimilate fully and quickly (or risk exclusion, perhaps literally), but assimilation takes generations because the *Leitkultur* cannot be assimilated in haste. Pautz (ibid.: 46–9) has suggested that this amounts to a modernisation of the ethnic German identity around the idea of an essentialist national culture, previously constructed around family (blood) descent. Such a construction is clearly an element in Sarrazin's perspective.

In conclusion, it is important to reiterate that while exclusionary constructions like Sarrazin's and PEGIDA's have achieved much public prominence recently, more welcoming constructions remain strong in Germany. It has moved forward towards a self-understanding as a country whose people are 20 per cent of 'migrant background'. 'Instituting Islam with a status comparable with that of a Christian church is under discussion' (Thränhardt 2014: 254). It is quite widely accepted that 'integration' cannot equate with 'assimilation'.

2.4 Sweden

At the end of 2015 Sweden, previously the most welcoming to refugees among EU states, alongside Germany, adopted much more restrictive measures. Sweden announced the deportation of 80,000 failed asylum seekers in early 2016. Historically and through to the end of 2015 Sweden had been the most generous European state in accepting asylum seekers and refugees, if one considers the number of asylum seekers per 100,000 of the population. In 2015 Sweden received over 1,575 applications per 100,000 inhabitants, compared to 520 in Germany and 42 in the UK. This huge disproportionality is obviously one factor behind the Swedish U-turn at the end of 2015. Overall from the 1970s, in contrast with Britain and France, 'humanitarian migration and family integration have consistently outpaced all other forms of migration to Sweden' (Fredlund-Blomst 2014).

Most Western countries' approach to refugees is two-faced. On the one hand commitments to human rights and international solidarity suggest an openness to accepting refugees, however many and wherever they come from. On the other hand, the settlement of refugees has become a quite large-scale form of immigration, which is constructed by some as undermining social cohesion and hard-won living standards. Nowhere are these contradictory perspectives more glaring than in Sweden. Within all the mainstream political parties there has been a sharp division of opinion between those supporting a liberal refugee policy and those who oppose it on 'communitarian' grounds (Schierup 1990: 563–4; Abiri 2000: 24–5). However, there has been something of a tacit compromise which, in effect, meant that refugee migration was a disguised form of labour migration, thereby accommodating both the supporters of international human rights and the needs of the economy for migrant workers (Schierup 1990: 562–3).

Sweden's comparative generosity towards refugees is part of a particular social construction of Swedish nationhood since the Second World War based on a moralistic, non-ethnic modernity. Key features have included a comparatively well-funded welfare state with a serious commitment to mitigating class and gender inequality, an early embrace of ethnic multiculturalism (from the 1970s) and international policies putting a strong emphasis on global human rights. Ramalingam (2012: 10) notes that

> aversion to anti-immigrant sentiment in Sweden is visible in the unwritten codes of conduct dictating the public debate on immigration policy . . .

Norman Ginsburg

[mainstream political] parties have deliberately chosen to not exploit the immigration issue and . . . have not responded to the reality of anti-immigrant views among Swedish citizens.

A good example of the 'welcome culture' is that, since the 1990s, while most states 'decreased asylum seekers' social rights and right to work . . . Sweden *increased* such rights' (Andersson and Nilsson 2009: 168). Two possible reasons for this are, first, that Swedes are more strongly attached to universal social rights in general, and are 'determined to protect them even for marginal groups' (ibid.: 183); and, second, Sweden is a comparably more 'child centred' society with a long history of progressive, interventionist family policies, which translates into a particular concern with the wellbeing of children with an immigrant background.

Brochmann (2014: 287) suggests that in Norway, Denmark and Sweden 'public discourse has been somewhat simplistic and polarised between the restrictionists . . . and the admissionists'. While Denmark has been the most restrictionist, it has also always had some resonance in Sweden. This came to the fore in the mid-1970s when economic migration was 'halted' and again in the 1990s when political migration was restricted under pressure of numbers and lack of sharing by other rich EU states. Restrictionism is a social construction with several strands in Sweden, not unlike those elsewhere, with a particular emphasis on concern about possible threats to the welfare state and social cohesion.

Ethnic segmentation of the labour market in Sweden is long-established. Migrant workers (and their wives and children) have generally been recruited into less attractive, low paid jobs in industry and the services sector, while native Swedes have had privileged access to professional and managerial status. Refugees, unsurprisingly, have found it much harder to find paid employment. Official unemployment figures register much higher rates for the foreign born, reaching 16.3 per cent in 2013, compared to 6.4 per cent for the Swedish born (Statistics Sweden 2014: 74). According to one official study quoted by Schierup *et al.* (2006: 207) "Africans" and "Asians" are – everything else equal (education, age, marital status, gender, time of residence in Sweden, and so on) – four times more likely to be unemployed than the native-born'. There is evidence of a range of racialised processes in the labour market which contribute to this, in addition to the structural decline in formal employment opportunities. Racialised minorities are often excluded from the social networks through which workers are recruited, and employers are prone to having inappropriate requirements of job applicants, e.g. for a high level of spoken or written Swedish. Such institutional processes are bolstered by negative ethnic stereotyping by 'actors in gatekeeper positions' within the public and private sectors, which have a direct impact on both the recruitment and subsequent treatment of minority workers (Rydgren 2004: 707–12). Second-generation migrants, particularly those with a non-European background, with comparable educational backgrounds and linguistic skills to native Swedes experience much higher levels of unemployment (ibid.: 704). There has developed a concentration of minority groups in poor neighbourhoods both in the inner-city and on edge-city estates, linked to the rise in unemployment, the arrival of larger numbers of asylum seekers and generally increasing socio-economic polarisation. Linked to this there has been considerable political and media anxiety about such 'segregation'.

Fredlund-Blomst (2014) describes these processes of socio-economic exclusion continuing on into the 2010s, and lying behind rioting by minority ethnic young people across some Stockholm suburbs in May 2013. In a similar vein Schierup *et al.* (2014: 1) link the rebellions to 'the consequences of securitisation and police repression, institutional racism, the corrosion of citizenship and the structuring of inequality in Swedish cities.'

In this socio-economic context, it is not surprising that the restrictionist construction has slowly gained ground based on a perception that minorities are over dependent on the welfare state and are failing to integrate both economically and culturally, as well as thinly disguised Islamophobia and racism. According to Brochmann (2014: 289) 'the public's focus has been increasingly on the implicit constituents of *duty* attached to the principle of a generous welfare system', that is, the duty to support the welfare state by regular employment and taxpaying. Of course this should be turned around to point the finger at the failings of the welfare state, not least in employment and housing.

While opinion surveys continue to suggest that anti-immigrant sentiment is lower among Swedes than in any other EU state, there has been a gradual rise in such views since the increase in the number of asylum applicants from the early 1990s. One concrete indicator of this is that over the 2000s there was a significant increase in the detention and deportation of asylum seekers, which inevitably carries with it the aura of criminalisation and punishment – the most negative possible social construction (as discussed by Khosravi 2009).

Anti-immigrant restrictionism is exemplified above all by the rise in support for the far right, most notably in the form of the explicitly anti-immigrant Sweden Democrat (SD) party. SD achieved an unprecedented 12.9 per cent of the vote in the 2014 election with 49 seats (14 per cent) in parliament. Though the centre-left government coalition and the centre-right opposition parties have kept SD very much at arm's length, SD hold a parliamentary balance of power between left and right. The rise of SD and the much increased number of asylum applications in 2014–15, alongside the failure of the EU to share the burden, explain the abrupt policy U-turn against refugees in 2016, leading some to conclude that the idea of Sweden as a sanctuary is dead (Brown 2015). That would be a great exaggeration, but there is no doubt that the comparatively welcoming construction on political migration has waned in the context of the problems of socio-economic integration faced by people 'with an immigrant background'. Institutional racism has become inscribed into the housing and labour markets (Schierup and Ålund 2011: 51). Another facet is new immigration policies emerging in the 2000s which, reflecting EU discourse, have shifted towards facilitating temporary labour migration from within the EU, instead of having refugees as a 'disguised' form of labour migration. So Fortress Europe (see sections 2.6 and 2.8) is making its impact in Sweden.

Norman Ginsburg

2.5 Hungary

More explicit hard-nosed opposition to Germany's stance has come from central European countries, particularly the Visegrad states – Czech Republic, Hungary, Poland and Slovakia. Hungary has led the way with explicit exclusionism – an authoritarian, barbed wire strategy, which may in part reflect the fact that in 2015 Hungary received the second largest number of 'migrants' per inhabitant, only bested by Sweden, and considerably more than Germany. But the Hungarian response also reflects the movement of its mainstream politics towards explicit racism and Islamophobia. Since 2010 the conservative coalition governments in Hungary have been dominated by the Fidesz party under the leadership of Viktor Orbán. Orbán has developed a popular nationalism with anti-Semitic undertones. He is

> master of a quasi-mystical oratory that constantly speaks of racial and cultural survival . . . marking out insiders and outsiders . . . whipping up fears about the Roma, Muslims and African migrants, and revulsion against the abject poor – all in the name of the Christian-national idea.
>
> (Fekete 2016: 2)

Popular sentiment sees Hungary as threatened by Western liberalism in general as well as 'Muslim jihadism and "the New York–Tel Aviv axis" (it is widely believed the latter is sending the former into Europe to weaken and subjugate it), not to mention "Gypsy criminality" . . . the Roma being "the biological weapon of global Jewry"' (Tamás 2015). However, it is important to note that, despite the prominence of Orbán and even worse the far right Jobbik Party, many Hungarians 'maintain their humanity' by supporting Roma citizens and refugees (Fekete 2016: 11).

One of the key factors explaining the rise of quasi-fascism in Hungary is the persistence of high levels of unemployment since the 'restructuring' of the economy after the end of communism in 1989. Over 30 per cent of jobs went in three years from 1989 to 1992. This precipitated massive emigration. The severe economic crisis in Hungary after 2008 brought another wave of emigration. In the two-year period 2013–15 '600,000 Hungarians (of a population of nine million) left the country for Britain and Germany, mostly young skilled workers and university graduates' (Tamás 2015). Tamás (2015) suggests that one of the reasons for Hungarian hostility to the present mass 'migration' from outside the EU is the phenomenon of 'competitive migration'. Hungarians do not want to be elbowed out of job opportunities in North West Europe, not least because the remittances from Hungarians working abroad are vital in sustaining its people and its economy. Such views are widely held across the former communist states in Central and Eastern Europe.

Towards the end of 2015 other Visegrad leaders were lining up behind Orbán, most notably Donald Tusk, the Polish President of the EU's European Council. In a newspaper interview he 'described Ms. Merkel's welcoming approach to migrants as "dangerous" and endorsed the view long promoted by

Mr. Orbán – that most of the asylum seekers entering Europe were not Syrians fleeing war, but economic migrants seeking jobs' (Higgins 2015). This is certainly one of the most distorted official constructions on the crisis, which brings us to the complex and contradictory role of the EU in the story.

2.6 The European Union (EU)

Most EU member state governments appear to be trying to keep the crisis at arm's length, unable to agree on sharing the burden with Germany, Sweden, Italy and Greece. Greece (together with Italy) is literally in the front-line in receiving would-be migrants from across the Aegean Sea. It has been threatened with expulsion from Schengen for not reinforcing the border adequately. This would leave it unable to move people on into the rest of the EU. Greece has experienced massive cuts in public social expenditure under EU austerity measures since 2010 and very high unemployment, and it has a comparatively small population (11 million). The pressures on Greece could become so fierce that the far right waiting in the wings could take a decisive advantage.

Without the demagoguery of Orbán, the British government has maintained a firm hostility to refugees during the crisis, refusing to accept more than small numbers, and in effect using the threat of leaving the EU as a means of silencing EU efforts to share the burden. 'From the outset the UK Government has been strongly opposed to proposals [from the EU] for mandatory relocation and resettlement schemes' (Gower and Smith 2015: 16). The government minister responsible for immigration insisted in July 2015 that the EU must ensure that refugees 'cannot travel further than their point of arrival and must return them without delay to their country of origin' (ibid.: 16).

Public discourse and policy making around political migration and asylum issues in Europe takes place almost entirely at the nation state level. Hence there is little public discussion at EU level, except in the European Parliament which has a low profile. The 2015 refugee crisis has brought the suspension of EU rules on asylum and of the Schengen passport-free zone alongside desperate efforts to 'share the burden'. Prior to 2015, the role of the EU was confined to supporting the management of the external border, and moving slowly towards common policies on asylum applications and equitable distribution of asylum seekers and refugees across the Union.

Regarding EU discourse on migrants from outside the EU, whatever their status – political, economic, undocumented, trafficked – the predominant con-struction has been exclusionary and restrictionist. For critics and some admirers this is encapsulated in the notion of 'Fortress Europe' – meaning the collective maintenance of a strong external border, while conceding some managed economic migration and some political migration for recognised refugees.

> For more than two decades now, the EU has been conducting the most extensive, sophisticated and far-reaching border enforcement programme in history . . . Militarised border patrols on land and sea; 400,000 police and border guards and the creation of a new European border agency Frontex;

computerised databases and surveillance technologies at the border; the 'externalisation' of the EU's border enforcement to neighbouring countries; quota-driven deportations; an escalating tempo of detention, immigration raids, identity checks and police harassment.

(Carr 2012: 1)

The financial cost of maintaining the fortress is impossible to estimate as most of the funding comes from individual member states. According to Amnesty (2014: 9)

the Directorate-General for Home Affairs of the European Commission allocated almost €4 billion for the period 2007–2013 under the Solidarity and Management of Migration Flows Programme (SOLID) to support member states' activities on asylum, integration, return of third country nationals and border control. Almost half of this was allocated for activities, equipment and technological infrastructure focusing on control of the external borders of the Schengen area. Just 17 per cent was allocated to support asylum procedures, reception services and the resettlement and integration of refugees.

This suggests a prioritisation of exclusion over support for migrants. The human cost of Fortress Europe has been documented by Carr (2015), Harding (2012) and Amnesty (2014). It has been estimated that from 2000 to 2013 over 23,000 people died in the attempt to reach Europe.

What social constructions of 'the problem' legitimate the physical construction and brutal reinforcement of the fortress? There are a number of strands here. First, there is the problem identified as 'illegal immigration' facilitated by 'people smugglers' and 'traffickers', 'criminals' who exploit the vulnerable, linked to the alleged criminality of refugees once they reach Europe's shores. De Giorgi (2010: 154) describes how 'in Europe in the last two decades the populist rhetoric of the war against immigration has been hegemonised by the myth of immigrant crime and of immigrants as a dangerous class'. This is

often framed in a racialized language that postulates self-evident links between some nationalities or ethnicities and specific types of criminal activity (e.g. Eastern Europeans and violent crime, Northern Africans and drug trafficking, sub-Saharan women and prostitution, Roma people and property crimes), fear of immigrant crime and deviance has been constantly amplified by political parties and mainstream media.

Essentially this transfers the label 'criminal' onto migrants themselves.

Another linked 'problem' concerns the 'securitisation' of migrants – the issue of migrants as a security risk, which became much greater after 9/11 of course. But even before 9/11 political scientists like Huysmans (2000: 751) had identified the development of the fortress as 'the social construction of migration into a security question'. Lahav (2013: 239–41) and Balzacq et al. (2015: 15–18) cite strong research evidence suggesting that, unsurprisingly, anti-migrant opinion and political discourse is closely linked with alleged security risks associated with migrants.

A third element, linked to securitisation and a wider threat to European/Judaeo-Christian culture, is that many migrants are Muslims. This is constructed in coded discourse about the alleged failures of some 'migrants' and some people of migrant heritage to integrate or assimilate into European culture and society. Perhaps the clearest example of this at a transnational, European level came in 2010/11. First, responding to the Sarrazin controversy (see section 2.3), in October 2010 the German Chancellor, Angela Merkel, told a Christian Democratic party meeting that

> the tendency had been to say, 'let's adopt the multicultural concept and live happily side by side, and be happy to be living with each other'. But this concept has failed, and failed utterly.

This was followed by the UK Prime Minister David Cameron's speech in Munich in February 2011 in which he said that 'multiculturalism had created segregated communities behaving in ways that run completely counter to our values'. Finally, a few days later the French President, Nicholas Sarkozy, declared on national TV that even the alleged, strongly integrationist multiculturalism of France had failed:

> The truth is that in all our democracies we've been too concerned about the identity of new arrivals . . . our Muslim compatriots should be able to live and practice their religion like anyone else . . . but it can only be a French Islam and not just an Islam in France.

These remarks by the leaders of the three most powerful EU states combine the construction of migrants as Muslim Others who either do not belong or must assimilate more deeply in European culture and society. This, of course, flies in the face of the successful integration of most Muslims into French, British and German societies. The responses of the three centre-right leaders are clearly responses to the rise of the far right and anti-immigrant populism in all three countries.

Another element in the construction of exclusionism at the EU level is that migrants and refugees are alleged to be a drain on the resources of the advanced welfare states, which lie at the heart of the European Social Model. Despite the solid evidence that migrants are net contributors to the welfare state through taxes and social insurance contributions, 'welfare chauvinism' has gained ground across the EU, particularly since the 2008 financial crisis and subsequent austerity measures. 'Welfare chauvinism' describes the notion that only members of the national community should benefit from the welfare state, particularly benefits for people of working age, but perhaps also extended to publicly funded provisions in housing, healthcare and social care, etc. The 'national community' is usually left undefined, but it customarily excludes migrants from other EU states and beyond. Welfare chauvinism is particularly prominent in the politics of the far right, but it also extends into the heart of the mainstream.

> Welfare chauvinism in its extreme is a preference for excluding immigrants from any welfare provision whatsoever. In weaker versions, it can stand for a preference for relegating immigrants to lower benefit levels or for employing relatively high barriers to inclusion.
>
> (Mewes and Mau 2013: 230)

Using the 2008 European Social Survey, van der Waal *et al.* (2013) suggest that welfare chauvinism in North West Europe is less virulent in five 'social democratic' states (Denmark, Finland, the Netherlands, Norway, Sweden) compared with five 'liberal'/'conservative' states (Ireland, UK, Belgium, France, Germany). As they admit, however, this is to some extent belied by the fact that Denmark has 'practically installed a two-tier welfare system, in which immigrants have less access to welfare benefits and services than the native population' (ibid.: 178). There has certainly been a recent upsurge in welfare chauvinism in Sweden (Norocel 2016) and Finland (Keskinen 2016), as well as Denmark (Jørgensen and Thomsen 2016).

One of the clearest and most recent examples of welfare chauvinism reaching the EU level was the British government's efforts to withdraw eligibility for tax credits and family benefits from workers migrating from other EU member states. This was one of the UK's four key conditions in the renegotiations of British EU membership in 2016. A compromise agreement was reached, which is now redundant in the light of the Brexit decision.

Putting all these strands together creates a powerful antidote to welcoming constructions, whether based on the economic needs for migrant workers or human-rights advocacy on behalf of refugees. Exclusionary constructions are not just articulated by the far right; they penetrate deep into the mainstream of European society and politics.

The absence of explicit EU discourse on refugees and other non-European migrants is in sharp contrast with discourse on labour migration *within* the fortress. It is worth examining in a little detail the positive social construction of migration for citizens of the member states. 'Free movement' of citizens of EU member states is one of the four fundamental freedoms underpinning the EU, the other three being the free movement of capital, goods and services – the essence of the 'single market'. In a speech in 2014 the then President of the European Commission (unelected head of the EU's civil service) José Manuel Barroso explained very clearly the key elements of this positive social construction of economic migration. First there are the economic benefits: 'Flexible and mobile labour markets help deal with economic changes and asymmetric shocks' (Barroso 2014: 8). This means, for example, that workers can move from declining economic regions with high unemployment to regions and industries where demand for labour is strong. Barroso suggests that this should not be a burden on the receiving states because 'those who move to work tend to put way more into the tax system than they take out in benefits' (ibid.: 8). He does not mention the more negative impact on the sending states. Recognising that the migration of less-skilled workers seeking lower paid jobs is often more controversial within the receiving states, he invokes universal human rights:

> There must be no first and second class citizens in Europe, where only the highly skilled are able to move and work freely while the low-skilled are not. This would be a kind of social stratification, which is against all the principles of fairness and against the principle of non-discrimination.
>
> (ibid.: 8)

Barroso reminded his audience in London that 'people's perception of free movement' was very positive; 'in all opinion polls across Europe, it consistently comes out as the one thing people see as one of the EU's greatest achievements' (ibid.: 8). This is certainly one of the most popular sides of the EU, particularly looked at from the point of view of poorer states with lesser economic opportunities such as the post-communist states in central Europe that joined during the 2000s. Barroso refers to the citizens of these states specifically as having been 'subject to totalitarian regimes, who could not even apply for a passport, who could not leave their own country. So freedom of movement is a great progress in human civilisation' (ibid.: 8).

2.7 Brexit

On June 23rd 2016 the UK electorate voted by a small margin to leave the EU. The 'social problems' associated with migration featured prominently in the 'Leave' campaign and were one of the key factors, probably the most significant one, in the success of that campaign. The result has been widely understood and constructed specifically as an explicit rejection of the 'free movement' of workers within the EU. At first glance this may seem perverse in view of the facts that net immigration into the UK over the last 15 years has been lower than in Italy, Spain, Germany and France, and that the UK has received the highest proportion of non-EU migrants among all the EU member states. However 'free movement' became associated for many with worsening socio-economic conditions in the UK since the financial crisis of 2008:

> Real wages fell sharply between 2008 and 2014, with those on low wages suffering the biggest falls. There is little evidence to suggest that EU immigration as opposed to a deep recession caused this, but in the popular mind there is a causal link between migrants and falling wages.
>
> (Tilford 2015: 1)

EU migration is also linked with the severe shortage of affordable housing and deteriorating health and schooling services. The collision between, on the one hand, social changes apparently linked to migration and, on the other hand, austerity cuts in the welfare state, increasing class inequalities and the growing

Norman Ginsburg

divide between 'north and south' in England manifested itself in the Brexit result. By in effect holding a referendum on EU immigration, the government also managed to give voice and legitimacy to long-held xenophobic sentiment in the UK. 'Complaining about Polish immigration is not seen as racist in the way complaining about black or Asian immigration is' (ibid.: 2) so 'free movement' has morphed with more covert racism towards refugees and non-European migrants. This came out most clearly with a UKIP (United Kingdom Independence Party) poster towards the end of the referendum campaign, which pictured a crowd of non-European refugees at the EU border. The poster was condemned by the official 'Leave' campaign, but the message had a wide resonance.

2.8 Conclusion

The present 'migrant crisis' has demonstrated very clearly the fault lines, dilemmas and divisions in European societies' approach to the question of immigration. We have contrasted 'welcoming', 'open borders', universal human-rights constructions with restrictionist, Fortress Europe, nationalistic constructions. This is a somewhat simplistic binary – there are clearly many constructions which compromise between these two poles. Indeed the 'liberal dilemma' consists in how to combine them somehow into coherent policy and discourse both at the EU level and in the individual member states. The scale of the present crisis has clearly made this extremely difficult at the EU level; the tentative moves towards a common European public discourse on immigration and asylum since the late 1990s have suffered a setback. Restrictionism, often with clear traces of Islamophobia and/or racism, seems to have become more prominent across the continent in the last two decades, demonstrated most clearly by the rise of anti-immigration populist politics, including but not confined to the far right. Yet 'welcoming' constructions have been bolstered by Chancellor Merkel's stand, and have much support across civil society, even though their voices are less strident, threatening and histrionic than those on the far right. It is widely understood that migration 'push' pressures are here to stay, fostered by Western foreign policy foolishness, climate change and increasing inequality between Europe and its neighbouring regions. The 'pull' pressures in the West of Europe are equally impressive – ageing societies with a demand for labour of many different kinds. The exclusionists cannot wish these away. Nor can they easily dismiss the moral obligations which underpin the 'welcoming' construction, the absence of which was bemoaned by Pope Francis on July 8th, 2013 on the Italian island of Lampedusa, which has received so many of those fleeing social chaos on the other side of the Mediterranean:

> We have lost a sense of responsibility for our brothers and sisters . . . The culture of comfort which makes us think only of ourselves, makes us insensitive to the cries of other people, makes us live in soap bubbles which, however lovely, are insubstantial . . . We have fallen into globalised indifference.

> (https://w2.vatican.va/)

The only moral and humane alternative, as Bauman (2015) says, is to

> reject the treacherous temptations of separation; indeed, making such separation unfeasible by dismantling the fences of 'asylum-seekers camps' and bringing the annoying differences, dissimilarities and self-imposed estrangements into a close, daily and increasingly intimate contact – hopefully resulting in a *fusion* of horizons instead of their induced yet self-exacerbating *fission*.

References

Abiri, E. (2000) 'The changing praxis of "generosity": Swedish refugee policy during the 1990s', *Journal of Refugee Studies* 13(1): 11–28.

Amnesty (2014) *The Human Cost of Fortress Europe*, London: Amnesty International.

Andersson, H.E. and Nilsson, S. (2009) 'Asylum seekers and undocumented migrants' increased social rights in Sweden', *International Migration* 49(4): 167–88.

Balzacq, T., Léonard, S. and Ruzicka, J. (2015) '"Securitization" revisited: Theory and cases', *International Relations* 30(4): 494–531.

Barroso, J.M. (2014) *Reforming Europe in a Changing World*, February 14th speech, London. http://europa.eu/rapid/press-release_SPEECH-14-131_en.htm; last accessed January 21st, 2017.

Bauman, Z. (2015) 'The migration panic and its (mis)uses', *Social Europe*. www.socialeurope.eu/2015/12/migration-panic-misuses/; last accessed January 21st, 2017.

BMI (2005) *Immigration Law and Policy*, Berlin: Bundesministerium des Innern (BMI, Federal Ministry of the Interior). www.bmi.bund.de/SharedDocs/Downloads/EN/Broschueren/Zuwanderungspolitik_und_Zuwanderungsrecht_en.pdf?_blob=publicationFile; last accessed January 21st, 2017.

Bosswick, W. (2000) 'Development of asylum policy in Germany', *Journal of Refugee Studies* 13(1): 43–60.

Bremmer, I. (2015) 'The refugee crisis – and the different ways European countries are dealing with it – has shown the EU's cracks', *Time Magazine*, September 11th.

Brochmann, G. (2014) 'Scandinavia', pp. 288–301, in Hollifield, J., Martin, P. and Orrenius, P. (eds) *Controlling Immigration: A Global Perspective*, Stanford (CA): Stanford University Press.

Brown, A. (2015) 'When Sweden shut its doors, it killed the dream of European sanctuary', *The Guardian*, November 27th.

Carr, M. (2012) 'The trouble with Fortress Europe' www.opendemocracy.net/matthew-carr/trouble-with-fortress-europe; last accessed January 21st, 2017.

Carr, M. (2015) *Fortress Europe*, London: Hurst.

Norman Ginsburg

De Giorgi, A. (2010) 'Immigration control, post-Fordism, and less eligibility', *Punishment and Society* 12(2): 147–67.

Fekete, L. (2016) 'Hungary: Power, punishment and the "Christian-national idea"', *Race & Class* 57(4): 39–53.

Foroutan, N. (2013) *Identity and (Muslim) Integration in Germany*, Washington, DC: Migration Policy Institute.

Fredlund-Blomst, S. (2014) 'Assessing immigrant integration in Sweden after the May 2013 riots', *Migration Policy Institute Online Journal*, January 16th. www.migrationpolicy.org/article/assessing-immigrant-integration-sweden-after-may-2013-riots; last accessed January 21st, 2017.

Gibney, M. (2004) *The Ethics and Politics of Asylum*, Cambridge: Cambridge University Press.

Gower, M. and Smith, B. (2015) *Migration Pressures in Europe*, London: House of Commons Library – Briefing Paper CBP 7210, September 8th.

Harding, J. (2012) *Border Vigils: Keeping Migrants Out of the Rich World*, London: Verso.

Higgins, A. (2015) 'Hungary's migrant stance: Once denounced, gains some acceptance', *New York Times*, December 20th.

Huggler, J. (2015) 'Refugees will change Germany', *Daily Telegraph*, September 8th.

Huysmans, J. (2000) 'The European Union and the securitization of migration', *Journal of Common Market Studies* 38(5): 751–77.

Jørgensen M. and Thomsen T. (2016) 'Deservingness in the Danish context: Welfare chauvinism in times of crisis', *Critical Social Policy* 36(3): 330–51.

Keskinen, S. (2016) 'From welfare nationalism to welfare chauvinism: Economic rhetoric, the welfare state and changing asylum policies in Finland', *Critical Social Policy* 36(3): 352–70.

Khosravi, S. (2009) 'Sweden: Detention and deportation of asylum seekers', *Race and Class* 50(4): 38–56.

Lahav, G. (2013) 'Threat and immigration attitudes in liberal democracies', pp. 232–53, in Freeman, G., Hansen, R. and Leal, D. (eds) *Immigration and Public Opinion in Liberal Democracies*, New York: Routledge.

Menz, G. (2013) 'European employers and the rediscovery of labour migration', pp. 105–23, in Jurado, E. and Brochmann, G. (eds) *Europe's Immigration Challenge*, London: IB Tauris.

Mewes, J. and Mau, S. (2013) 'Globalization, socio-economic status and welfare chauvinism: European perspectives on attitudes toward the exclusion of immigrants', *International Journal of Comparative Sociology* 54(3): 228–45.

Norocel, O. (2016) 'Populist radical right protectors of the *folkhem*: Welfare chauvinism in Sweden', *Critical Social Policy* 36(3): 371–90.

Pautz, H. (2005) 'The politics of identity in Germany: The *Leitkultur* debate', *Race and Class* 46(4): 39–52.

Piwoni, E. (2015) 'Claiming the nation for the people: The dynamics of representation in German public discourse about immigrant integration', *Nations and Nationalism* 21(1): 83–101.

Ramalingam, V. (2012) *The Sweden Democrats: Anti-immigration Politics and the Stigma of Racism*, Oxford: Working Paper 97, Centre on Migration, Policy and Society (COMPAS), Oxford University. www.compas.ox.ac.uk/2012/wp-2012-097-ramalingam_anti-immigration_politics_sweden/; last accessed January 21st, 2017.

Rydgren, J. (2004) 'Mechanisms of exclusion: Mechanisms of ethnic discrimination in the Swedish labour market', *Journal of Ethnic and Migration Studies* 30(4): 697–716.

Schierup, C.-U. (1990) '"The duty to work": The theory and practice of refugee policy in Sweden', *New Community* 16(4): 561–74.

Schierup, C.-U. and Ålund, A. (2011) 'The end of Swedish exceptionalism? Citizenship, neoliberalism and the politics of exclusion', *Race and Class* 55(1): 45–64.

Schierup, C.-U., Hansen, P. and Castles, S. (2006) *Migration, Citizenship and the European Welfare State*, Oxford: Oxford University Press.

Schierup, C.-U., Ålund, A. and Kings, L. (2014) 'Reading the Stockholm riots – A moment for social justice?', *Race and Class* 55(3): 1–21.

Schuster, L. (2003) *The Use and Abuse of Political Asylum in Britain and Germany*, London: Frank Cass.

Statistics Sweden (2014) *The Labour Market among Foreign Born 2005–2013*. www.scb.se/en_/Finding-statistics/Statistics-by-subject-area/Labour-market/Labour-force-surveys/Labour-Force-Survey-LFS/Aktuell-Pong/23272/Behallare-for-Press/374972/; last accessed January 21st, 2017.

Tamás, G.M. (2015) 'The meaning of the refugee crisis', *Open Democracy*, September 21st. www.opendemocracy.net/can-europe-make-it/g-m-tam%C3%A1s/meaning-of-refugee-crisis; last accessed January 21st, 2017.

Thränhardt, D. (2014) 'Commentary – Germany: From ideological battles to integration consensus', pp. 251–5, in Hollifield, J., Martin, P. and Orrenius, M. (eds) *Controlling Immigration: A Global Perspective*, Stanford, CA: Stanford University Press.

Tilford, S. (2015) 'Britain, immigration and Brexit', *CER Bulletin*, Issue 105, Centre for European Reform. www.cer.org.uk/sites/default/files/bulletin_105_st_article1.pdf; last accessed January 21st, 2017.

Van der Waal, J., De Koster, W. and Van Oorschot, W. (2013) 'Three worlds of welfare chauvinism? How welfare regimes affect support for distributing welfare to immigrants in Europe', *Journal of Comparative Policy Analysis: Research and Practice* 15(2): 164–81.

chapter 3

Migration and integration

Matt Scott

3.1 Introduction: Kondriatieff revisited

In recent years the dilemmas of the Syrian exodus have raised challenges not seen for seventy years, as the 'imagined community' (Anderson 2006) of Europe has struggled to come to terms with the scale of the problem. At the time of writing the media has been saturated with contrasting images including football crowds and concerned citizens extending a warm welcome, a dead Syrian child washed up on a Turkish beach off the coastal town of Bodrum, to Hungary's four-metre-high border fence spanning the 110 kilometre border with Serbia. There have been acute flows of refugees at other times in the past. However, the current situation and the measures taken in response are exceptional. A briefing by *The Economist* magazine (12 September 2015) notes that the world's insti-tutional approach, which was born in Europe seven decades ago, must now be revisited and that the continent must 'relearn its lessons'.

Whilst the millions that were displaced as result of World War Two do not match the hundreds of thousands currently seeking entry it is possible to discern certain symmetry to events; the Soviet economist Nikolai Kondriatieff, a victim of Stalin's purges, identified economic business cycles marked by 50–60 year bouts of crisis, which became known as Kondriatieff waves. Today it is con-ceivable that the European social problem of immigration is marked by a similar cataclysm. The German Chancellor seems to think so. Angela Merkel has claimed the surge of refugees was the biggest crisis to face the European Union (EU), more serious than the recent threat of a Greek departure and related questions about the stability of the euro. This view is reinforced by *The Economist* magazine (ibid.) which notes that the Geneva Conference and Refugee Convention marked a 'never again' moment in post war history. The consensus that defined a refugee as someone who had a 'well-founded fear of being persecuted' clearly applies to those fleeing Syria, Afghanistan, Eritrea and Libya. Yet these same people are met with a makeshift European policy response, marked by national differences that appear to deepen the crisis. The result is to place into question the viability of Europe itself as a coherent political entity.

Guy Standing (2014) locates the problem within the interpretation of rights to freedom of movement under Article 13 of the Universal Declaration of Rights, which upholds a right to leave a country (emigrate) but not to enter another country (immigrate). To Standing this is a 'recipe for leaving emigrants without rights anywhere and without protection by national laws' (ibid.: 4). He argues that the denial of rights to migrants are a part of a wider effect of globalisation whereby civil, political, cultural, social and economic rights are attenuated, even withdrawn, creating a subclass of citizen, a denizen, with a more limited range of rights. This redrawing of the meaning of citizenship calls into question not only what it means to be a citizen but also the functionality of the state. Just as the coherence of Europe as a political entity is being questioned, the same question hangs over individual governments if citizens lack protection and opportunities to flourish.

The controversy surrounding immigration is often reduced to instrumental terms – whether there is an overall gain or loss that arises. Whilst it might be argued that simple measurements cannot capture the complexity of social reality, the framing of popular understanding is inevitably drawn in this direction. In November 2014 academic research hit the headlines. A report on 'The Fiscal Effects of Immigration to the UK' (Dustman and Frattini 2014), published by the Royal Economic Society in *The Economic Journal* revealed that EU migrants contributed £4.96 billion more in taxes in the years to 2011 than the costs of their use of public services. The story departed from the conventional wisdom of our times which perceives immigration, Europe and European migration as a threat, rather than a potential social and economic advantage as suggested by the figures. In this sense the media firestorm that ensued typified the emotive and contradictory impulses at play when considering the topic. Immigration rages across the 'imagined community' of Europe as a fractious debate enforced by increasingly draconian laws and populism, where putative 'common sense' views (Isaacs *et al.* 2014: 15) simplify complex social forces. Each country provides its own nuance to this story. In Greece the Golden Dawn represent a fascist threat, whereby police brutality mixes with outright murder. In Germany the non-citizenship of Turkish guest workers, who may spend generations in the country, illustrates another facet of national unease and exclusion. More socially progressive Nordic states also seek to crack down, in ways that would have been inconceivable in more liberal times.

Since it is all but impossible to remain above the fray, my own standpoint is pro-immigration, built around greater levels of government-backed measures to invest and manage existing services. For the purposes of this chapter I will endeavour to reflect the range of views and social constructions as widely and accurately as possible whilst recognising the emotive and frequently extreme polarisation which makes an even-handed approach itself problematic.

Matt Scott

It is a quirk of our neoliberal era that whilst the economic benefits of immigration are consistently reported as favourable, the cluster of semi-federated states across Europe, that otherwise might increasingly defer to market wisdom, push back on this issue. There may be strong evidence, albeit fiercely contested (Collier 2013), supporting net economic gain but the wider social and political context has generated a number of perspectives and commentary, from the xenophobic to the multicultural, with an increasingly sceptical media narrative across Europe amplifying the insular political mood music.

Whilst migration is clearly recognisable as a social problem uniquely fashioned by the traditions, history and hence 'path dependency' of each nation state it will be argued that a double movement can be discerned, whereby forces of convergence play a decisive long-term role. The existence of multiple actors complicates the simplistic narratives of politicians and media outlets resulting in a gap between the shrill rhetoric of national defiance, the ensuing punitive policy responses and what actually happens. It is in its complexity that European migration can best be understood, as an evolving tension only partially managed, at one and the same time harnessing dynamic forces of national renewal, countering demographic decline and labour market shortages whilst simultaneously advancing questions of what it means to belong, of citizenship and welfare entitlements. Thus European migration is both problem and solution, and within this irreducibility creates the competing understandings of both Europe and European nations as they have come to know themselves, by defining themselves for and against, yet ultimately, inescapably part of a wider humanity. Hence European migration is a constant not an aberration of human history accompanying all manner of social, economic and technological change. But perhaps, in the twenty-first century, it has never been as pervasive or politically significant (Castles *et al.* 2014: 317).

This chapter looks at the way in which migration has been defined and the competing social constructions at play, drawing on recent history and policy responses, with special reference to a range of commentators and contemporary examples. It will be argued that at the heart of debates on migration there are always the centrifugal and centripetal forces of exclusion and integration. But if the analysis remains at the superficial level of push–pull theory, it risks being 'a platitude at best' (Skeldon 1990: 125–6); it is vital that we consider a range of factors and detail how they critically interact with each other. We need to go beyond functionalist and neoclassical migration theories which have privileged the overall balancing of factors, and the narrowly cast rationality of the migrant, to a richer sense of the identity, social networks and agency that sustains the migratory process. This complex social dynamic has given new impetus in an era of rampant globalisation, leading to an explosion of transnational communities (Vertovec 1999). Likewise transnationalism is characterised by initiatives from above and below, for example from multinationals, whose wealth is often larger than nation states, and at the other end of the spectrum, from grassroots neighbourhood activity and increasingly from virtual networks. This has important implications for national identity and politics and is itself a form of agonistic pluralism (Mouffe 1999). On this reading agonistic pluralism is an inescapable part of the political process, which can never achieve a fully inclusive rational consensus but may also deepen democratic practice. Thus pluralism, and the conflict it engenders, may have positive uses. In the case of migration, such agonism mobilises passions which adhere to competing social constructions that are inherently conflictual with no once-and-for-all resolution but instead a tension that is the hallmark of pluralist democracy.

3.2 Definitions

There are two terms that require immediate attention in order to illuminate migration as a European social problem, both of which are far from straightforward. Europe is both geographically and politically contested, to the extent that Jean Monet, often described as the father of modern Europe, speaking in the immediate aftermath of World War Two proclaimed that 'Europe has never existed, one has genuinely to create Europe' (quoted in Davies 1997: 10). On the other hand migration is frequently confused with related terms, including asylum and labour movement within the member countries of the EU. Thus both terms are inherently malleable.

Europe is usually understood as consisting of western and central Europe, including countries outside the EU but not extending to Russia, although the credentials of Russia as European have been considered and Russia, including as the Soviet Union, has shaped Europe, never more so than in the previous century. Thus ambiguity about the precise parameters of Europe should be sustained, mirroring the uncertainties of migration that recur rather than neatly revolve themselves.

Europe is likewise often taken as shorthand for the EU and yet its semi federated structure lacks the political boundaries of similar trade rivals, notably the USA and China and this economic partnership with its partial supranational dimension is at the heart of many concerns, with parties in many nations seeking to 'leave Europe'. Not all European countries are part of the EU, so Europe as a term must extend beyond it, and yet the EU at times eclipses all other categories, and thus becomes a defining institutional term.

Migration as it is properly understood can only refer to countries outside the EU, given the rights of free movement of all EU citizens, and yet this distinction is rarely made in contemporary discourse, leading to a general assumption of migrants as coming from any other nation. Third Country Nationals, those from outside the EU, therefore represent a constituency of migrant. This is a clear and important distinction that acknowledges the rights of free movement between those within and those outside of the EU. Within this category there are important differentiations including labour, family and irregular migration and also asylum and refugee flows. The Geneva Convention of 1951 enshrines the right for protection for this latter group and hence refugees and asylum seekers should be seen as outside the coverage of migration, given the emergency – typically armed conflict – that removes choice. In popular parlance, however, migration frequently confuses these important distinctions and in the minds of many concerned citizens the social problem of migration becomes coterminous with EU labour mobility, asylum and refugees.

3.3 Post-war immigration regimes

Over the centuries prior to World War Two Europeans moved outward, 'conquering, colonising and settling in lands elsewhere on the globe' (Castles *et al.* 2014: 102). Amidst the rubble of reconstruction rapid economic growth took hold, attracting growing numbers of migrants often from former colonies and elsewhere. Joppke (1999) has suggested three different models: settler regimes, exclusionary regimes and postcolonial regimes by way of delineating patterns of migration. The former was comparatively at ease with long-term settlement, typified by new world countries but less prevalent in Europe. In contrast exclusionary regimes emphasised the temporary nature of the arrangement with European examples including Germany, Austria and Switzerland, each with their own guest worker programmes, premised on ethnic separation. Whereas postcolonial regimes were also deeply racialised and proactively recruited workers, in countries such as France, the UK and the Netherlands the link with former colonies delivered citizenship.

These regimes are 'ideal types' whose relevance has become less pronounced as the memory of the colonial era grows more distant and the world market moves on. In terms of chronology Castles *et al.* (2014) discerned three successive phases. From 1945 to the early 1970s there was a phase of rapid growth. This was followed by a second phase which saw a sharp interruption of growth and migration and the adoption of policies of deregulation, flexible labour and privatisation. Migrants who had initially been exhorted to take up jobs found themselves without work but often remained resident and increasingly brought families over to share their lives, as the arrangement became more fixed. The service sector gained prominence throughout the 1980s, with opportunities for both high- and low-skilled migrants. The fall of the Berlin Wall (1989) opened up Central and Eastern Europe as a new wave of migration ensued. By the mid-1990s, a third phase of migration was identifiable where migrants from Eastern Europe were joined by those from Africa and South America. These new forms of migration primarily involved migrant workers meeting labour needs during the economic booms of the 1990s and 2000s but also featured growing irregular migration that was both economic and political in nature. As numbers of those claiming asylum rose, from the mid-1990s EU member states more actively collaborated to deter settlement. During this time, the Fortress Europe epithet took hold and has remained a feature ever since. Despite the 2008 global economic crisis labour migration has generally continued in many countries.

3.4 Europe: EU treaties

European migration is regulated and administered by a unique overarching framework of policy: EU treaties. These structures define migration in routine and often mundane ways, albeit with heavy criticism from both the populist media and human rights groups, on the one hand for failing to address concerns of 'swamping' (*The Guardian* 26 October 2014), on the other, for demeaning and degrading treatment at odds with human dignity. An example of the latter is Amnesty International's recent highlighting of instances of abuse in Cyprus which exploited EU laws, forcibly separating mothers from their young children (Amnesty 2014). Amidst an increasingly sceptical climate of opinion European migration is often presented as an issue on which nation states are powerless to act in the face of supranational legislative structures, by EU treaties that inform and trump national measures. In fact the paradox of Europe's borders is that their administration is constantly shifting. Amidst a raft of EU legislation there are multiple levels of policy setting and intensive cooperation, where sovereignty bargains are often struck. The same nations that protest about an erosion of sovereignty will at other times use it as a bargaining chip, hence the need for dissonance between words and actions.

EU immigration policies can be traced back to the 1985 Schengen Agreement, originally signed between five member states (Belgium, France, Luxembourg, the Netherlands and West Germany) to gradually abolish common border controls. Whilst free movement of people had been a core part of the original Treaty of Rome (1957), border controls still remained a point of contention with little progress made until Schengen sought to harmonise arrangements amongst a smaller grouping, which has since grown – covering a population of over 400 million, including twenty-six states, some of whom are not EU members.

The clarification of free movement and harmonisation of labour markets was followed by a focusing of attention on social concerns, such as the Maastricht Treaty (1992) and in particular the Social Chapter, which was drafted as the Social Charter of Fundamental Workers Rights by the Commission of the European Communities. This included freedom of movement, working conditions and social protection in order to ensure consistency and best practice across the EU. Alongside the Charter, there was a Social Action Programme which consisted of policy initiatives necessary to implement the Charter's aims. This met with further changes in June 1997 via the Treaty of Amsterdam. By way of indicating how social and economic considerations meshed together and the perils for policy making that ensued, one of the rationales for the Chapter was to avoid the competitive advantages secured by individual countries by operating a less generous social policy or less regulated labour market, dubbed 'social dumping', leading to exported unemployment. The implementation of the harmonisation of social labour markets has often clashed with national sentiment as the practicality of what citizenship actually means is scrutinised for migrants and Third Country Nationals alike.

The Lisbon Treaty, ratified in December 2009 is the most recent development of already existing provisions aimed at creating a common migration policy since the Amsterdam Treaty of 1999. The detail of operations can be seen in the Tampere, Hague and Stockholm Action Plans, from 1999–2014, where the EU plays a key role in setting the migration agenda and hence realising convergence of policy across European nations. Prior to this the Maastricht Treaty of 1992 did much to forge a common political identity, building broader citizenship rights and to which the Treaty of Amsterdam added rights of freedom, security and justice. Whilst the 1999 EU Council in Tampere stressed the positive role of partnerships that promoted human and political rights, fair treatment and full application of the Geneva Convention, it was also accompanied by Frontex – the European Agency for Management of External Borders. Frontex typifies the fortress aspect of EU policy, gathering intelligence via Eurosur, the European border surveillance system. Ruben Andersson (2014: 96–7) writes that Eurosur 'created new battles along new fronts' and rather than decentralising powers tended to play 'an increasingly pivotal role at Europe's external borders, appropriating the data dutifully fed into the system by border guards'.

3.5 Inside and outside: integration and exclusion

The salience of integration and exclusion has been touched upon in the previous section on recent iterations of EU policy. From this we begin to see the social problem of European immigration become organised around two foci: border and integration issues. The boundaries of Europe are at once porous and permeable, given the EU commitment to open borders within the EU member states, yet more frequently carceral and exclusionary to non-European countries, notably African and Asian ones. Thus the epithet 'Fortress Europe' is often used to describe the wider European stance on immigration indicative of resistance and barriers, whereas 'integration' is seen as a twin strategy which seeks to ameliorate cultural differences that might otherwise become divisive and hence socially undesirable. Immigrants are encouraged to 'fit in', to adapt and adopt a recognisably new identity redolent of the host country.

Competing constructions: the reluctant criminal?

Migration is often perceived to threaten established social norms, to destabilise or undermine the homeland, its traditions and institutions. Real and imagined threats are constructed around issues of crime, terrorism, disease, welfare, jobs and an existential loss of identity. Whilst there is little doubt over the misery visited on many outside Europe due to civil wars, extreme poverty and environmental catastrophe, this is no guarantee of refugee and asylum status, which may be either denied outright, interminably delayed or be highly conditional. A popular discourse asserting 'common sense' constructions of this reality often feature in parts of the media, framing such issues as fundamentally insoluble, and hence advocate that 'charity begins at home'. Irregular migration arises due to illegal forms of entry which may also extend to legitimate migrants whose visa or related documents have lapsed and hence become over-stayers. Irregular, illegal and undocumented migration came to prominence across western European countries in the 1980s; however, whilst laws are broken, the factors causing transgression have a tragic dimension. One story amongst many is of a cargo ship which set sail from the port of Tartus in Syria on 1 October 2014, which was abandoned by its crew on 2 January 2015 off the coast of southern Italy, in dangerous seas, having acquired 450 migrants, many of whom were Syrian refugees smuggled on board what was termed a 'ghost ship'. A few days previously 800 migrants on a Moldavian registered ship were rescued by Italian lifeguards under similar circumstances. In this way people smugglers gamble with the lives of desperate people seeking to effect irregular migration. Since the start of the Syrian war in March 2011 an estimated 9 million Syrians have been displaced, with over 3 million fleeing to neighbouring countries (Turkey, Lebanon, Jordan and Iraq). One BBC journalist, Richard Hamilton ('Europe's ethical dilemma over migrants', BBC 2015), noting the reluctance of many governments (including the British Foreign Office) to support search and rescue operations that would only encourage migrants, asked 'is Europe turning its back on the migrants?' (ibid.).

By definition irregular migration is defined by the terms set out for legitimate migration and the reliance on cheap and flexible labour, but is also conflicted by concerns about work and welfare. The irregular migrant cannot fulfil the terms of entry and will lack valid documents, including visas, and be without secure residence or job. Boswell and Geddes (2011: 131) note that it is important to 'identify migrant agency within debates about irregular flows'. Whilst some migrants are 'horribly exploited' others make a 'conscious decision in order to seek a better life' (ibid.). Several commentators have noted that migration operates as a business or industry where smugglers and authorities compete with one another either on the margins or outside the law, and is underpinned by strong social ties and familial networks. In the case of trafficking sex workers and other forms of enslavement personal agency is clearly diminished; although bound up in the same effort to thwart state law, they cannot be considered as calculated acts of economic opportunism or advancement, yet are invariably bound up in the same tangle of enforcement and criminal constellations.

The migrant as terrorist

In the wake of the 11 September 2001 attacks, with repercussions in Europe including the 11 March 2004 Madrid train bombings, the 7 July 2005 London bombings and a number of other incidents and foiled plots, the need for greater precautionary and proactive measures to manage risk were embraced. It is important to note that such terrorist attacks were invariably not perpetrated by migrants. However, they did contribute to negative constructions and hostility towards migrant individuals and communities. In 2002 a report written on behalf of the European Monitoring Centre on Racism and Xenophobia noted that

> Islamic communities and other vulnerable groups have become targets of increased hostility since 11 September. A greater sense of fear among the general population has exacerbated already existing prejudices and fuelled acts of aggression and harassment in many European Member States.
>
> (2002: 5)

Matt Scott

Amidst a climate of fear, terrorism generated a form of moral panic (Cohen 2011), though of a different order to many contemporary panics. Migrants became linked with this hazard in the public mind, far beyond the relatively small networks of individuals thought to be involved, as media coverage cued a cascade of ever stricter policy responses (Tirman 2004; Huysmans 2006). And yet others have suggested the approach has been more nuanced, with governments adopting a more considered and cautious approach, resisting the securitisation of migration policies (Boswell 2007) and focusing on the value of social cohesion, diversity and trade.

Securitisation and surveillance

Whilst the knee jerk rush to exclude, contain and control migrants can easily be overstated, it is harder to escape the sense of heightened surveillance which, as understood by the work of Foucault (1977), adds depth to the concept of securitisation. Andersson (2014: Chapter 6) vividly describes the Ceuta and Melilla migrant camps as 'gaps in the migration circuit, in which a regime, seemed to regulate migrants as a population while disciplining them as bodies' (ibid.: 215). These camps house migrants seeking entry into Europe, based in what are both free ports and autonomous cities of Spain, located on the north coast of Africa. They can be characterised as 'the observatory of the enclave – the turnstiles and camp cards, the patrols and surveillance cameras. Reprieve but no escape . . . a world of multiple fences' (ibid.: 212). Yet Andersson notes the 'Foucauldian view . . . of discipline preparing irregular migrants for their marginal role in European labour markets' is only able to project power 'unevenly and imperfectly' (ibid.: 238). Foucault (1977) famously adopted Bentham's panopticon, a circular building where inmates could be observed by a single watcher, as extended now to society at large, in armies, schools, hospitals, factories and, in the context of European migration, detention centres. However, rather than assume such power is absolute and all-seeing it is more likely to have only partial success in its ability to control and exclude.

The migrant as health risk

As well as being portrayed as 'criminals' and 'terrorists' migrants are sometimes feared to be harbouring disease, and given a specifically pathological construction that threatens public health. Tuberculosis and HIV/AIDS are linked to poverty both within and beyond the EU, as the European Academies Science Advisory Council has pointed out in their statement on the impact of infectious diseases in Europe (EASAC 2006). Whilst unable to draw on consistent data sets the Council noted that migrants were a vulnerable group and hence timely access to health services was vital. However, given the fortress mentality such a priority was likely to be obstructed by exclusionary practices. The irony is that many migrants frequently go on to work in health care, often in the more low paid roles, and hence prop up a vital service that might otherwise cease to function.

At its most blatantly prejudicial, the health concerns of migration are elided with overt racism. The Far Right has long deployed rhetoric that has described migrants as a pestilent swarm. Under the Nazi regime Germany identified the Jewish 'race' in especially virulent terms and Neo-Nazis across Europe have continued to adopt thuggery and racist rhetoric. In the May 2012 national elections the Greek neo fascist party Golden Dawn ran on the slogan 'so we can rid our land of filth'. In the 2014 European Elections it won 9.4 per cent of the vote, even with its leadership in prison.

The migrant as threat to welfare and work

Simply put, migration is often motivated by the possibility of accessing work, typically at a higher rate of remuneration. Around one-third of the world's 86 million transnational migrant workers reside in Europe, including EU nationals and Third Country Nationals, many in low-skilled jobs. Labour migration is itself very diverse, ranging from high to low skills and from short-term to long-term stays. High-skilled migrants have typically travelled to Belgium, Denmark, Ireland, Luxembourg, Poland and Sweden whereas those with low skills have travelled to Austria, Germany, Spain and Greece. Likewise labour migration is sectorally specific; it is concentrated around a range of forms of employment, and is also gendered. Likewise it is spatially specific, located in urban or rural areas and may be regulated by a work permit or 'green card'.

The case for labour migration is often made most powerfully by economists who argue that economic growth should be the paramount concern, and workers who are willing to do dirty, difficult or dangerous jobs ensure the labour market functions better. The success of the West in driving up living standards resulting in an ageing population is a further strain that requires extra human resources. This is one key example where migrant workers improve public finances by working in health care. Marx recognised the tendency for capitalism to seek out flexible labour that could be conscripted by the owners of capital and described migrants as a reserve army of labour, willing to move to access jobs. One immediate issue arises when migrants therefore compete with indigenous workers, whose jobs are consequently at risk from people often willing to work for less remuneration.

Another alleged threat related to work is the entitlement it bestows in accessing welfare benefits and the fear that migrants take up benefits without making a contribution or paying their way. Whilst there is evidence that migrants are less likely to take up benefits than the indigenous population, the perception that they cynically exploit a nation's hospitality in order to live on benefits, which is largely a pernicious myth, is widely believed. This has coincided and arguably contributed to a weakening of support for aspects of the welfare state (Castles and Schierup 2010: 283–7). The degree to which access to benefits should be conditional is played out not only in terms of indigenous populations who might otherwise 'game' the system but also migrants who might be similarly tempted. The term 'welfare' or 'benefit tourists' was coined in the 1990s with particular political application to the perceived threat from the enlargement of the EU in 2004, and led to benefit restrictions in a number of countries, despite evidence that migrants tended to pay their way (Timmins 2009).

3.6 Family migration

Family migration has become more pronounced in recent years across Europe as migrant workers, typically men, seek to reunite their families. Since the 1970s this form of immigration has contributed to a significant proportion of the overall numbers and particularly challenged liberal states who privilege the rights of individuals and families. Migrant children, husbands and wives are often protected in international law and by many national laws and this entitlement can be exercised in order to bring families together, thus further embedding one aspect of integration.

From the mid-1950s the West German government began to recruit foreign workers with recruitment offices set up in Mediterranean countries in order to meet the demands of industrial growth. German employers had to pay a fee and provide accommodation and the arrangement was seen as temporary, staying for short periods. Labour and residence permits were granted for finite time periods, valid only for specific jobs and areas. Migration of dependants was discouraged along with a range of regulations via bilateral agreements signed between West Germany and migrant home countries: first Italy, then Spain, Greece, Turkey, Morocco, Portugal, Tunisia and Yugoslavia, with figures reaching 2.6 million by 1973. Although workers were brought in groups with the expectation of a rapid return, longer-term settlement took place, even though citizenship was frequently withheld. This led to criticisms both in terms of social justice and the denial of human rights, including the rights of families and children, but also the need to ensure integration of de facto communities. Although strongly associated with Germany, both before and after reunification, formal guest worker programmes also arose in Belgium, Holland, Sweden, Norway, Denmark and Finland.

Citizenship

Silverman (1992) notes the foreigner is no longer from somewhere else but is from here, a colleague at work, a neighbour in the same flats. It becomes harder to sustain rigid identities in an era of economic liberalisation and globalisation, where labour mobility is on hand to meet demographic shortfalls and political instability in other parts of the world and has immediate impact. The citizen is a hybrid with whom legal and political frameworks have yet to catch up. The citizen may be someone born in the country, with relatives or increasingly seen as worthwhile – a South African millionaire or Russian oligarch. Thus citizenship becomes conditioned by net worth with the corollary that those not contributing, who claim rights such as benefits, without working and paying taxes, are often denied citizenship and residency.

Both at the national and European level this fragile concept with its tenuous constructions can act as an inclusionary or exclusionary force. Kleinman refers to EU citizenship as a 'weak and nebulous concept' (2002: 201) more bound up in rhetoric than legal and social reality. On one level there is no European 'state' in which citizenship can be placed, but increasingly the evolving policies frame rights and responsibilities. Whether within the EU or outside it citizenship is therefore not only a matter of national definition, which is the dominant factor, underlining the path dependency of each state, but also informed by the policy convergence of the EU.

T H Marshall (1950) made the point that citizenship implies not only civil and political rights such as freedom of speech and the right to vote but also social rights, which increasingly came to the fore in the twentieth century and which more recently have seen a push back from neoliberals who have targeted a culture of dependency and passivity. Thus migrants' access or exclusion from citizenship and its attendant rights has become part of a wider debate about the meaning and merits of welfare as a form of social protection and entitlement.

3.7 Integration revisited

In September 2010 the French Senate voted 246–1 in favour of a ban on face-covering Islamic veils in public, on the basis that it encouraged citizens to 'live together'. The ban was upheld by judges at the European Court of Human Rights (ECHR) in 2014. The Belgian government introduced a similar ban in 2011 and was party to the French defence arguing that the laws were aimed at 'helping everyone to integrate'. Isabelle Niedlispacher, representing the Belgian government declared both the burqa and niqab were 'incompatible' with the rule of law. She added 'It's about social communication, the right to interact with someone by looking them in the face and about not disappearing under a piece of clothing' (*The Guardian* 1 July 2014). Other neighbouring countries have eschewed such measures that intrude into private life and traditionally protected freedoms of religion and expression but may insist on other disciplines that imperfectly inscribe national belonging. The UK citizenship tests to identify national dishes and sporting heroes frequently defeat a majority of the indigenous population yet the innovation introduced by New Labour in 2005 been retained by David Cameron, despite his own difficulties in answering a set of the same questions whilst in the US on the David Letterman Show (*The Guardian* 27 September 2012).

Whilst integration is widely understood to be desirable, the practical means of categorising it continue to challenge administrations keenly aware of wider public concerns as evidenced by the rise of populist political parties across Europe. In various forms immigration is greeted with a measure of defensiveness and hostility: if immigrants cannot be kept out they must become more recognisably indigenous. Yet also within the more recognisably unwelcoming stance there exists a subset of views that embrace immigration as a means of cultural richness, alongside economic vitality. The proponents of multiculturalism and cosmopolitanism emphasise the undesirability, in the face of globalisation, of retreating behind national borders (Gilroy 2000; Parekh 2002; Madood 2012).

Matt Scott

Managed migration

The fortress and the open borders within Europe can be seen as a balancing act, which each country uniquely manages, seeking to assuage fears and secure prosperity. Rob Sykes writes (Sykes and Alcock 1998: 256) that 'it is not impossible that both a European 'fortress' excluding 'outsiders' and a system of internally-focused policies for the benefit of ethnic minority EU citizens may be coupled together'. Boswell and Geddes (2011: 225) note that EU policy is underpinned by 'competing and contradictory interests', thus policy making and delivery is rarely wholly transparent or rational. What Pressman and Wildavsky (1982) identified as policy failure, a refrain frequently echoed by many commentators, invites us to write of the whole of migration policy-making as irredeemably and systemically flawed. Joppke (1998) describes a challenge to state power, noting the clash between migration and sovereignty in the 'thwarting of formal law making authority' (ibid.: 267) but seeing 'legal constraints in combination with obligations' (ibid.: 282) as driving European states to accept immigration. However, more recently theorists have asserted an increasingly subtle interpretation. Rather than politicians and officials being powerless they have adapted to irreconcilable demands. Nils Brunsson (2003) discerned a process of 'talk', 'decision' and 'action' whereby each stage could be decoupled and hence that policy making should not be seen as uniform, seamless or linear. If talk or rhetoric was designed to appeal to different constituents then implementation also saw a range of interests come to the fore, albeit ones of a less populist hue. It was not that policy making was simply messy but that it sought to broker and resolve conflicting pressures behind closed doors in ways that were perhaps necessarily opaque, given the reluctance of public figures to own up to crafting mundane compromises. Thus Hall (1984) notes a tendency towards 'deliberate malintegration' and what Sykes and Alcock note can be a 'rational approach to unrealistic demands' (1998: 48).

Foucault (1977) understood the polyvalence of power, including the possibility for resistance as well as entrapment through micro disciplines, extended across society, in armies, schools, hospitals, factories and, in the context of European migration, detention centres and the work of Frontex. The disciplinary gaze, most obviously typified by CCTV cameras in public spaces, spans a range of administrative technology that is able to generate a form of social quarantine. But it is perhaps in his work on governmentality, taken up by Rose (1999) where the State appears to withdraw, with citizens left to regulate themselves, and scrutinise their identity and conduct as a form of decentralised governance, where migrants may struggle to attain levels of reflexivity as the price of entry.

An uncertain convergence

Each European country has its own historical understandings that have traditionally shaped its response to migration so that, despite the overarching EU framework, national laws and institutional arrangements have a decisive bearing resulting in different integration regimes for migrants across Europe (Carmel 2012: 36). The precise balance between path dependency and a wider convergence is open to debate but the fact that there is interplay between endogenous and exogenous factors is undeniable. Each European country is both the product of its own history and its political institutions, which have produced unique responses to migration alongside discernible regional similarities.

For example, the new immigration countries of Portugal, Spain and also Greece have seen vast levels of emigration tip back. Between 1850 and 1950 3.5 million Spaniards sought work overseas with 1.5 million migrating to Argentina. However since 2000 the trend has reversed, with Spain's population rising by 12 per cent due to immigration, with large numbers from South America. Likewise movement east to west has arisen in recent years from Romania and Bulgaria. The movement of return from overseas including from former colonies is also reflected in Portugal, long a country of net migration. Unlike Germany, Portugal has embraced family migration with this category featuring in 62 per cent of all permanent migration according to OECD research in 2006, with Germany scoring 26 per cent. Both Spain and Portugal also experience another variant of migration – sunset migration, whereby retirees from colder European climates prioritise more congenial weather.

3.8 Conclusion: migration, poverty and globalisation

It is possible to view worsening poverty as one of the most salient issues with regard to migration. In order to escape hardship and poverty migrants more frequently arrive at the 'lower end of the labour market with few prized skills, who have to fight for jobs with immigrants, can lose out by being made to accept lower wages, poorer working conditions and higher chances of unemployment' (Chang 2014: 439). Inequality ensues and with this a sense of grievance that can feed numerous constructions, enabling what Freire (1970) identified as horizontal forms of violence, violence against ones neighbours, peers or class rather than an effective challenge of the underlying structural causes that promote and maintain such unequal conditions. Ha-Joon Chang notes that

> free market economists wax lyrical about the benefits of open borders . . . [b]ut there is an economic transaction they don't talk about in the same way – immigration, or cross border movement of people . . . [they] do not even seem to realise that they are being inconsistent when they advocate free movement of everything except people.

> (2014: 436)

Whilst the global market has tended to exert a homogenising influence, social problems go far beyond the study of economics (Isaacs *et al.* 2014). One underlying feature, however, when considering the social problem of European migration is the institutional response initiated by a European Community

Matt Scott

(now EU) that was created to facilitate trade, alongside other post-war concerns. The post-war labour market demand caused economic migration to soar, and subsequent booms and recessions have been linked to clear cycles of increasing and decreasing immigration rates (Castles *et al.* 2014: 123). The commodification of migrant labour coupled to a highly segmented market that demanded a range of skills has meant a highly dynamic, interdependent and symbiotic relationship has evolved.

Whilst inequalities are generated within Europe, the darker side of this arrangement is a disregard of the turmoil at the edges of the frontiers, in Libya and Syria for example. Chang writes that with regard to the countries of Europe, 'immigrants add to cultural diversity, which may stimulate both the natives and immigrants into being more creative in bringing new ideas, new sensitivities and new ways of doing things' (2014: 439) thus going beyond a narrow economic frame to encompass wider cultural dynamism.

In a recent interview in the *New Statesman* (10–16 June 2016) Kofi Annan, former UN secretary general, argued with regard primarily to the Syrian crisis, that 'a community of 500 million people could have absorbed one to two million refugees' and that 'smaller and less prosperous nations have done much more' – that it need not be such a divisive social problem. He noted that the forces of globalisation 'cannot be dealt with by one country alone' but require 'nations to join together'. Dani Rodrik (2011) has argued that the challenges of globalisation generate the need for trade-offs which are presented in the form of a 'trilemma' whereby only two of three outcomes (1. economic integration, 2. national sovereignty, 3. democratic politics) are ever wholly achievable. The social problem of European migration continues to be ever more central to the relative arguments for and against each of these areas. Whereas Annan noted that the EU arose 'from the rubble of two world wars' and argued that retrenchment in national sovereignty risked the 'peace and prosperity of Europeans', the contentious nature of European migration has seen a questioning of the benefits of openness and, with it, the sense that the role of the EU itself, and the 'imagined community' of Europe, is at a crossroads.

Bibliography

Amnesty International (2014) www.amnesty.org/en/news/cyprus-abusive-detention-migrants-and-asylum-seekers-flouts-eu-law-2014-03-18, accessed 5 January 2015.

Amnesty International (2015) *The Human Cost of Fortress Europe* www.amnesty.org/en/library/asset/EUR05/001/2014/en/48cb6136-cefc-4fd0-96cd-cd43b46eb5a8/eur050012014en.pdf, accessed 5 January 2015 (no longer available).

Anderson, B (2006) *Imagined Communities: Reflections on the Origins and Spread of Nationalism* London: Verso.

Andersson, R (2014) *Illegality, Inc. Clandestine Migration and the Business of Bordering Europe* Oakland, CA: University of California Press.

BBC (2015) www.bbc.co.uk/news/world-europe-30660777, accessed 22 January 2017.

Boswell, C (2007) 'Migration Control in Europe after 9/11: Explaining the Absence of Securitisation', *Journal of Common Market Studies*, 45(3), 589–610.

Boswell, C and Geddes, A (2011) *Migration and Mobility in the European Union* Basingstoke: Palgrave MacMillan.

Brunsson, N (2003) *The Organisation of Hypocrisy: Talk, Decision and Action in Organisations*, 2nd edn, Copenhagen Business School Press.

Carmel, E (2012) 'Migration Governance in the EU', *Journal of Poverty & Social Justice* 20(1), 31–9.

Castles, S and Schierup, C (2010) Ch. 19, in Castles, F, Leibfried, S, Lewis, J, Obinger, H and Pierson, C (eds) *Oxford Handbook of the Welfare State* Oxford: Oxford University Press, 278–91.

Castles, S, De Haas, D and Miller, M J (2014) *The Age of Migration*, 5th edn, Basingstoke: Palgrave MacMillan.

Chang, H J (2014) *Economics: The User's Guide* London: Penguin.

Cohen, S (1972) *Folk Devils and Moral Panics: The Creation of Mods and Rockers*, 3rd edn, London: Routledge.

Cohen, S (2011) *Folk Devils and Moral Panics* Abingdon, Oxon: Routledge.

Collier, P (2013) *Exodus: Immigration and Multiculturalism in the 21st Century* London: Allen Lane.

Davies, N (1997) *Europe: A History* London: Pimlico.

Dominiczak, P (26 October 2014) 'Towns in the UK are "Swamped" by EU Migrants, Cabinet Minister Warns', *Daily Telegraph*.

Dustman, C and Frattini, T (2014) 'The Fiscal Effects of Immigration to the UK', *The Economic Journal* 124 (Feature Issue), F565–8.

The Economist (Magazine) (12 September 2015) Briefing, The Syrian Exodus.

European Academies Science Advisory Council (EASAC) (2006) 'Impact of Migration of Infectious Diseases in Europe' (statement) www.easac.eu/fileadmin/PDF_s/reports_statements/Migration.pdf, accessed 5 January 2015.

European Monitoring Centre on Racism and Xenophobia (2002) 'Summary Report on Islamophobia in the EU after 11 September 2001' http://fra.europa.eu/sites/default/files/fra_uploads/199-Synthesis-report_en.pdf, accessed 5 January 2015.

Fassman, H and Münz, R (1994) *European Migration in the Late Twentieth Century* Aldershot: Edward Elgar Publishing.

Foucault, M (1977) *Disciple & Punish* London: Penguin.

Freire, P (1970) *Pedagogy of the Oppressed* London: Penguin.

Ghatak, S and Showstack Sassoon, A (eds) (2001) *Migration and Mobility: The European Context* London: Palgrave.

Gilroy, P (2000) *Between Camps: Nation, Culture and the Allure of Race* London: Allen Lane.

Glover, S, Gott, C, Loizillon, A, Portees, J, Price, R, Spencer, S, Srinivason, V and Willis, C (2001) *Migration: An Economic and Social Analysis* London: Home Office.

The Guardian (27 September 2012) www.theguardian.com/politics/2012/sep/27/david-cameron-letterman-late-show, accessed 3 January 2015.

The Guardian (1 July 2014) www.theguardian.com/world/2014/jul/01/france-burqa-ban-upheld-human-rights-court, accessed 3 January 2015.

The Guardian (26 October 2014) www.theguardian.com/uk-news/2014/oct/26/british-towns-swamped-immigrants-michael-fallon-eu, accessed 16 March 2017.

Hall, P (1984) 'The Patterns of Economic Policy: An Organisational Approach', in S Bornstein, D Held and J Kreiger (eds) *The State in Capitalist Europe* London: Allen and Unwin, 31–53.

Huysmans, J (2006) *The Politics of Insecurity: Fear, Migration and Asylum in the European Union* London: Routledge.

Isaacs, S, Blundell, D, Foley, A, Ginsburg, N, McDonough, B, Silverstone, D and Young, T (2014) *Social Problems in the UK* London: Routledge.

Joppke, C (1998) 'Why Liberal States Accept Unwanted Immigration', *World Politics*, 50(2), 266–93.

Joppke, C (1999) *Immigration and the Nation State* Oxford: Oxford University Press.

Kleinman, M (2002) *A European Welfare State?* Basingstoke: Palgrave.

Madood, T (2012) *Multiculturalism: A Civic Idea*, 2nd edn, Cambridge: Polity.

Marshall, T H (1950) *Citizenship and Social Class and Other Essays* Cambridge: Cambridge University Press.

Mouffe, C (1999) Deliberative Democracy or Agonistic Pluralism? *Social Research*, 66(3), 745–58.

New Statesman (Magazine) (10–16 June 2016) The Questionnaire: 'Big Challenges Cannot be Dealt with by One Country' Gordon Brown talks to Kofi Annan.

OECD (2006) *International Migration Outlook* Paris: Organisation for Economic Co-operation and Development.

Parekh, B (2002) *Rethinking Multiculturalism: Cultural Diversity and Political Theory* London: Harvard University Press.

Pressman, J and Wildavsky, A (1982) *Implementation*, 2nd edn, Berkeley, CA: University of California Press.

Rodrik, D (2011) *The Globalisation Paradox: Why Global Markets, States and Democracy Can't Coexist* Oxford: Oxford University Press.

Rose, N (1999) *Powers of Freedom: Reframing Political Thought* Cambridge: Cambridge University Press.

Silverman, M (1992) *Deconstructing the Nation: Immigration, Racism and Citizenship in Modern France* London: Routledge.

Skeldon, R (1990) *Population Mobility in Developing Countries: A Reinterpretation* London: Belhaven Press.

Standing, G (2014) *A Precariat Charter: From Denizens To Citizens* London: Bloomsbury.

Sykes, R and Alcock, P (1998) *Developments in European Policy* Bristol: The Policy Press.

The Telegraph (26 October 2014) www.telegraph.co.uk/news/uknews/immigration/11188602/Towns-in-the-UK-are-swamped-by-EU-migrants-Cabinet-minister-warns.html, accessed 5 January 2015.

Timmins, Nicholas (Public Policy Editor) (22 July 2009) 'Wave of EU Migrants Pay their Way', *Financial Times*.

Tirman, J (ed.) (2004) *The Maze of Fear: Security and Migration After 9/11* New York: New York Press.

Vertovec, S (1999) 'Conceiving and Researching Transnationalism', *Ethnic and Racial Studies*, 22(2), 445–62.

Matt Scott

chapter 4

Religion and multiculturalism

Jeffrey Haynes

4.1 Introduction: religion and secularisation in Europe

Religion is now socially and politically active in Western Europe (in this chapter 'Europe' refers to Western Europe) in ways which until recently were unthinkable, following the fast post-World War II pace of secularisation. This 'return of religion' to social and political concern has coincided with and is often focused on the recent growth of Muslim communities in many European countries, including Britain, France and The Netherlands. The consequence is that 'Islam' is now central to debates about religion and multiculturalism in Europe. To understand what is happening in this regard necessitates entering the debate about multiculturalism, pointing to a remodelling and re-assumption of our understanding in Europe of Islam's public persona. This chapter examines the issue of religion and multiculturalism in Europe, through a focus on Islam.

Europe is filled with secular countries. A country is secular when religion is publicly marginalised. Secularisation implies that traditional religious organisations, including for example in the UK the state church, the Church of England, no longer having the *right* to be actively or regularly engaged in public life. Secularisation does not however necessarily imply that Europeans are necessarily becoming less interested in spiritual matters. Rather, secularisation refers to: (1) dwindling social and moral influence of many religious leaders and institutions, especially if they are established and traditional, such as the Church of England; and (2) government policies pursued without clear heed to specifically religious injunctions or interdictions.

In Western Europe, the public role of religion, especially established Christian churches, has recently diminished significantly. There is now a compartmentalisation of societies and consequent reduction in churches' social and political significance. One school of thought believes that this is a continuous trend (Hirst, 2003). Another contends that religion is still institutionally and politically powerful in many European societies (Berger, 1999). Recent opinion polls indicate that many – perhaps most – Europeans still perceive themselves to be differentiated or affected by religious and/or cultural criteria, which in Europe is traditionally Christianity; some are of relevance to social and political outcomes, manifested in various ways (Davie, 2000). They include:

- *Catholic/Protestant divisions, especially in Northern Ireland and to an extent in Germany.* In the former, religious-cultural divisions are the main social basis of competing political parties, such as the Catholic/nationalist Sinn Fein and the Protestant/loyalist Democratic Unionist Party and Ulster Unionist Party.
- *Religious differences – roughly along right–left political lines – internal to the main confessional traditions.* In Britain, for example, there is the cross-party, socially conservative Movement for Christian Democracy, while both Germany and Italy have Christian Democratic political parties, notable for social conservatism.
- *A variety of church–state relationships.*

Such concerns are only intermittently important in domestic social and political contexts in a few European countries. Of more general regional concern are the social and political roles of Islam, including:

- *The impact of globalisation on the religious, social and political position of Europe's Muslim minorities.* For most European Muslims, Islam is an important basis of identity that can impact upon religious, social and political concerns.
- *Fears of Islamic extremism.* This issue was highlighted following the infamous 11 September 2001 New York and Pentagon attacks, and the Madrid and London bombings in March 2004 and July 2005 respectively. In France, in addition, a focus on extremist Islam was provided by the Paris riots of October–November 2005. Some commentators claimed that the riots were indicative of a new trend in France: alienated youths from Muslim backgrounds did not see themselves primarily as French but as Muslims, part of the global Islamic *ummah* ('community'), empowered and radicalised by extremist ideas.
- *Muslim Turkey's bid to join the European Union.* Fears of Islamic extremism encourage some Europeans to oppose Turkey's bid to join the European Union. Would Europe's 'Christian cultural identity' be destroyed by admission of Turkey, with its 80 million – mostly Muslim – people? Would it open up Europe to increased infiltration from Islamist extremism?
- *Blasphemy issues.* Blasphemy – that is, irreverence towards supposed holy personages, religious artefacts, customs and beliefs – has become a key civil liberties issue in many European countries in recent years, especially in relation to Islam.

Jeffrey Haynes

This chapter analyses the relationship between religion, multiculturalism and political and social developments in Europe through a focus on Islam and explains why these issues are now publicly important despite the continuing advance of secularisation.

4.2 Religion and multiculturalism in Europe

The issues raised above highlight that while, in Europe, the religious, social and political have to a considerable degree disengaged from each other, due to a process of secularisation, we are also now seeing a 'return of religion' to social and political significance. To some extent there is a paradox here: on the one hand, there is a continuing process of decline of institutionalised religion's social and political significance. A potential consequence of this is that many established religious elites appear to have lost much of their once highly significant social, cultural and political importance. This is underlined by the fact that, in Europe, political rulers now no longer require endorsement of their policies (whether directly or indirectly) from religious elites, although this is not to say that political leaders – such as Britain's former prime minister, David Cameron, or the German chancellor, Angela Merkel – do not *prefer* to have their support if possible. On the other hand, a new set of concerns has emerged, linked to the growth of Muslim communities in Europe, which poses new questions about the social and political role of religion, especially Islam, in the context of a debate about multiculturalism.

> During the last decade the debate on multiculturalism has taken shape as a legitimising paradigm of the Western democracies, and of the European Union itself. It has developed into a cultural-political cornerstone of societies *simultaneously in full transition towards economic globalisation on the one hand,* and *potentially prey to the advent/resurgence of far-right and/or fascist political organizations on the other hand.*
>
> (emphasis added; Zemni, 2002: 158)

Globalisation changes the power, authority and sovereignty of the state, by weakening the authority of national governments. Nevertheless, it is impossible to deny that, despite significant changes in recent decades, Europe's states still retain much power (Haynes *et al.*, 2011). Hirst and Thompson (1999) examine the legitimacy of democratic states in their ability politically to represent their citizens, that is, all the people who live within the confines of the states. Consequential to a high degree of cultural homogenisation, various peoples living together in a national territory are said to be able to identify both with the state and each other. On the other hand, it is also suggested that the more ethnically or religiously diverse the inhabitants of a country are, the more potentially complicated becomes the task of both representation and legitimacy.

Rosenau's (1997) concept of 'the Frontier' highlights a factor that potentially complicates homogenisation. This refers to a new or newly relevant divide emerging from the fact that many nations – including many in Europe – now include often significant numbers of people whose origins are in countries with which the state has 'foreign affairs', including, in the European context, states in North Africa and South Asia. And, since domestic and foreign politics increasingly engage with the same issues, the result is that traditional distinction between the two previously autonomous spheres dissolves (Haynes, 2013), in some cases replaced by a new dividing line between citizens.

In Europe, the concept of 'the Frontier' is said to be relevant to the relations between Muslim minority and non-Muslim host populations. The issue came into sharp focus following Western involvement in Afghanistan (from 2001) and Iraq (from 2003). Both events had serious political repercussions for the then leaders of both countries: President George W. Bush in the USA and Prime Minister Tony Blair in Britain. For example, many among Britain's nearly three million strong Muslim community saw the actions as fundamentally 'anti-Muslim' (Pew Global Attitudes Project Report 2005a).

Further problems emerged in Europe following the publication of the infamous Muhammad cartoons in a Danish newspaper, *Jyllands-Posten* (in English, *The Morning Newspaper/The Jutland Post)*. A controversy erupted after 12 cartoons were published in the newspaper on 30 September 2005. Several of the cartoons portrayed the Prophet Muhammad and some seemed to equate him with terrorism. The purpose, the newspaper claimed, was to contribute to a continuing debate regarding criticism of Islam and self-censorship. The effect, however, was almost certainly not what the newspaper intended, as publication of the cartoons was followed by public protests from Danish Muslim organisations, which helped to disseminate knowledge about them around the world. The controversy swiftly grew, with newspapers in over 50 countries reprinting some or all of the cartoons. The result was often violent protests in many countries, especially in the Muslim world. Both *Jyllands-Posten* – whose office received a bomb threat in January 2006 – and Denmark became a focus of Muslim anger. Demonstrators in the Gaza Strip (Palestinian territory) burned Danish flags, Saudi Arabia and Libya withdrew their ambassadors to Denmark, Danish goods were boycotted across the Middle East and many Middle Eastern and Asian countries saw violent clashes, with demonstrators attacking the Danish and Norwegian Embassies in Tehran and thousands of protesters taking to the streets in Egypt, the West Bank, Jordan and Afghanistan (Bright, 2006). Overall, the main complaint expressed by critics of the cartoons was that they were both Islamophobic and blasphemous. Their purpose was to humiliate a marginalised Danish minority and more generally to insult Islam. In February 2006 Denmark's prime minister Anders Fogh Rasmussen announced that the 'Prophet Muhammad cartoons' controversy was Denmark's worst international crisis since World War II *Times Online*, 2006)

Overall, the 'Prophet Muhammad cartoons' controversy focuses on how the topic of Islam and the position of Muslims in European countries generates intense debate both in Europe and around the world, while also highlighting the issues of religion and multiculturalism.

Multiculturalism is much more than the de facto acknowledgement of the living together of people with different religious traditions, ethnic loyalties or

Jeffrey Haynes

national affiliations. *Multiculturalism is the basis of a (supra-national) societal project with universal aspirations.* In that sense defining multiculturalism has become a stake of political conflict, one of the irreversible references for self-respecting democracies (emphasis added; Zemni, 2002: 158).

The linked issues of identity and multiculturalism are controversial in Europe, including among many 'second' or 'third' generation Muslims – offspring of immigrant parents or grandparents. Many Muslims today, especially among the young, confront religious and national identity issues in ways that differ from their parents' often more fixed cultural personalities (Cesari, 2010). This contrasts with the position a few decades ago when Islam was virtually unknown in Europe, when the faith was physically manifested in few mosques in a handful of major population centres. The situation began to change with the expansion of Muslim migration in the 1970s, when the issue of multiculturalism also began to surface.

Initially, Muslim immigrants were principally defined by the host society *vis-à-vis* their economic function (for example, in Germany where Turks were referred to as *gastarbeiter*, or 'guest workers'), their skin colour, or their nationality, and to a lesser extent by culture and/or religion. According to Nonneman (1996: 382), 'this reflected the migrants' own perception of their place in their European surroundings, and their relative lack of concern with opportunities for socio-religious expression within the context of the host society'.

In Europe today Islam is mainly associated with immigrant communities of fairly recent origin. Increased Muslim immigration largely occurred in the 1970s and 1980s, a time of European regional economic recession and an international environment characterised by international friction between Muslims and the West following Iran's revolution (Cesari, 2010). Over time, growth in numbers of Muslims continued consequential to growing numbers of children born to Muslim immigrants, and to a lesser extent to conversions among the host population.

In his study of construction of Hong Kong identity after Hong Kong's incorporation into China in 1997, Mathews (2000) offers a methodological approach to globalisation and identity that can usefully be applied to Muslims in Europe. Mathews distinguishes between, on the one hand, the state as constructor of culture in the nationalistic sense of 'the people's way of life', related to institutionalised practices; and, on the other, the de facto global 'cultural supermarket', as producer of free-floating culture-items, objects of individual choice. Today, an individual can construct self-identity in relation to both aspects and, in addition, can choose between self-identity as an 'authentic national culture', or a 'completely different' culture, or 'something in between', by combining, for example, ethnicity or religion and associated values. In the Hong Kong example, identity is Chinese ethnicity *plus* democracy/rule of law/human rights/freedom/gender equality, associated with the colonial legacy of British-ruled Hong Kong, as opposed to authoritarian 'isolationist' China. Simultaneously, mainland Chinese moving to Hong Kong may identify themselves with the latter's values, which differ from those of most indigenous inhabitants of Hong Kong (ibid.). In addition, personal and group mobility and global culture-shopping can encourage development of transnational communities whose values and identities are constructed in dialectical relation to both new countries and countries of origins, and therefore cannot be explained simply in terms of one over the other (Kennedy and Roudometof, 2002; Roy, 2004) In sum, from this viewpoint, it is possible to argue that ethnicity/religion and culture constitute 'forms' of self-identity which can be filled with different 'value-contents'.

Referring to the religious and cultural dimensions of Islam, it is clear that the consequence of decisions taken three or four decades ago by European governments has led to a changing Muslim presence, from one of numerically small, often-autonomous groups of migrant workers to larger, more complex, social communities. Over time, regularised contacts and interactions between Muslim immigrants and host societies increased. By the late 1980s, there were collectively about five million Muslims in Britain, France and Germany – countries where male Muslim 'guest workers" families were allowed to join them. Today, there are more than ten million Muslims living in Western Europe (Fetzer and Soper, 2005: 1). Over time, many second- or third-generation Muslims have become increasingly politicised. That is, born in Europe, many were familiar from the start with egalitarian Western assumptions about political participation. In some European countries – for example, Britain and France – it was relatively easy to acquire citizenship. An effect of accompanying expectations was that many Muslims demonstrated increased willingness to agitate for what they perceived as their social, cultural, religious, political and economic rights.

Some Muslims, including those sometimes called 'Islamists' – that is, people who believe that it is appropriate to link 'Muslim values' to political outcomes – see Western individualistic liberalism as both unauthentic and antipathetic to their culture and religion (Marty and Appleby, 1997; Hirst and Thompson, 1999; Roy 2004, 2010). The French author and analyst of the Muslim presence in Europe, Olivier Roy, argues that to counter European constructions of Islam, which he contends often do not get beyond presumptions of 'Islamic fundamentalism' or 'Islamist extremism', it is necessary to raise public awareness of the 'normal' behaviour of most European Muslims significantly. According to Roy (2004), many Muslims in Europe 'do all those things [Islamic] fundamentalists say Muslims should not do', including selling and drinking alcohol, voting for secular parties, having non-Muslim friends and marrying non-Muslims, while still considering themselves to be good Muslims.

Roy's contentions raise an important question: To what extent – if at all – is there an inevitable and unbridgeable incompatibility between Muslims-in-Europe, their values, norms and beliefs, and the typically secular organising principles of non-Muslim European societies? Esposito (2002) and Ayubi (1991) contend that there is no fundamental incompatibility – because Islam is primarily pragmatic, with separation, on the one hand, between religious/cultural principles and institutions and, on the other, between the temporal ruler and the state. As a result, there are not only grounds for expectations of compatibility between Islamic precepts and the 'world of nation-states' but also no impracticable obstacles of principle to a reasonable degree of compatibility between 'Islamic'

Jeffrey Haynes

and 'Western' practices regarding citizenship and the nature of socio-political organisation. 'European Muslims' reactions (themselves varying strongly) may often be less a matter of "Islamic practice" than of a cultural minority's sense of discrimination leading to a search for rallying points' (Nonneman, 1996: 384).

This is not to suggest that Muslims in Europe are necessarily complaisant about the norms, values and practices they encounter. Muslim leaders often express concern for the development of their faith and its adherents, especially in relation to the moral wellbeing and education of the young. For many Muslims, Western society is essentially meaningless, rootless and characterised by crime, juvenile delinquency, riots, collapse of marriages and sexual promiscuity (Ahmed, 1992; Leiken, 2012). In addition, some Muslims believe that the values and norms of Islam could provide an alternative, appropriate lifestyle to correct European secular societies' focus on materialism and individualism that can lead to self-ishness. Sometimes the goal can be achieved, it is believed, by adopting a political programme of 'Islamicisation' via what Roy (2004) calls 'neo-fundamentalism'. Others take a different path: they pursue Islamic authenticity via extremism or even terrorism (Leiken, 2012). Roy's term, 'neo-fundamentalism', refers primarily to the idea of a transnational Islamic community constructed largely via the Internet and focusing on Europe's Muslims. It equates Muslim identity with Islamic (*Sharia*) law. At the same time, it breaks with traditional Islamic jurisprudence whereby Muslims are obliged only to follow *Sharia* ritual, not its legislative dimensions (Roy, 2004). The result is that the call for *Sharia* law among Europe's Muslims can have widely different implications for understanding and behaviour.

For example, a professor at the University of Oxford, the Swiss-Muslim intellectual and scholar, Tariq Ramadan, advocates liberal reform of *Sharia*. At the same time, Ramadan also seeks to challenge existing European (secular) models of citizenship by explicitly making *Sharia* the guiding principle for Muslim citizens of Europe. Finally, he also calls for European Muslims to represent the oppressed South against European/Western neo-liberal imperialism. His goal is to create an independent 'Western Islam', anchored not in the historic traditions of Islam but rooted in the multicultural reality of the Europe of today, which seeks to draw on the strengths and values of both Islam and Europe. In doing this, Ramadan urges a fresh reading of Islamic sources in order to interpret them for a Western context and enable a new understanding of universal Islamic principles that could open the door for greater Muslim integration into European societies. The point is that Ramadan's notion of a novel Muslim identity, rooted in 'Muslim values' but also reflecting multicultural ideals, is a message with profound implications for what it means to be a Muslim in Europe (Ramadan, 2003: 172ff.). Ramadan offers a striking vision of a new Muslim identity, which rejects once and for all the idea that Islam must be defined in opposition to the West.

Ramadan also seeks to identify how the inherent principles of Islam can be put to wider purpose in European societies, while contending that Muslims can – indeed *must* – be faithful to their principles and arguing that they can and should feel at home in Europe. In *Western Muslims and the Future of Islam* (2003),

Ramadan focuses on Islamic law (*Sharia*) and tradition in order to analyse whether Islam is in conflict with Western ideals. According to Ramadan, there is no contradiction between them. He also identifies several key areas where Islam's universal principles can be 'engaged' in Europe, including education, inter-religious dialogue, economic resistance and spirituality. As the number of Muslims living in Europe increases, the question of what it means to be a European Muslim becomes increasingly central to the cultural, social and political future of Europe. Finally, while the media are focused on radical Islam, Ramadan claims that a silent revolution is sweeping Europe's Muslim communities, with growing numbers of Muslims actively seeking ways to live in harmony with their faith. The next section of the chapter examines Ramadan's ideas about multiculturalism in the context of Muslims living in Britain and France – European countries that have different ideas about multiculturalism and the place of Islam.

4.3 Britain

Britain is home to nearly three million Muslims, amounting to around 5 per cent of the total population of over 60 million people. British Muslims have various roots, with communities in the UK comprising people whose parents or grandparents came originally from: Pakistan, Bangladesh, North Africa, sub-Saharan Africa, Cyprus, Malaysia, the Middle East and, most recently, Eastern Europe (primarily Bosnia-Herzegovina). Until the 1960s, Islam was a relatively obscure religion in Britain; there were only a few mosques in major cities, including Cardiff, Liverpool, Manchester, South Shields and London's East End. The situation changed with the expansion of Muslim labour migration in the 1970s. At this time, as a result of a change in immigration policy, British governments halted further labour immigration, while allowing family unification. As a result, the Muslim presence in Britain changed from one of primarily migrant workers to social communities in a fuller sense. As a result, contacts significantly increased between Muslim families and the British host society.

During the 1980s, some Muslims – especially among the second generation, offspring of first-generation immigrants and their spouses – became increasingly politicised and in some cases politically active. Such people, with British citizenship and familiar with British assumptions about political participation, began to demand what they saw as their rights. At the same time, a backlash began against some British Muslims from some sections of existing British society. This was in part a consequence of increased fears of 'Islamic extremism', often linked to Iran's 1979 revolution, and more generally with increased Islamic militancy in many parts of the Muslim world. Some sections of British public opinion believed that British Muslim communities were hotbeds of 'Islamic extremism', posing a threat to peace and social stability (Leiken, 2012).

Some British Muslims, especially from among the young, began increasingly to identify with struggles of fellow Muslims in Israel-controlled Palestine and elsewhere, with some radicals organising themselves into 'a huge web of Islamic associations of various shades of feeling and opinion' (Kepel 1994: 37; also see, Ramadan, 2003 and Leiken, 2012). Such organisations included the Young Muslims, *Al Muntada al Islami*, Muslim Welfare House, *Al-Muhajiroun* and *Hizb ut Tahrir*; collectively they represented a range of Islamist positions. *Hizb ut Tahrir* is often regarded as one of the most radical of such groups (www.hizb.org.uk/). *Hizb ut Tahrir*, an Arabic term that translates as 'the Party of Liberation', is a radical political organisation with members throughout the Muslim world and in countries – including Britain – with significant Muslim populations. Taqiuddin an-Nabhani, an Islamic jurist, formed the organisation in Jerusalem in 1953. *Hizb ut Tahrir* calls for separation of Muslims from Western society, while employing 'anti-Israel, anti-homosexual, anti-liberal rhetoric' (see many relevant articles and postings at www.hizb.org.uk/).

Some Muslims in Britain are attracted to *Hizb ut Tahrir* and other radical groups because of their deep sense of injustice. Ansari (2002: 1) argues that such sentiments have increased over time because of

> a huge rise in the number of attacks on Muslims in Britain, increasing threats to civil liberties in the name of security measures, a resurgence in the activities of the far-right in Britain and elsewhere in Europe, and a crackdown on refugees fleeing persecution.

> (Ansari, 2002: 1)

Reflecting such concerns, many British Muslims are said to be concerned primarily about two main issues, one domestic and one external. The first relates to the defence of Muslim culture and religion, especially in relation to their children's education in Britain. The second is linked to issues of terrorism and international security, especially prominent and focused following the US–British assault on Afghanistan in 2001, the campaign in 2003 to oust Saddam Hussein in Iraq and the continuing but inconclusive bid to pacify the country's insurgency.

The education of their children is a key issue for large numbers of Muslim parents in Britain. In many cases this is linked to a strong desire to safeguard their religion and culture in a strongly secular society. Many British Muslims want segregated education – believed to be necessary in order to prevent young Muslims drifting away from their faith and culture (Travis, 2004). Many Muslim parents also demand that their children's school curriculum should include: teachings of Islam, with associated school prayer facilities; celebrations of the main Muslim festivals, *Eid ul Fitr* and *Eid ul Adha*; and exemption from what many see as inappropriate sex education for children. They also want schools to offer *halal* food and to allow wearing of appropriately 'modest' clothing, especially for girls (Goulborne and Joly, 1989: 92–4). But despite Muslim demands, which have been made over many years, these conditions are not met in British state schools. As a result, increasing numbers of Muslims now withdraw their children from UK state education, with numbers of Muslim schools in Britain growing from 24 in the mid-1990s to around 140 in 2011 (Abrams, 2011). These schools collectively educate well over 10,000 Muslim children (Abrams, 2011). A 2004 opinion survey of 500 British Muslims indicated that, if available, nearly half would send their child to a Muslim school rather than a conventional – that is, secular – state school. Since only a small fraction of Muslim children are already in Muslim schools, this represents a huge latent demand for separate religious schooling. The demand is said to be greatest among men, younger families and the more affluent (Travis, 2004; Abrams, 2011).

An opinion survey in March 2004 found that many British Muslims expressed little desire to integrate fully with the host culture and people, a view partly founded in anti-Western resentment at US and UK involvement in Iraq, seen by many simply as a 'war on Islam'. The poll also showed that many British Muslims saw George W. Bush and Tony Blair's 'war on terror' also as a facet of a more general 'Western' conflict with Islam as a faith and Muslims as a group of people. Finally, nearly two-thirds (64 per cent) believed that Britain's stringent anti-terrorist laws were being used unfairly against Britain's Muslim community (Travis, 2004). While it is not fully clear what their motives were, it seems highly likely that Britain's home-grown Islamist bombers who struck on 7 July 2005 with four bomb attacks in London killing over 50 people were motivated at least in part by a deep sense of grievance and injustice at what they perceived as punitive Western policies against Muslims in Afghanistan, Iraq, Israel's occupied territories, and elsewhere.

This section has described how the likelihood of the achievement of the kind of aims expressed by Tariq Ramadan for Western Muslims may be seriously undermined by the existence of grievances, both domestic and international. Unless they are resolved, Muslim criticisms of the status quo might significantly undercut chances of the development of a 'Western Islam' advocated by Ramadan and other figures, including Olivier Roy (2004, 2010).

4.4 France

Between five and six million Muslims are thought to live in France, twice as many as the UK. It is thought that about half have French citizenship – although precise figures are unavailable. This is because the French state is officially secular and officials are forbidden to ask citizens questions about their religion or ethnicity. It is often asserted, however, that while still preponderantly Catholic, France now has more Muslims than Jews or Protestants, historically the country's most significant religious minorities. Overall, Islam is now almost certainly the country's second religion in terms of numbers of followers (Caeiro, 2006: 71).

Growth in the numbers of Muslims in France came, as in Britain, initially by immigration. Most came from France's former North African colonies, including Algeria and Morocco. Although present from around the time of World War I, Muslims arrived in significant numbers in France only in the 1960s. At this time, the government granted asylum to hundreds of thousands of Algerians who had fought on the French side in Algeria's 1954–62 war of independence. During the same decade, France also invited immigrant manpower – including many Muslims – to meet the needs of the country's then booming economy. The economic boom soon fizzled out but by the 1970s there were substantial numbers of Muslims in most of France's main towns and cities.

Like Britain, France has had a policy of 'zero immigration' since the 1970s. However, France's Muslim population still increases because of relatively high birth rates, an unknown number of illegal entrants, particularly from North and sub-Saharan Africa, and a legal exception that allows the reunion of immigrant families. The purpose of the exception makes clear French policy in regard to its Muslims: to legitimise them in French society by integrating them into it. This policy contrasts with that of Britain, where governmental strategy has long been that of 'multiculturalism', that is encouraging development of separate cultures in an overall context of 'Britishness', informed by 'British values'.

Successive French governments have claimed to want to integrate the country's Muslims into French society, by seeking to develop Muslims' sense of 'Frenchness', informed by 'French values'. This implies reducing overt signs of 'Muslim-ness', especially particularistic forms of dress for females, such as the *hijab* ('Islamic veil'). The so-called 'headscarves of Creil affair' erupted in late 1989, centring on the desire of several young Muslim women to wear Islamic headscarves at school in the seaside town of Creil. The affair was portrayed in the French media as an attempt to introduce 'communalism' into schools, a traditionally neutral sphere. To explain the passion that this issue raised it is important to note that France is the country where the Enlightenment began, leading to the presumption that the common ground for the French is their 'rationality', implying that religion takes a decidedly secondary position. Now, many French people are highly secular, perceiving visible signs of what they see as religious identity (such as the *hijab*) to be highly disturbing – because they believe it undermines basic French values of secularism (Caeiro, 2006: 78–80; also see Barras, 2012).

As in Britain, Islamic networks grew in France during the 1980s and 1990s. Members were composed of mainly students and other young people, whose parents were mostly from Algeria or Morocco. Some Islamic activists wanted to stage a trial of strength by confronting the French state on the sensitive ground of *laïcité* (secularism) (Kepel, 1994: 40). The issue seemed to strike a chord with many French Muslims who, it appeared, also wanted 'positive discrimination' in favour of Muslim girls in French state schools. Student militants appointed themselves as the spokesmen of 'Islam', seeking to negotiate 'positive discrimination' for practising Muslims enabling them to withdraw, in some contexts, from French law and replace it with *Sharia* law. The Islamic militants found powerful allies in the campaign from other religious entities, including leaders of the Roman Catholic Church in France and some Jewish rabbis. These non-Muslims supported the campaign because they were also religious people, determined to seek protection of their faiths in the face of what they regarded as an increasingly strident *laïcité* (ibid.: 41). Eventually, despite the protestations of the religious groups, the French national assembly voted overwhelmingly in February 2004 in favour of a ban on the *hijab* and other 'conspicuous' religious symbols in state schools, despite warnings from religious leaders that the law would persecute Muslims and encourage 'Islamic fundamentalism'. The national assembly voted 494–36 in favour of banning 'conspicuous' religious symbols in schools, including the Christian cross. The law, ratified by the senate in March 2004, came into effect the following September (Henley, 2004). Seventy-eight per cent of French people favoured such a prohibition, as did smaller majorities in Germany (54 per cent) and The Netherlands (51 per cent) (Pew Global Attitudes Project Report, 2005a).

As in the UK, Muslims' domestic concerns in France overlapped with international issues, including the invasions of Afghanistan and Iraq in 2001 and 2003 respectively. Unlike the British government, however, that of France was strongly opposed to the invasion. Did France's large Muslim minority help determine French policy? Such a question is hard to answer, but it does seem clear that the then president – Jacques Chirac – welcomed (1) the renewed bond between the Muslim community and the rest of the French population that resulted from a common opposition to the war in Iraq, and (2) the boost to his personal popularity that he would no doubt gain from the anti-war stance.

Given this apparent meeting of minds between President Chirac and the Muslim communities of France over opposition to the invasions, how can we explain and account for serious riots primarily involving youths of Muslim origin that erupted in Paris in October 2005, and which soon spread to other French towns and cities? Two broad arguments have been expressed to explain why the riots occurred. One is linked to the perceived impact of globalisation, the other to domestic factors. According to Watson and Jones (2005),

> *The world watches in trepidation as the wildfires of chaos sweep from France across Europe. We are witnessing the fruits of globalization. Rampant unchecked immigration policies and the enforced fusion of multiculturalism form the backbone of the New World Order's systematic purge of the sleeping middle class.*
>
> (emphasis added)

This view expresses what might be called the 'clash of civilisations' argument, whereby the riots were seen in the context of a polarised conflict between 'Western civilisation' and 'Islamic extremism'. However, according to de Koning (2006), many of the rioters seemed more in tune with American rappers and spoke in French, not Arabic. Yet this did not prevent a number of prominent French people, including a well known intellectual and academic, Alain Finkielkraut, and the then Interior Minister, former president, Nicolas Sarkozy, claiming that the riots were linked to the 'inability' of Muslims to live according to French norms and values. In this view, those who believed that the source of the riots was to be found outside Islam were naïve.

Those who claimed that the 2005 French riots were rooted in domestic factors expressed a second view. Some argued that it was the result of unemployment, a consequence of the country's adhesion to the European Social Model with attendant high wages for those lucky enough to be in work, but also leading to

Jeffrey Haynes

high unemployment, especially among Muslim youths in the *banlieues* (suburbs) of major cities, including Paris (Astier, 2005). Few – certainly not from the peaceful majority in the suburbs whose cars and schools were torched – argued that violence was a legitimate way to express grievances. Yet, what for many was beyond question was that the rioting was *not* an affirmation of a distinct religious or ethnic identity, buoyed by a transnational network of Islamist extremists. According to a French sociologist, Laurent Chambon, the riots were not about 'youth gangs inspired by radical Islam'. Instead, they were part of a movement against the 'precariousness' of everyday life in the French *banlieues*, that is, the riots were the product of alienation and existential angst not Islamist radicalisation (de Koning, 2006: 30).

Overall, few if any French commentators found plausible evidence for an ethnic or religious component to the protests. 'Very few in the suburbs are saying: black (or brown) is beautiful. Their message is the exact opposite: neither the colour of our skins nor our names should make us less than fully French' (Astier, 2005). Nor were the riots prompted by religion. On the other hand, many among the urban youths who rioted would define themselves as Muslims, in a way that they would not have done ten or fifteen years ago (de Koning, 2006). In addition, it may well be that that the 2004 ban on the wearing of the headscarf in public schools – more accurately, the 'law on religious signs' (for the display of Christian as well as Muslim signifiers were prohibited) – was a factor. On the other hand, very few French Muslims challenged the separation of church and state. Mohammed Elhajjioui, a youth in Lille, claimed that the headscarf ban negated the original, tolerant spirit of French-style secularism which guarantees religious freedom (Astier, 2005). Prior to 2004, courts had upheld the right of girls to wear headscarves in schools. Yet a sense of *religious* grievance was not in evidence during the period of unrest, a six-week time when nearly 3,000 rioters were arrested. Certainly, there was no call by French Muslim leaders, with virtually all mosques appealing for calm (Caeiro, 2006). In short, the *banlieues were* seething with anger, but that anger had little or nothing to do with a desire to be recognised as separate. Indeed, the separateness of the youths from mainstream French society appeared to be endured with resentment, certainly not proclaimed with pride. According to de Koning (2006), the riots and accompanying violence did not express a rejection of French ideals as such, rather a deep sense of frustration that those ideals were not being put into practice for such people. What seems clear was the exact opposite of what Alain Finkielkraut claimed: the violence of October and November 2005 revealed how *unsuccessful* extremist Muslim groups had been in significantly penetrating the urban youth culture of the *banlieues*. In short, Islam is not the problem; the problem is that the majority of the residents of the *banlieues* are Muslim and/or black and because of this many have been discriminated against for long periods, especially in the search for employment. The youths were rebelling because they still dreamt of being accepted as French, not because they wanted to separate themselves from mainstream French society. In other words, the riots were the result of a refusal to be marginalised, a manifestation of 'a deep acceptance of fundamental French values expressed in the "coupling of liberty and equality"'. However, if French society supported Sarkozy's

> push to crush the violence by cleansing the ghettos of their 'troublemakers', the next 'intifadah of the cities' could well be in honor not of Marianne, France's national emblem and the personification of liberty and reason, but of Musab al-Zarqawi and his successors.
>
> (LeVine, 2005)

Note however that while some rioters were Muslims, with origins in North and sub-Saharan Africa, 'Islamic extremism' was not a driving force, although anger, frustration, alienation and unemployment were. Few if any lessons appeared to be learnt by the French state from the 2005 riots. During the 2012 presidential campaign both the National Front candidate, Marine le Pen, and her rival, the incumbent president, Nicholas Sarkozy, vied with each other to make Islam and Muslims 'the problem' during outspoken comments about *halal* meat, which became a metaphor for wider concerns about the presence of millions of Muslims in France.

Halal meat became a topic of debate in early 2012, when Le Pen made the erroneous claim that all meat in the Paris region is now prepared according to Islamic methods. It is not labelled as such, she claimed, with the intention of misleading non-Muslim customers. The inference was that a sop to French Muslims and an attempt to pull the wool over the eyes of non-Muslim French regarding the allegedly growing influence of Muslims and Islam in the country. Yet, as officials later confirmed, although Paris region abattoirs mainly supply local Muslim butchers, this does not imply that all or even most of the meat consumed Paris is *halal*; in fact, most comes from outside the region and is neither kosher nor *halal*. While Sarkozy initially criticised Le Pen for creating a 'false controversy', he was soon content to reignite the controversy, in what some saw as a cynical ploy to increase his electoral attractiveness to 'anti-immigration' voters ahead of the presidential election in April 2012.

4.5 Conclusion

Our brief surveys of Britain and France indicate that Islamic extremism is a marginal tendency, seemingly of interest only to small groups of Muslim militants without much in the way of popular support. Figures including Tariq Ramadan and Olivier Roy make the point that Islam can be divided into 'good' and 'bad' versions, driving a more general call for an 'Enlightened' Islam. This implies a Muslim *aggiornamento* (liberalisation) as a prerequisite to the integration of Muslims into Western societies – setting the necessary conditions not for a privatisation of the faith but for a public Islam (Ramadan, 2003; Roy, 2004, 2010; Peter, 2006).

The chapter also looked at the issue of multiculturalism. We saw that a successful policy of 'multiculturalism' must do much more than acknowledging – perhaps only rhetorically – that people need to make comprises and be tolerant

Jeffrey Haynes

in order to live together when exhibiting different religious traditions, ethnic loyalties and/or national affiliations. Instead, as the examples of both Britain and France show, it is necessary for multiculturalism truly to be an ideological aspiration, based on a collective project with shared aspirations. Seeking to define and operationalise multiculturalism, in various European countries, including Britain and France, has become a focal point of social concern, an issue that Europe's democratic countries need to resolve for their individual and collective wellbeing.

Bibliography

Abrams, F. (2011) 'Islamic schools flourish to meet demand', *The Guardian*, 28 November. Available at www.guardian.co.uk/education/2011/nov/28/muslim-schools-growth, accessed 1 April 2012.

Ahmed, A. (1992) *Postmodernism and Islam: Predicament and Promise*, London: Routledge.

Ansari, H. (2002) *Muslims in Britain*, London: Minority Rights Group International.

Astier, H. (2005) 'We want to be French!', *Open Democracy*, 22 November. Available at: www.opendemocracy.net/debates/article.jsp?id=6&debateId=28&articleId=3051, accessed 5 June 2006.

Ayubi, N. (1991) *Political Islam. Religion and Politics in the Arab World*, London: Routledge.

Barras, A. (2012) *A Rights-Based Discourse to Contest the Boundaries of State Secularism? The Case of the Headscarf Bans in France and Turkey*, London: I.B. Tauris.

Berger, P. (ed.) (1999) *The Desecularization of the World: Resurgent Religion in World Politics*, Grand Rapids/Washington, DC: William B. Eerdmans/Ethics & Public Policy Center.

Bright, Arthur (1 February 2006) 'Firestorm over Danish Muhammad cartoons continues', *Christian Science Monitor*.

Caeiro, A. (2006) 'An anti-riot fatwa', *ISIM Review*, 17(Spring): 32.

Casanova, J. (1994) *Public Religions in the Modern World*, Chicago and London: University of Chicago Press.

Cesari, J. (ed.) (2010) *Muslims in the West after 9/11. Religion, Politics and Law*, London: Routledge.

Davie, G. (2000) *Religion in Modern Europe*, Oxford: Oxford University Press.

Esposito, J. (2002) *Unholy War*, New York: Oxford University Press.

Fetzer, J. and J. C. Soper (2005) *Muslims and the State in Britain, France and Germany*, Cambridge: Cambridge University Press.

Goulborne, H. and D. Joly. (1989) 'Religion and the Asian and Caribbean minorities in Britain', *Contemporary European Affairs*, 2(4): 77–98.

Haynes, J. (2013) *An Introduction to International Relations and Religion*, 2nd ed., London: Pearson.

Haynes, J., P. Hough, S. Malik and L. Pettiford (2011) *World Politics*, London: Pearson.

Henley, J. (2004) 'French MPs vote for veil ban in state schools', *The Guardian*, 11 February.

Hirst, P. and G. Thompson (1999) *Globalization in Question*, Cambridge: Polity.

Hirst, R. (2003) 'Social networks and personal beliefs', in G. Davie, P. Heelas and L. Woodhead (eds), *Predicting Religion*, Aldershot: Ashgate, pp. 86–94.

Kennedy, P. and V. Roudometof (2002) *Communities Across Borders*, London: Routledge.

Kepel, G. (1994) *The Revenge of God*, Cambridge: Polity.

de Koning, M. (2006) 'Islamization of the French riots. Interview with Laurent Chambon', *ISIM Review*, 17(Spring): 30–1.

Leiken, R. (2012) *Europe's Angry Muslims*, New York: Oxford University Press.

LeVine, M. (2005) 'Assimilate or die. Do the French riots portend a coming cultural backlash against globalization?', Mother Jones. Available at http://motherjones.com/commentary/columns/2005/11/assimilate_or_die.html, accessed 5 June 2006.

Marty, M. and Appleby, R. Scott (eds) (1997) *Religion, Ethnicity and Self-identity: Nations in Turmoil*, Salzburg: Salzburg Seminar Books.

Mathews, G. (2000) *Global Culture/Global Identity*, London: Routledge.

Nonneman, G. (1996) 'Muslim communities in post-Cold War Europe: Themes and puzzles', in I. Hampsher-Monk and J. Stanyer (eds), *Contemporary Political Studies 1996, Volume One*, Glasgow: Political Studies Association, pp. 381–94.

Peter, F. (2006) 'Towards civil Islam? A comparison of Islam policies in Britain and France', *Recht van der Islam*, No. 23.

Pew Global Attitudes Project (2005a) 'Islamic extremism: Common concern for Muslims and Western publics', 14 July. Available at http://pewglobal.org/reports/display.php?ReportID=248, accessed 10 December 2005.

Pew Global Attitudes Project Report (2005b) http://features.pewforum.org/muslim/number-of-muslims-in-western-europe.html (no longer available).

Ramadan, T. (2003) *Western Muslims and the Future of Islam*, Oxford and New York: Oxford University Press.

Rosenau, J. (1997) *Along the Domestic-Foreign Frontier*, Cambridge: Cambridge University Press.

Roy, O. (2004) *Globalised Islam. The Search for a New Ummah*, London: Hurst.

Roy, O. (2010) *Holy Ignorance*, London: Hurst.

Times Online (London) (2006) '70,000 gather for violent Pakistan cartoons protest' 15 February. Available at www.timesonline.co.uk/tol/news/world/asia/article731005.ece, accessed 20 July 2011.

Travis, A. (2004) 'Desire to integrate on the wane as Muslims resent "war on Islam"', *The Guardian*, March 16.

Jeffrey Haynes

Watson, P. and Jones, A. (2005) 'The fruits of globalization: Rotten to the core. France erupts as rampant immigration reaps its vengeance'. Available at www.prisonplanet.com/articles/november2005/081105rottentothecore. htm, accessed 5 June 2006.

Zemni, S. (2002) 'Islam, European identity and the limits of multiculturalism', in W. Shadid and P. Van Koningsveld (eds), *Religious Freedom and the Neutrality of the State: The Position of the European Union*, Leuven: Peeters, pp. 158–73.

part II

Inequalities

chapter 5

Inequalities in European cities

Jane Lewis

5.1 Introduction

This chapter examines the evidence that European cities are becoming more unequal and more socially and spatially segregated and divided. Social problems are concentrated in cities and this chapter points to the growth of inequality, poverty, unemployment and social exclusion in European cities and to the increasing concentration of social problems in poor neighbourhoods within cities throughout Europe. Europe's cities face increasing challenges, not least to social cohesion, from this growth in inequality and poverty. After examining some of the trends in inequality, the chapter looks at some of the underlying causes of the growth in social and spatial inequality both within and between European cities – including recent economic and labour market changes, changes in the social class and ethnic structure of cities and the restructuring of housing and the welfare state. The chapter also highlights some of the implications of these challenges for urban and social policy, examining growing concerns that while urban planning, housing and urban regeneration policies have frequently led to a revitalisation of declining city and especially inner city areas, they have also further reinforced social and spatial divisions and inequalities in European cities.

While it is clearly too early to say what the impact of Brexit will be on inequalities in UK cities, there are a number of important points emerging. First, many commentators, including the FT City Network of senior leaders in the financial services in London (Jenkins 2016), have argued that widening inequalities in the UK was one of the key factors underlying the 'Leave' vote, with many voters who have not benefitted from economic growth and who suffer the impacts of widening income inequalities, insecure employment and austerity policies and who felt they had little to lose voting to leave the EU (McInroy 2016).

This was especially true in cities in the north and midlands. Second, what evidence there is at this early stage suggests that the poorest may find themselves worse off and that Brexit may create even greater income inequality (Jenkins 2016). There are also concerns that the housing crisis may worsen with the building of new and affordable homes likely to be stalled, banks more cautious in their lending and rents continuing to rise more quickly than incomes (Easton 2016).

5.2 Diverse European cities: dynamic and shrinking cities

Almost three-quarters (73 per cent) of the population in Europe live in towns and cities and Europe is one of the most highly urbanised regions of the world (Burdett *et al.* 2015). This chapter will examine inequalities *within* cities across Europe but starts with an examination of inequalities *between* the different cities in Europe. The recent history of European cities is a diverse one and while inequalities between the countries, regions and cities of Europe have a long history, evidence suggests inequalities between cities in Europe are intensifying. The recent EU URBACT (2011) report *Cities of Tomorrow* identifies three types of European city based on differences in population and economic growth:

- *economically dynamic cities with strong population growth* through the in-migration of both highly skilled and less qualified migrants – particularly larger Western European cities;
- *cities with a strong economy but stagnant population* – small and medium-sized European cities – again particularly in Western and Northern Europe;
- *cities experiencing demographic and economic decline* – mostly Central and Eastern European cities in Poland, Bulgaria, Hungary, Slovakia and Romania, eastern German cities, some southern European cities and former industrial cities in Western Europe.

The discussion below highlights key differences between dynamic and shrinking cities across Europe.

Economically dynamic European cities

From the 1970s and 1980s, cities and especially inner cities throughout Western Europe experienced economic decline caused by deindustrialisation (the collapse of manufacturing industries and employment) and the suburbanisation and spatial decentralisation of both population and jobs. Unemployment increased, vast tracts of cities became derelict and redundant and the future of cities was dominated by debates of urban decline and crisis.

More recently, however, a 'contrasting view has emerged that identifies cities as sites of economic dynamism and engines of national prosperity' (Turok and Mykhnenko 2007). There has been a major shift over the past decade with cities increasingly recognised as the economic hubs, the engines of economic growth,

Jane Lewis

innovation and creativity of the globalised early twenty-first century economy – a shift reflected in both academic and government policy thinking (Florida 2002, 2005; Buck *et al.* 2005; Glaeser 2011; Cabinet Office 2011). It is widely recognised that cities 'outperform their national contexts for productivity, competitiveness, innovation and economic growth' (Burdett *et al.* 2015: 8). Concerns over the future of European cities hit by crisis and economic decline, by deindustrialisation and mass unemployment, in the 1970s and 1980s has to a certain extent (and for some cities) been replaced by a focus on the dynamic city, the resurgent city and the revitalisation and renaissance of the city as many cities throughout western and northern Europe in particular have once again experienced a growth in population, economic productivity and employment. As Turok and Mykhnenko (2007) highlight:

> This view of cities has been readily endorsed at national and European policy levels to the point where it can be described as a new conventional wisdom.
>
> (ibid.: 165)

Since the 1990s, there has been a major growth in employment in the knowledge-intensive financial and other professional services, in ICT and the digital industries, in media and other creative industries, most of which is concentrated in cities.

These growth sectors of the 'new economy' have been the focus of recent debates on the future of cities. The 'creative city' concept has become an increasingly significant influence on urban policy across European cities. Florida (2002, 2005) argues that to be competitive, cities must attract the 'creative class' (scientists, artists, teachers, entrepreneurs, gays, youth, bohemians) who he argues are key to economic growth in contemporary cities and who are attracted to those cities that offer the best 'qualities of place' – which for Florida includes 'talent, technology and tolerance' and diversity (which we return to later in the chapter and which may certainly be threatened by Brexit in the UK). For many the growth of this new knowledge economy and of the professional and managerial occupations and jobs it has created has led to the rise of a 'new middle class' whose lifestyles, cultures and consumption have transformed cities and whose growth in economically dynamic cities is one of the key underlying causes of the growing inequalities which are the subject of this chapter (Lees 2014).

Shrinking European cities

However, while some European cities have experienced economic and population growth over the past two decades, this has not been the case for all European cities. European cities are, of course, very different and have different historical, political, economic and cultural contexts. Some cities have fared better than others, while some particularly former industrial cities and most particularly many cities in Central and Eastern Europe have experienced population and economic decline alongside a growth in unemployment and poverty. These can be termed 'shrinking cities'.

Recent research suggests 42 per cent of large European cities and 75 per cent of Eastern European cities are shrinking (Turok and Mykhnenko 2007; Haase *et al.* 2013). A recent study of population change in 310 European cities over the period from 1960 to 2005 found over one-third (116) of the cities had experienced population decline lasting between 5 and 15 years (Turok and Mykhnenko 2007). Most of the cities experiencing population decline were in Central and Eastern Europe, particularly in Russia, Poland, the Ukraine and Romania. Population decline in these cities is the result of both out-migration (largely to cities in northern and Western Europe) and a fall in birth rates, reflecting economic and employment decline, in large part a consequence of their transition to capitalist, market economies (ibid.).

Turok and Mykhnenko's (2007) study also found 13 European cities had suffered sustained population decline lasting 25 years or more, all of which were former industrial cities – three in the UK (Liverpool, Newcastle and Glasgow) and seven in Germany (including the Ruhr, Saarbrucken and Leipzig). This pattern of continued population and economic decline in former industrial cities is a pattern which is also highlighted in recent reports in the UK with cities such as Sunderland, Hull and Swansea continuing to experience population and economic decline (Centre for Cities 2014; Lee *et al.* 2013). The EU URBACT (2011) report *Cities of Tomorrow*, argues that population decline and economic stagnation are a major challenge for many European cities.

The 2008 global recession and subsequent shift to what Peck (2012) argues is a new era in which 'austerity urbanism' permeates policy thinking and practice has hit particular cities and poor neighbourhoods within cities everywhere especially hard. Burdett *et al.* (2015) point to the growth in youth unemployment in some southern European cities (ibid.: 18). Cities in Greece and Spain have been especially hard hit by the economic crisis and austerity, with youth unemployment rates of 60 per cent in Athens and Barcelona and 55 per cent in Malaga, Spain. This compares with far lower youth unemployment rates of 1 per cent in Cambridge, 2.5 per cent in Edinburgh, 6 per cent in Copenhagen and Helsinki and 7 per cent in Hamburg and highlights the growing inequalities that exist between European cities (Burdett *et al.* 2015).

As an indicator of economic wealth, a look at Gross Domestic Product (GDP) rates per capita further highlights the growing inequality between cities in Europe. Copenhagen, Dublin, London and Groningen in the Netherlands all have a GDP per capita of over 54,000 Euros while the equivalent figures for non-capital cities in Bulgaria and Romania are between 2,000 and 5,000 Euros. Cities with GDP per capita over 50,000 Euros are concentrated in northern and Western Europe (Burdett *et al.* 2015).

5.3 Social and spatial inequalities within European cities

There is, however, a common trend characterising both growing and shrinking cities across Europe, with cities throughout Europe becoming increasingly socially and spatially unequal and segregated since the 1980s (Colini *et al.* 2013).

Evidence suggests that income inequality and polarisation have been increasing in Europe since the 1980s and that income inequalities in cities are bigger than they have been for generations (Tasan-Kok *et al.* 2014; Dorling 2011). There is a growth of poverty and inequality in London (MacInnes *et al.* 2011) and throughout European cities including Stockholm, Paris and Rome (Harsman 2006; Mudu 2006; Cassiers and Kesteloot 2012). Cities in Eastern and Central Europe, as well as in Western Europe are experiencing increasing social and spatial divisions and polarisation.

Inequalities in income and in wealth have a spatial dimension, indeed 'spatial segregation' can be seen as 'the projection of the social structure on space' (Haussermann and Siebel. 2001 in Cassiers and Kesteloot. 2012) and cities are spatially segregated in terms of both social class and ethnicity (Van Kempen and Murie 2009; Wacquant 2008). While European cities are less spatially segregated than US cities, it remains the case that:

> Today almost all European cities face growing problems of spatial segregation. Although Europe still has relatively less polarised and segregated urban structures compared to cities in other parts of the world, segregation affects prosperous, growing and shrinking cities alike.
>
> (Colini *et al.* 2013: 10)

In many European cities income inequalities and poverty are increasing, the poor are getting poorer and there is an increasing concentration of poverty, unemployment, poor housing, low educational attainment and poor health within particular poor neighbourhoods (EU 2011). Such poor neighbourhoods differ in their location and composition in different cities. In France, the UK and in many northern, Central and Eastern European cities, poor neighbourhoods are predominantly social housing neighbourhoods but while in some cities these may be predominantly located on the periphery of cities such as in France, in others social housing is overwhelmingly concentrated in the inner city such as in many cities in the UK, although there are large social housing estates with high levels of deprivation on the outskirts of large cities, such as Liverpool and Glasgow, throughout the UK too.

It is of no surprise that 'In even the richest of our cities, social and spatial segregation are growing problems' (EU 2011). Indeed, recent research conducted by the Joseph Rowntree Foundation (Lee *et al.* 2014) highlights the fact that economic growth does not always reduce poverty and that many of the most economically successful cities have experienced increasing poverty rates even during periods of economic growth (ibid.). The contrast between rich and poor is especially striking within larger economically dynamic cities where the growth of high-end knowledge-intensive jobs exists alongside persistent urban poverty. Indeed, cities throughout Europe which have been successful in capturing new investment and jobs in the knowledge and financial industries are those with the greatest inequalities. Numerous recent studies in the UK, for example, highlight the fact that inequalities are highest in cities in the south of England – in London in particular and in Reading and Milton Keynes which have the highest levels of wage inequality and employment polarisation – whereas smaller cities and those that have experienced industrial decline have the most equal labour markets (ibid.). Lee *et al.* (2014) argue that:

> The main driver of urban inequality is affluence. Cities with higher than average wages and knowledge-based economies tend to be more unequal.

Studies show that London (and inner London in particular) is the most unequal region in the UK (Aldridge *et al.* 2015). The *London Poverty Profile 2015* highlights the fact that 'One of the main drivers of inequality in London is the disparity in wages between high paid and low paid workers' and that 'London has the most unequal pay distribution of any part of the UK, wholly due to very high pay at the top end' (ibid.: 33).

As Hall also highlights:

> the contrast is between the very high-earning, highly-educated, highly-skilled, highly specialised individuals working in the knowledge economy, especially in industries like financial services or the media, and very poorly paid recent immigrants to the cities doing basic service jobs.
>
> (2013: 20)

Hall also points to the socio-spatial inequalities throughout many cities in the UK:

> This inequality is reflected in the new geography of the [Core] Cities. Their central business districts are the chief locations for the growth of the knowledge economy, together with their university campuses. Sometimes city centre growth washes out into regenerated inner-ring locations, such as Salford Quays in Greater Manchester. But large areas of the middle and outer rings of these cities have failed to make the adaption, leaving many of their inhabitants unemployed and deeply deprived . . . This is why, despite their prosperity, these cities still record extraordinarily high levels of deprivation.
>
> (2013: 20–1)

Such increases in inequality and segregation clearly threaten social cohesion and present key challenges in cities throughout Europe (Cassiers and Kesteloot 2012; Colini *et al.* 2013; EU 2011).

5.4 Case studies of growing social and spatial inequality and segregation in European cities

Recent research highlights the growing social and spatial inequalities and spatial segregation in European cities. Research by Zwiers *et al.* (2015) in large cities in

Jane Lewis

the Netherlands shows increasing social and spatial polarisation in all four cities of Amsterdam, The Hague, Rotterdam and Utrecht:

> the socio-spatial structure of Amsterdam has turned more or less inside out: the inner-city neighbourhoods have experienced significant upgrading, while the neighbourhoods at the outskirts of the city have experienced down-grading . . . While all four cities do not show the same patterns (which can be explained by the different histories and contexts of each city): the overall picture is that these cities have become increasingly polarized in terms of social status. The maps show that average status neighbourhoods are disappearing from the cities.
>
> (Zwiers *et al.* 2015: 9–10)

This study of large Dutch cities shows growing social and spatial polarisation – with growth 'of the top and bottom end of the neighbourhood distribution in terms of social status, at the expense of the middle' (Zwiers *et al.* 2015: 10). This process of social and spatial polarisation taking place in many dynamic European cities reflects social class changes in central city neighbourhoods in particular, in which a new middle class in gentrified housing live alongside poorer households, many in social housing, with the middle and lower income groups all but squeezed out. Such social class polarisation is also highlighted in a recent study of Islington, North London (NEF 2013).

Despite the different histories of the post-socialist Eastern and Central European cities, evidence suggests similar outcomes and patterns (EU 2011). In Czech Republic cities, for example, the wealthy have moved into inner city areas and suburban locations while the poor, including migrants and the elderly, increasingly live in social housing estates:

> The housing estates . . . have changed from mostly middle-class young family housing in the 1960s to the 1980s, into residences for elderly people and increasingly, for migrants . . . Exclusionary enclaves have emerged in old working class districts and housing estates in declining old industrial regions. At the same time, gentrification is changing certain attractive historical cores as well as certain selected inner-city districts.
>
> (ibid.)

Similarly, a recent study of 15 German cities found increasing social polarisation and argued that social segregation in German cities grew between 1990 and 2005 (Friedrichs and Triemer 2009 in Colini *et al.* 2013).

Against Divided Cities in Europe (Colini *et al.* 2013) highlights growing spatial segregation in a number of European cities including Berlin (Germany), Malmo (Sweden), Vaulx-en-Velin (France) and Naples (Italy) but also points to the way in which this manifests itself differently in each city. The report indicates that while in Berlin there are a number of areas of deprivation, in Malmo there is a growing concentration of deprivation in the central urban area.

In Berlin, since the reunification of Germany in 1990, a patchwork of communities has emerged in the city based on ethnic, religious, social and economic divisions. Overall, about one-quarter of the population of Berlin has a foreign background, unemployment is high and at 25 per cent especially high in some neighbourhoods, rents have rapidly increased and about 20 per cent of the Berlin population has precarious or part-time employment (Colini *et al.* 2013). The ethnic and socio-economic divisions are reflected in the city with the most deprived areas located in the inner areas of the city.

Similarly, Malmo, Sweden's third largest city has experienced population and economic growth and yet is a city in which segregation is increasing. The most evident form of this segregation in Malmo is ethnic segregation in particular neighbourhoods. Migrants account for 40 per cent of the population in Malmo with 30 per cent having been born abroad:

> The newly arriving people are largely immigrants who live in over-crowded privately rented apartments . . . In the mid-20th century, the most deprived part was located next to the port. However, after the construction of the Oresund link to Copenhagen and massive investments in urban renewal, the harbour zone has turned from brownfield into a trendy residential and mixed-use area including offices, restaurants and university departments. As a result, disadvantaged groups have moved to other areas of the city. Today Malmo can be described as ethnically and socio-economically segregated, with middle-class neighbourhoods in the west and working-class neighbourhoods in the south and east.
>
> (Colini *et al.* 2013:18)

The main signs of segregation in the poorer areas are unemployment, higher crime rates, overcrowding, low achievement at school, welfare dependency, youth crime, drug sales and burglary. There are four disadvantaged areas where the socio-economic segregation is stark. One of these is Rosengard (23,000 residents):

> this is the district with the highest unemployment. As many as 82 per cent of residents are unemployed (having no taxable income) and a large part of them are immigrants . . . Rosengard is the area where low income people end up living.
>
> (Colini *et al.* 2013:18)

Recent research in Birmingham, Britain's second largest city, highlights growing inequality in the city and the existence of deprived neighbourhoods side by side with more affluent areas mapping how austerity and welfare reform together with the unequal impacts of economic growth have widened the gap between poor (mostly inner city) and prosperous neighbourhoods in the city since 2010 (Gulliver 2016). Birmingham, the fifth most deprived local authority in England (and with 50 per cent of voters voting to leave the EU), saw local services cut by £560m between 2010 and 2015 with further cuts of

£250m planned over the following four years. The report highlights rising inequality in Birmingham exemplified by tenure changes (a fall in home ownership and a doubling in private renting in the five years since 2010) and a widening income divide between high and low earners with the differential between the average wage of the top and bottom 10 per cent of earners in Birmingham increasing by over 4 per cent from £34,985 in 2010 to £36,467 in 2015 (ibid.).

While each of these case studies has its own context – its own economic and cultural history – what these cities have in common is growing inequality and growing social and spatial segregation. In each city, there is a growing concentration of low income and especially ethnic minority communities in deprived neighbourhoods.

5.5 Hyper-diversity, migration and ethnicity

Alongside the segregation of European cities in terms of social class, there is also significant ethnic residential segregation in European cities, as highlighted in the examples above. While it is the case that European cities are less ethnically segregated than US cities (and much of the literature on ethnic segregation examines US rather than European cities), European cities exhibit high levels of ethnic residential segregation and ethnic minority groups are concentrated in the poorest neighbourhoods in cities across Europe. The pattern of ethnic segregation in European cities differs greatly between cities and countries. In French cities, for example, there is a concentration of ethnic minority population in the peripheral social housing estates of Paris, Lyons and the other major cities, whereas in the UK the black and ethnic minority population is more highly represented in social housing estates in the inner city areas of London, Birmingham, Manchester and of other towns and cities. Also, in some European cities it is argued that ethnic segregation is declining while in others it is increasing. Malmo in Sweden, for example, 'is a city in which segregation is rising and its most evident form is the ethnic segregation in key neighbourhoods' (Colini *et al.* 2013).

One key change taking place in European cities is that they are becoming increasingly ethnically diverse. The phrases hyper-diversity and super-diversity have recently been used to capture this growing ethnic diversity in contemporary European cities (Tasan-Kok *et al.* 2014). Taking London as an example, Hamnett (2003: 109) notes that 'In the 1960's the population of London was still predominantly white and British born . . . the scale of the transformation is remarkable'. In the 2011 Census, 55 per cent of the population of London identified as 'Non-White British' (as compared with 40 per cent in 2001), just under three million people in London were born outside the UK and a total of 107 languages were spoken (Aldridge *et al.* 2015).

In London, certain ethnic minority groups are concentrated in particular neighbourhoods. The population of Bangladeshi heritage has been concentrated in Tower Hamlets in East London since the 1970s while Southwark has a large

Black African population and Lewisham a large Black African/Black Caribbean and Black Other population. However, Johnston *et al.* (2002: 226) shows that 'the degree of ethnic residential segregation typical of US cities is almost entirely absent from London – which has no ghettos and few polarised enclaves' and that most of London's ethnic minorities live in mixed areas. Indeed, evidence suggests that ethnic residential segregation is both changing and declining in London (and more widely throughout UK cities), with many settled ethnic minorities communities moving from inner to outer London. In 2011, for example, the Indian/Pakistani/Bangladeshi heritage communities accounted for over 30 per cent of the total population in the outer London boroughs of Harrow and Redbridge. In East London, Butler and Hamnett (2011) have documented major changes in both the social class and ethnic composition of the population over the last 20 years, indicating that middle-class black and minority ethnic residents are increasingly moving to the outer East London boroughs of Redbridge, Havering and Barking:

> If the marker between the outer London boroughs and Essex used to be one of social class, it is increasingly one of ethnicity. The non-white populations of Inner East London (particularly Newham's Asians) have been moving steadily outwards.
>
> (Butler and Hamnett 2011: 9)

Analysis from the 2011 Census indicates ethnic segregation has decreased within most cities in England and Wales (with inequalities increasing most in rural and coastal areas with small ethnic minority populations:

> Increasing residential mixing in inner and outer London and major urban centres is the dominant pattern of change in segregation. In outer London, for example, segregation decreased by 12 per cent for the Bangladeshi ethnic group. Large cities such as Leicester, Birmingham, Manchester and Bradford have seen a decrease in segregation for most groups.
>
> (Catney 2013)

This evidence of a decline in ethnic residential segregation in UK cities contradicts some of the debates which became prominent in the mid-2000s in which Pakistani communities in northern cities in particular were seen as self-segregated, leading 'parallel lives' and as having failed to integrate into British society. This view was made explicit in 2005 when Trevor Phillips, Head of the Commission for Racial Inequality, argued that Britain was 'sleep-walking to segregation', to ethnic enclaves and potential conflict (Woods and Leppard 2005). Phillips argued that ethnic communities in Britain were increasingly concentrated in 'ghettos' and that there was evidence of a growing ethnic divide in UK cities.

As highlighted above, this view is at odds with the evidence which suggests a decline in ethnic segregation in UK cities. Finney and Simpson (2009), for example, show that in Bradford, while much of the black and Asian population is concentrated in particular parts of the city, there are changes and the reality is complex and dynamic with many Asian families moving to more affluent areas in the city and more recent migrants from Eastern Europe and Africa moving into poorer areas – a dynamism and diversity that suggested something more complex than isolated ghettos (ibid.). Indeed, Sriskandarajah (in Woods and Leppard 2005) argues that there is no simple pattern of ethnic segregation but a 'churning' of ethnic populations and that segregation in UK cities reflects socio-economic class rather than ethnicity.

Similarly, Wacquant (2008) argues that ethnic segregation is not the same everywhere but is a 'historical matrix of class, state and space characteristic of each society at a given epoch' (ibid.: 2). Wacquant (2008) argues that analysis needs to integrate 'the roles of the labour market, ethnic division and the state' and that ethnic residential segregation reflects 'race and class in the context of the double retrenchment of the labour market and the welfare state' (ibid.: 2–3). In other words, for Wacquant (2008), ethnic residential segregation reflects a complexity of factors which includes race, social class, the restructuring of labour markets and the restructuring of welfare states, the outcome of which will be different in different cities. Wacquant's (2008) research compares ethnic segregation in Chicago's South Side with the social housing estates on the periphery of Paris and argues that in US cities ethnic segregation reflects a more specifically racial dimension than in the social housing estates in Paris where marginalisation is primarily caused by the social-class position of the more ethnically heterogeneous population supported by a stronger welfare state than in US cities, which have weak welfare state support 'which results in sharply higher levels of blight, isolation and hardship in America's dark ghetto' (ibid.: 5).

As Wacquant (2008) suggests, there are different patterns of ethnic segregation in different cities and while in the UK there is evidence of a decline in ethnic segregation, this is not the case in other European cities where ethnic segregation is increasing. There is also a difference between segregation and diversity. Most European cities are becoming increasingly ethnically diverse. In Europe cities are more demographically and ethnically diverse than ever before as a result, in part, of the significant recent growth in migration (further examined in Ginsburg's chapter above and at the heart of the UK's Brexit vote). Increasing ethnic diversity has also produced conflicting responses. While many celebrate diversity and employers welcome migration as an important source of both skilled and unskilled labour, for others there is 'too much' diversity in European cities and increasing diversity is seen as a challenge to social cohesion (again a debate that featured heavily in the UK's Brexit campaign and vote). As Tasan-Kok et al. (2014: 34) indicate, 'some stress that diversity constitutes a threat to an imagined social order and the legitimacy of welfare state systems across the EU' (ibid.). Indeed, Tasan-Kok et al. (2014) argue that policy climates across Europe have been shifting with a hardening of positions on migrants and diversity particularly in the context of economic recession and austerity. 'Too much diversity' is a perspective which has permeated policy debates and interventions from migration to urban policies across Europe. Again it is too early to discuss the impact of the UK's vote to leave the EU on the free movement of people within the UK and the wider EU countries, but this was a key factor underlying the 'Leave' campaign and vote in the UK.

Ethnic residential segregation has also been a focus of concern in cities in the Netherlands, where there has been a shift in policy since the 2000s (Musterd and Ostendorf 2008) with government voicing concern that the concentration of ethnic minorities in certain neighbourhoods hampers their integration:

> Concentration is especially disadvantageous for integration because it results in an accumulation of social problems which may eventuate in a state of affairs that is very difficult to handle . . . Concentration is also disadvant-ageous because it makes the ethnic dividing lines more visible in a more concerted way. That harms the image of the ethnic minorities . . . Finally, concentration is particularly disadvantageous for the possibilities of meeting and contacts between persons from different origin groups . . . the diminishing contacts with native Dutch indirectly influence the social chances of ethnic minorities.
>
> (Cited in Tasan-Kok *et al.* 2014: 44)

The Dutch government have introduced social-mix policies in low income and ethnic minority dominated social housing neighbourhoods in order to encourage more middle-income households to poor neighbourhoods.

While it is widely argued that the increasing hyper-diversity of European cities raises key challenges (Tasan-Kok *et al.* 2014; Syrett and Sepulveda 2012) and that ethnic segregation is a key policy challenge for European cities, there is also a large literature highlighting the advantages of diversity to the economic competitiveness of cities (Fainstein 2005). Florida (2002) (whose work has had a significant influence on urban policy-makers in cities across Europe including Berlin, Liverpool and Copenhagen) argues that diversity (in a wide sense including gay couples, bohemians and foreign-born populations) and tolerance contribute to the attraction of knowledge workers and increases the 'creative capital' of cities.

5.6 Case study: poverty and inequality in London

It is perhaps no surprise that London, a global city with a large growth in knowledge and financial industries since the 1990s, is the most unequal city in the UK with the highest proportion of both rich and poor people. Inner London in particular has the highest proportion of people in the top and the bottom deciles in terms of income. Wealth is even more unequal than income, with the richest 10 per cent of households accounting for two-thirds of wealth in London (MacInnes *et al.* 2011). *London's Poverty Profile 2015* indicates:

> Whatever aspect of inequality we look at – income, pay or wealth – London is the most unequal part of the country. This inequality is not due to those at

the bottom being exceptionally worse off in London. Inequality in London is being driven by the wealth of those at the top, which is much higher in London in every aspect. This is not new or surprising.

(Aldridge *et al.* 2015: 38)

London's Poverty Profile 2015 indicates that 'the level of inequality in London has remained consistently high since the mid-1990s' (ibid.: 32).

Poverty is also high in London with 27 per cent of Londoners living in poverty after housing costs are taken into account (GLA 2011; Aldridge *et al.* 2015). What is both significant and new, however, is that the majority of people living in poverty in London are in working families, which highlights the growing issue of in-work poverty in London. The number of people in a working family in poverty in London has increased by 70 per cent (from 700,000 to 1.2 million) in the last ten years (Aldridge *et al.* 2015). Nearly one in every five jobs in London pays below the London Living Wage. Low income is at the heart of poverty and the measure of poverty used here is income poverty, in which a household is considered to be in income poverty if it has an income below 60 per cent of the national mean (ibid.). High and rapidly growing costs of housing are also a major contributor to high levels of poverty in London and so the measure of poverty used is what is known as the After Housing Costs (AHC) income. As the *London's Poverty Profile 2015* report suggests

it is high housing costs that act as a real block to reducing poverty in London, and it is rent, particularly private rent, which is the issue – more people in poverty in London live in the private rented sector than the social rented sector.

(Aldridge *et al.* 2015: 12)

Poverty and deprivation are not, of course, evenly spread across the city and London accounts for six of the ten local authority areas in the UK with the highest proportion of households living in poverty – Tower Hamlets, Newham, Hackney, Brent, Southwark and Barking and Dagenham. As the recent GLA (2011) report *Poverty: The Hidden City* highlights:

It is clear from this that the most deprived areas within London are concentrated in an arc to the east and north of the City, from Newham through Tower Hamlets, Hackney and Islington up into Haringey and the outer London boroughs of Enfield and Waltham Forest.

(ibid.: 14)

In Tower Hamlets, 53 per cent of children lived in poverty in 2008, a figure which compares with 12 per cent in the affluent west London borough of Richmond upon Thames (GLA 2011). Similarly, 47 per cent of pensioners received Pension Credit in Tower Hamlets, twice the London average, compared with a rate of 10 per cent in Bromley (MacInnes *et al.* 2011). In terms of health inequalities, the *London Poverty Profile* report indicates that the highest rates of premature deaths were in inner South and East London with rates in Hackney, Lambeth, Tower Hamlets, Islington, Newham and Southwark more than twice that for Kensington and Chelsea, and Richmond. Poor mental health is also much more common in the more deprived parts of London.

At a local level, research on the inner North London borough of Islington points to growing social polarisation within the borough:

> In terms of income, occupation, qualifications and housing tenure, Islington shows signs of being a socially polarised borough. Overall, the picture is one of rich families with highly qualified and high-earning adults at one extreme and poor families often without work and living in social housing at the other. This picture of polarisation is nuanced however by a transient middle group of highly mobile young professionals who are earning middle-incomes but who are not asset wealthy and are struggling to lay down roots in the area.
>
> (NEF 2013: 31)

The study highlights the role of the housing market in producing and reinforcing inequality:

> The role of the housing market is central in producing and reproducing the unequal and polarised social make-up of Islington.
>
> (NEF 2013: 31)

The study highlights that Islington has a polarised income distribution – with a high proportion of residents living on benefits and a large proportion earning very high incomes (a total of 70 per cent of employed residents are in top occupational jobs) (NEF 2013). The study also highlights the process of social polarisation taking place in the borough – poverty is increasing in Islington while middle-income families are being squeezed out and only the wealthiest are able to afford housing in the private sector:

> We predict that by 2020 a family will need to earn more than £90,000 a year to afford market rents in Islington. House buying will be out of reach for almost all but the very top earners. This will leave Islington polarised, with very wealthy families at the top, a youthful transient and childless sector in the middle and those on low incomes at the bottom, living in social housing.
>
> (ibid.: 5)

Housing is a key issue underlying the growth of inequality in cities. In London, house price and rent increases in the private sector, the growth of foreign investors in housing markets and a decline in social housebuilding alongside welfare reforms are causing a growing housing crisis, in particular a crisis of affordable housing (Booth 2014; Meek 2013; Lees 2008, 2014; Watts 2013). Evidence suggests that changes in housing and labour markets are resulting in the dual processes of gentrification, in which the 'new middle class' moves into inner

Jane Lewis

city' and previously working class areas, alongside the displacement (social cleansing) of poor (and middle-income) families, no longer able to afford to live in large areas of the city (Lees 2014; Watts 2013). Research on the impact of recent benefit changes (the benefit cap in particular), suggests that poorer families are being pushed out of inner London. The number of children entitled to free school meals, for example, has declined by 25 per cent in four inner London boroughs and by 16 per cent in inner London as a whole since 2010 (Taylor 2015). Such trends raise concerns over the displacement of the poor from inner London.

Large council housing estates have previously protected significant parts of inner London from gentrification. However, Watts (2013) argues that the current demolition and regeneration of council housing estates across London (such as the Heygate and Aylesbury estates in Southwark and the Woodberry Down estate in Hackney) and the development of large mixed-tenure neighbourhoods in their place is facilitating a widening of the processes of gentrification and displacement throughout inner London (Chakrabortty and Robinson-Tillett 2014; Watts 2013).

5.7 The drivers and causes of growing inequalities and segregation in European cities

Research into the social class and ethnic segregation of cities is not new. Over the past two decades or so, however, there has been renewed debate about the increasing social and spatial divisions in cities and a large literature has emerged on segregation and division within Western European cities (Musterd 2005; Van Kempen 2005; Musterd and Van Kempen 2009). There is also a growing literature on spatial segregation in Central and Eastern European cities (Marcinczak *et al.* 2012). Much of this literature points out that European cities are less segregated than US cities and that this can in part be explained by the different contexts in which they operate, especially the existence of stronger welfare states in much of Europe as compared to the US. However, austerity and the retreat of the welfare state in many European countries is seen as a key driver of growing inequalities in contemporary European cities and this is further examined below. Alongside the retreat of the welfare state, economic and labour market restructuring and changes in housing are all key drivers of the growing segregation of European cities. As a number of recent studies have highlighted:

> European cities have traditionally been characterised by less segregation and less social and spatial polarisation compared to . . . US cities. This has been specifically true for cities in countries with strong welfare systems. However, there are many signs that polarisation and segregation are increasing. The economic crisis has further amplified the effects of globalisation and the gradual retreat of the welfare state in most European countries.
>
> (EU 2011: 24)

Although segregation levels in Europe are not as high as on the other side of the Atlantic . . . socio-spatial inequalities also seem to be on the rise in urban Europe. This has been demonstrated for many cities, such as Stockholm, London, Paris, Rome, and Istanbul...these increasing inequalities are brought about by intensified processes of economic globalisation, capital and labour flexibility and welfare restructuring.

(Cassiers and Kesteloot 2012: 1909)

The following section examines some of the different and complex causes of growing socio-spatial inequalities in European cities.

Economic restructuring

For many, the growth in social and spatial inequality in European cities is linked to a new phase of (neo-liberal) capitalism which has produced new, intensified patterns and forms of social and spatial inequality and division in European cities (Harvey 1989; Davis 1990; Cassiers and Kesteloot 2012; Minton 2012; Lees 2014). As Tasan-Kok *et al.* argue:

. . . we are seeing the rise of new forms of 'enclave urbanism' . . . in which new powerful economic elites live in exclusive and increasingly gated and gentrified parts of the city. The global economy has created new super-elites consisting of a tiny number of staggeringly wealthy individuals . . . exclusive, top-end property in many cities has continued to soar in value. Again London provides the EU's most extreme example with research . . . showing that prime central London property has increased by 53% in value between March 2009–January 2013.

(2014: 26–7)

For many, it is economic restructuring which is the primary driver of growing socio-spatial inequalities in cities. It is argued that a new phase of capitalism, involving a shift from industrial to post-industrial city economies, has resulted in a growth of high paid and skilled jobs in the knowledge-intensive industries alongside the collapse of middle-income manual jobs in the manufacturing industry and a growth of low paid service sector jobs (Sassen 2011). Such shifts in industrial and occupational structure feed through to changes in social structure leading to a growing social polarisation in cities which is itself reflected in a growing polarisation of neighbourhoods between increasingly affluent and gentrified neighbourhoods and increasingly poor (and frequently social housing) neighbourhoods. This is a simplification of complex debates, but highlights how social and spatial segregation is seen by many as the outcome of economic change.

According to Sassen (1991), growing social and spatial polarisation is especially marked in 'global cities' such as London and Paris. Sassen (1991) suggests that, since the 1990s, globalisation has led to the emergence of a new hierarchy of cities, one in which the key command and control functions of the global economy are increasingly concentrated in a small number of 'global cities'. Sassen (1991) argues that in large global cities economic restructuring has involved the collapse of manufacturing and growth of knowledge-intensive industries, and led to a social and income polarisation with an increase in professional and managerial jobs, a decline in middle-income jobs in manufacturing and a growth in low paid jobs in the service industries. Economic restructuring is therefore seen as having produced a new social polarisation in global cities such as London, New York, Tokyo and Paris.

The impact of the restructuring of employment and of labour markets (the growth of labour market flexibility, casualisation and precarious employment) on social inequality and polarisation has also been highlighted in recent studies (Standing 2011). Pratschke and Morlicchio (2012) argue that economic and welfare state restructuring together with global migration have combined to create a growth in low paid employment in cities throughout Europe. Recent research also points to the existence across Europe of a 'migrant division of labour' in many European cities with migrants an increasingly important source of low paid labour (May *et al.* 2007).

However, much of the literature on growing spatial inequalities in European cities has focussed on the fact that cities faced with the same global economic pressures and changes exhibit different patterns of inequality and segregation and that an important element of the explanation of these differences is to be found in the differences between welfare states which is further discussed in the section below.

Welfare state restructuring

A recent EU report suggests that the increasing socio-spatial segregation taking place across European cities is being caused by 'a rolling back of state intervention, retrenchment of welfare support and weak social housing policies' (Colini *et al.* 2013: 5). In terms of socio-economic inequalities and particularly of ethnic segregation in cities, the differences between the more intense social polarisation and ethnic segregation in US cities as compared with European cities is frequently attributed to the relative strength of the welfare state (Wacquant 2008; Van Kempen and Murie 2009). However, in recent years austerity measures and the restructuring and weakening of the welfare state has become commonplace across Europe. As Van Kempen and Murie (2009: 383) point out, 'since the 1980s, all European welfare states have experienced some movement from managed to market led approaches'. Welfare states across Europe have been weakened by austerity measures over recent years and this has had a disproportionate impact on the poor and on widening inequalities in European cities.

It is important to point out, however, that while there are common pressures on cities, different cities within Europe show different manifestations of growing socio-spatial segregation which reflect their different welfare state contexts. It has been argued that while countries such as France, Germany and Sweden all have strong welfare states, they have shown different manifestations

inequalities in European cities

of growing socio-spatial segregation over recent years (Colini *et al.* 2013). This suggests the importance of a context-dependent or 'path dependency' approach to understanding socio-spatial inequalities and segregation in different European cities – an approach adopted by Zwiers *et al.* (2015) in their study of increasing socio-spatial polarisation in large cities in the Netherlands. Musterd and Ostendorf (1998) also argue that cities affected by the same global economic pressures have different patterns of segregation and that differences between welfare states are an important part of the explanation. Esping-Andersen's (1990) regime analysis in which he clusters different models of welfare states into three key welfare state regimes (conservative, social democratic and liberal, and sometimes a fourth, southern model), is useful in helping us understand different outcomes in different European cities and countries. It is argued that differences in welfare state models or regimes impact differently on the levels and form of inequality, particularly between the liberal model of the US and the more corporatist and social democratic models of the European welfare state. While neo-liberal austerity has been a path chosen by most European countries since 2008, the outcome has been less profound in the Nordic countries than in liberal and southern European states and this in part is seen as a consequence of the different welfare regimes in these countries.

Van Kempen and Murie (2009) argue that Esping-Andersen's typology of welfare states remains relevant to an understanding of socio-spatial segregation in European cities but also argue that differences in social housing policy and in urban planning (frequently not covered in comparative analysis of welfare state regimes) are of key importance in explaining socio-spatial divisions and segregation in European cities. In the Netherlands, France and the UK, for example, social housing is concentrated in specific areas in which low income households have become increasingly concentrated.

Housing markets, and urban policy and planning

Clearly housing markets and housing policy are major factors underlying social and spatial inequalities and segregation in European cities. Weak social housing policies alongside the reduction of welfare state support have been identified as key causes of the growing socio-spatial segregation in European cities (Colini *et al.* 2013).

Van Kempen and Murie (2009) highlight the fact that throughout Europe housing is market dominated. Thirteen EU member states have more than 75 per cent of housing in the owner-occupied sector, which includes most Central, Eastern and Southern European countries. While Southern European countries have long been dominated by private housing (owned and rented), in Central and Eastern Europe where there was a significant state housing sector in the past, deregulation and privatisation have led to major changes in housing since the 1990s. The other group of EU countries with relatively large social rented housing sectors largely consist of Northern European countries. In these countries, the location of social rented housing is a key factor underlying socio-spatial segregation in cities as low income households are concentrated in social

Jane Lewis

housing. When social housing is concentrated in certain areas 'spatial concen-trations of low income households can be expected' (Van Kempen and Murie 2009: 389). Recent years have also seen a 'residualisation' of social housing in all European countries with a large social housing sector including in the UK, Sweden and the Netherlands, in all of which social housing neighbourhoods have become increasingly dominated by low income households.

Van Kempen and Murie have therefore argued that patterns of social and spatial division within cities cannot be derived from economic change and growing income inequality or even welfare state regimes:

> While economic restructuring and the increased income inequality associated with the impacts of this are a key part of these dynamics, they are not sufficient to explain the different social and spatial patterns emerging in European cities. New social divisions emerging in European cities also relate to a new competition around housing, land and property investment.
>
> (2009: 391)

5.8 Policy responses to the growing segregation of European cities

Against Divided Cities in Europe (Colini *et al.* 2013) argues that social cohesion in European cities is threatened by the increase in social polarisation, itself the result of increasing income polarisation since the 1980s. The report examines the range of policies aimed at tackling the problems of segregation in European cities and highlights how difficult it is to deal with the complex problems of segregated and polarised cities. 'Area-based' initiatives targeting poor neighbourhoods are a common response but, as the report argues, frequently do not address the wider causes of segregation such as weak social housing policies and a shrinking welfare state or indeed of growing income polarisation and labour market inequality.

Policies which encourage social- and tenure-mix have become common among urban policy-makers in European cities as a way of tackling areas with high levels of social class and ethnic segregation and of reducing the concen-tration of low income households in large social housing estates (Colini *et al.* 2013). In many cities, particularly in the Netherlands, France and the UK, attempts have been made to tackle the problems of poor social housing neighbourhoods through a policy of demolition of existing social housing and the construction of new mixed-tenure housing to encourage greater social class mix. On large single-tenure social housing estates in the UK, regeneration schemes increasingly focus on the development of new mixed-tenure housing and communities as a means of tackling the problems of poor neighbourhoods (or perhaps more realistically as a financial model in which social housing is subsidised by new build housing for sale). Similarly, in 1997 in the Netherlands a national Urban Renewal Policy was implemented with the aim of upgrading the worst neighbourhoods through a policy of housing diversification in which social housing was demolished alongside the construction of new, more expensive rent and owner-occupied housing (Zwiers *et al.* 2015). Critics have argued that this is 'state-led gentrification' (Lees 2008, 2014). In the Netherlands, evaluation studies have shown that such urban regeneration policies, while improving the physical quality of poor neighbourhoods, fail to improve the lives of existing low income residents and that social-mixing policies have displaced low income and ethnic minority communities (Van Beckhoven *et al.* 2009). In South-East London, the redevelopment of the Heygate estate has been criticised as being 'all about the gentrification of the area, they've chosen to knock the estate down because it's in a prime location' (Moss 2011); Watts (2013) has documented similar processes taking place on social housing estates throughout London and in early 2016 Cameron announced extending this as a national policy initiative (Davies 2016).

Indeed, for some, urban regeneration policy in general is seen increasingly as a form of 'state-led gentrification'(Lees 2008). Porter and Shaw (2009) attempt to look beyond this 'dominant regeneration-as-gentrification approach' in their comparative study of regeneration across Europe (and globally) but conclude that 'the same processes of capital-centric regeneration, rising land values and the victimisation of the most vulnerable' appear to be the outcome of regeneration strategies everywhere (Hodkinson 2011: 272). Minton (2012) also argues that much regeneration policy is driven by a model 'based on a virtuous circle of property finance, shopping, spending and rising property values' and this 'is an approach which has seen large private centres take over towns and cities around Britain, created as citadels of finance or high-end retail which aims to attract the well-heeled ABC's of the region rather than the local communities around them' (ibid.: xiv).

Increasingly urban policy has tended to focus on economic competitiveness (Boddy and Parkinson 2004; Office of the Deputy Prime Minister 2006; Cabinet Office 2011). Policy-makers focus on making cities competitive in an increasingly global economy which involves making cities attractive to both new investment and highly skilled workers in the knowledge and creative industries (Florida 2002). Not only is this policy agenda one in which poverty and inequality are not seen as a priority but also, critics would argue, such policy priorities further reinforce inequality, polarisation and segregation in European cities.

5.9 Conclusion

This chapter has examined the growth of poverty and inequality, of social polarisation and segregation in European cities. It has argued that over recent years segregation and inequality have increased in most European cities, be they growing or shrinking cities. It has shown that European cities face challenges of growing poverty and inequality. The chapter has attempted to highlight some of the underlying causes of growing inequality and segregation in European cities. It has been argued that the drivers of growing inequality in European cities include economic restructuring, labour market change and welfare state, and wider housing and urban policy restructuring.

Jane Lewis

Bibliography

Aldridge. H, Born. TB, Tinson. A and MacInnes. T (2015) *London's Poverty Profile 2015*. London: Trust for London/New Policy Institute.

Boddy. M and Parkinson. M (eds) (2004) *City Matters: Competitiveness, Cohesion and Urban Governance*. Bristol: Policy Press.

Booth. R (2014) Londoner's miss out as homes built as 'safe deposit boxes' for foreign buyers. *The Guardian*. 27th December.

Buck. N, Gordon. I, Harding. A and Turok. I (eds) (2005) *Changing Cities: Rethinking Urban Competitiveness, Cohesion and Governance*. London: Palgrave.

Burdett. R, Griffiths. P, Heeckt. C, Moss. F and Vahidy. S (2015) *Innovations in European Cities*. London: LSE Cities.

Butler. T and Hamnett. C (2011) *Ethnicity, Class and Aspiration. Understanding London's New East End*. Bristol: Policy Press.

Cabinet Office (2011) *Unlocking Growth in Cities*. London: HMSO.

Cassiers. T and Kesteloot. C (2012) Socio-spatial inequalities and social cohesion in European cities. *Urban Studies*. 49(9) pp 1909–24.

Catney. G (2013) Has neighbourhood ethnic segregation decreased? *Dynamics of Diversity*. Centre on Dynamics of Diversity (CoDE). Manchester: University of Manchester.

Centre for Cities (2014) *Cities Outlook 2014*. London: Centre for Cities.

Chakrabortty. A and Robinson-Tillett. S (2014) The truth about gentrification: Regeneration or con trick? *The Guardian*. 18th May.

Colini. L, Czischke. D, Guntner. S, Tosics. I and Ramsden. P (2013) *Against Divided Cities in Europe*. Cities of Tomorrow – Action Today. URBACT II Capitalisation. May 2013.

Davies. C (2016) David Cameron vow to 'blitz' poverty by demolishing UKs worst sink estates. *The Guardian*. 10th January.

Davis. M (1990) *City of Quartz*. London: Verso.

Dijkstra. L and Poelman. H (2012) *Cities in Europe. The New OECD–EU Definition*. Brussels: European Commission.

Dorling. D (2011) *Injustice. Why Social Inequality Persists*. Bristol: Policy Press.

Easton. M (2016) Brexit and housing: Radical ideas wanted www.bbc.co.uk/news/uk-politics-uk-leaves-the-eu-36661425, accessed 4th July 2016.

Esping-Andersen. G (1990) *The Three Worlds of Welfare Capitalism*. Cambridge: Policy Press.

EU URBACT (2011) *Cities of Tomorrow. Challenges, Visions and Ways Forward*. Luxembourg: Publications Office of the European Union.

Fainstein. S (2005) Cities and Diversity. *Urban Affairs Review*. 41(1) pp 3–19.

Finney. N and Simpson. L (2009) *'Sleepwalking to Segregation'? Challenging the myths about race and immigration*. Bristol: Policy Press.

Florida. R (2002) *The Rise of the Creative Class*. New York: Basic Books.

Florida. R (2005) *Cities and the Creative Class*. New York: Routledge.

Friedrichs. J and Triemer. S (2009) *Gespaltene Städte?: Soziale und Ethnische Segregation in Deutschen Großstädten*. Wiesbaden: VS Verlag für Sozialwissenschaften.

Glaeser. E (2011) *Triumph of the City*. London: Macmillan.

Greater London Authority (GLA) (2011) *Poverty: The Hidden City*. Focus on London. London: GLA.

Gulliver. K (2016) *A Tale of Two Cities: Poverty and Prosperity in Birmingham*. Birmingham: Human City Institute.

Haase. A, Bernt. M, Grossmann. K, Mykhnenko. V and Rink. D (2013) Varieties of Shrinkage in European Cities. *European Urban and Regional Studies*. 23(1) pp 86–102.

Hall. P (2013) *Good Cities, Better Lives: How Europe Discovered the Lost Art of Urbanism*. London: Routledge.

Hamnett. C (2003) *Unequal City*. London: Routledge.

Harsman. B (2006) Ethnic diversity and spatial segregation in the Stockholm region. *Urban Studies* 43(8) pp 1341–64.

Harvey. D (1989) *The Condition of Postmodernity*. Oxford: Blackwell.

Harvey. D (2012) *Rebel Cities*. London: Verso.

Hodkinson. S (2011) Can we really ride the urban tiger of global capitalism? *City*. 15(2) pp 270–2.

Jackson. E and Butler. T (2015) Revisiting 'social tectonics': The middle classes and social mix in gentrifying neighbourhoods. *Urban Studies*. 52(13) pp 2349–65.

Jenkins. P (2016) City of London elite blame inequality for Brexit. *Financial Times*. 26th June.

Johnston. R, Forrest. R and Poulsen. M (2002) Are there ethnic enclaves/ghettos in English cities? *Urban Studies*. 39(4) pp 591–618.

Lee. N, Sissons. P and Jones K (2013) *Wage Inequality and Employment Polarisation in British Cities*. York: Joseph Rowntree Foundation. May 2013.

Lee. N, Sissons. P, Hughes. C, Green. A, Atfield. G, Adam. D and Rodriguez-Pose. A (2014) *Cities, Growth and Poverty: A Review of the Evidence*. York: Joseph Rowntree Foundation.

Lees. L (2003) Visions of 'urban renaissance'. In Imrie. R and Raco. M (eds) *Urban Renaissance?* pp 61–82. Bristol: Policy Press.

Lees. L (2008) Gentrification and social mixing: Towards an inclusive urban renaissance? *Urban Studies*. 45(12) pp 2449–70.

Lees. L (2014) The 'new' middle class, lifestyle and the 'new' gentrified city. In Paddison. R and McCann. E (eds) *Cities and Social Change*. pp 35–55. Sage: London.

Lymperopoulou. K and Finney. N (2016) Socio-spatial factors associated with ethnic inequalities in districts of England and Wales, 2001–2011. *Urban Studies*. DOI: 10.1177/0042098016653725.

MacInnes. T, Parekh. A and Kenway. P (2011) *London's Poverty Profile*. London: Trust for London/New Policy Institute.

Jane Lewis

McInroy. N (2016) Post-Brexit we need to build an economy for the many http://newstartmag.co.uk/your-blogs/post-brexit-need-economy-many/, accessed 4th July 2016.

Marcinczak. S, Musterd. S and Stepniak. M (2012) Where the grass is greener: Social segregation in three Polish cities at the beginning of the 21st century. *European Urban and Regional Studies*. 19(4) pp 383–403.

Massey. D (2007) *World Cities*. London: Polity.

May. J, Wills. J, Datta. K, Evans. Y, Herbert. J and McIlwaine. C (2007) Keeping London working: Global cities, the British state and London's new migrant division of labour. *Transactions of the Institute of British Geographers*. NS. 32(2) pp 151–67.

Meek. J (2013) Where will we live? *London Review of Books*. 36(1) pp 7–16.

Minton. A (2012) *Ground Control: Fear and Happiness in the Twenty-First Century City*. London: Penguin. Second edition.

Mollenkopf. J and Castells. M (1991) *Dual City: Restructuring New York*. New York: Russell Sage Foundation.

Moss. S (2011) The death of a housing ideal. *The Guardian*. 6th March.

Mudu. P (2006) Patterns of segregation in contemporary Rome. *Urban Geography*. 27(5) pp 422–40.

Musterd. S (2005) Social and ethnic segregation in Europe: Level, causes and effects. *Journal of Urban Affairs*. 27(3) pp 331–48.

Musterd. S and Ostendorf. W (1998) *Urban Segregation and the Welfare State: Inequality and Exclusion in Western Cities*. Routledge: London.

Musterd. S and Ostendorf. W (2008) Integrated urban renewal in the Netherlands: A critical appraisal. *Urban Research and Practice*. 1(1) pp 78–92.

Musterd. S and Van Kempen. R (2009) *Segregation and the Housing of Minority Ethnic Groups in Western European Cities*. London: Routledge.

Nathan. M (2015) After Florida: Towards an economics of diversity. *European Urban and Regional Studies*. 22(1) pp 3–19.

New Economics Foundation (NEF) (2013) *Distant Neighbours. Poverty and Inequality in Islington*. London: NEF/Cripplegate Foundation.

Office of the Deputy Prime Minister (2006) *State of the English Cities*, Volume 1. London: HMSO.

Peach. C (1996) Does Britain have ghettos? *Transactions of the Institute of British Geographers*. NS. 21(1) pp 216–35.

Peck. J (2012) 'Austerity Urbanism' *City* 16(6) pp 626–55,

Porter. L and Shaw. K (eds) (2009) *Whose Urban Renaissance? An International Comparison of Urban Regeneration Policies*. London: Routledge.

Pratschke. J and Morlicchio. E (2012) Social polarisation, the labour market and economic restructuring in Europe: An urban perspective. *Urban Studies*. 49(9) pp 1891–907.

Sassen. S (1991) *The Global City: New York, London, Tokyo*. Princeton, NJ: Princeton University Press.

Sassen. S (2011) *Cities in a World Economy*. London: Sage. Fourth edition.

Standing. G (2011) *The Precariat: The New Dangerous Class*. London and New York: Bloomsbury Academy.

Syrett. S and Sepulveda. L (2012) Urban governance and economic development in the diverse city. *European Urban and Regional Studies*. 19(3) pp 165–88.

Tasan-Kok. T, Van Kempen. R, Raco. M and Bolt. G (2014) *Towards Hyper-Diversified European Cities: A Critical Literature Review* www.urbandivercities.eu, accessed 23rd January 2017.

Taylor. M (2015) 'Vast social cleansing' pushes tens of thousands of families out of London. *The Guardian*. 28th August.

Turok. I and Mykhnenko. V (2007) The trajectories of European cities, 1960–2005. *Cities*. 24(3) pp 165–82.

Van Beckhoven. E, Bolt. G and Van Kempen. R (2009) Theories of neighbourhood change and neighbourhood decline: Their significance for post-WWII large housing estates. In Rowlands. R, Musterd. S and Van Kempen. R (eds) *Mass Housing in Europe: Multiple Faces of Development, Change and Response.* pp 20–53. Basingstoke: Macmillan.

Van Kempen. R (2005) Segregation and housing conditions of immigrants in Western European cities. In Kazepov. Y (ed.) *Cities of Europe, Changing Contexts, Local Arrangements, and the Challenge to Urban Cohesion.* pp 190–209. Oxford: Blackwell.

Van Kempen. R and Murie. A (2009) The new divided city: Changing patterns in European cities. *Tijdschrift voor Economische en Sociale Geografie*. 100(4) pp 377–98.

Wacquant. L (2008) *Urban Outcasts: A Comparative Sociology of Advanced Marginality*. Cambridge: Polity Press.

Watts. P (2013) 'It's not for us': Regeneration, the 2012 Olympics and the gentrification of East London. *City*. 17(1) pp 99–118.

Woods. R and Leppard. D (2005) Are we sleepwalking our way to apartheid? *Sunday Times*. 18th September.

Zwiers. M, Kleinhaus. R and Van Ham. M (2015) *Divided Cities: Increasing Socio-Spatial Polarization within Large Cities in the Netherlands*. The Institute for the Study of Labour (IZA). Discussion Paper No. 8882.

chapter 6

Precarious work and unemployment in Europe

Brian McDonough

6.1 Introduction

Work in Europe is characterised by insecurity and precariousness. The financial crisis of 2008 has exacerbated social inequalities; increased job insecurity; intensified the exploitation of marginalised groups; fuelled the deterioration of work–life balance; and elevated levels of stress and health problems in the workplace. This chapter draws upon several key ideas which situate the precarious nature of work in Europe, showing how marginalised groups become stigmatised (Goffman 1990) and routinely exploited in terms of gender (Bolton and Muzio 2008); age (Raito and Lahelma 2015; Riach and Loretto 2009); nationality (Behtoui and Neergaard 2010) and disability (Fevre *et al.* 2013; Riach and Loretto, 2009). This chapter argues that Europe is entering an 'age of insecurity' (Sennett 2006), in which there are undependable forms of employment and risky working conditions, situated in economic insecurity and social instability. Drawing on the work of Standing (2015) and others, this chapter shows that a new set of working conditions and parameters is prevalent in Europe today – one which is fuelled by neo–liberal economic policies and which has created new forms of precarious work across nearly all sectors of employment (ibid.). This chapter draws upon the idea of 'the precariat' (developed in Standing's 2015 work) and broader notions of precarious work insofar as it helps with our analysis of work conditions across contemporary Europe.

Many of the issues most pertinent to work have already been addressed to some extent in previous chapters of this book. For example, Lewis explained that, in many European cities, inequalities in pay are increasing – the poor are getting poorer and there is an increasing concentration of poverty, unemployment, poor housing, low educational attainment, poor health, and poor public and private services within particular poor neighbourhoods (see Chapter 5). This chapter extends some of these discussions, but focuses primarily on work, unemployment and the precarious nature of work as a social problem.

6.2 Work, social status and social identity

Work is central to people's lives in Europe. The kind of work we carry out, how much we earn and where we work are integral aspects of our everyday lives. For most of us living in Europe, work occupies a larger part of our life than any other social activity. Most of us must work to earn a living, but even those of us who do not 'work' (i.e. are not employed) are affected by the work of others – such as dependants who are either too young or old to work, or those who are recipients of benefits or pensions. Thus work affects all of us, either directly in terms of what we do for work or indirectly via the sorts of work our parents, spouses and off-spring have or did. Work also determines our social worth and status (Kirk and Wall 2010). Throughout our working lives we will often be judged and rewarded on the basis of 'what we do' for work. The kind of job we have will likely dictate a number of things such as the quality of our housing (a flat, terraced house, semi-detached house or mansion), the quality of our education (such as public or private schooling, or whether or not we go to university) and the quality of our health (the sort of food we eat or healthcare services we receive). The kind of work we do also affects our lives more broadly. It influences the sorts of people we meet, the friends we have and the social activities we engage in, many of which continue over the course of our lives. Our work, therefore, says a lot about who we are. It is part of our social identity (ibid.). This relationship between our work and social identity is nothing new. For thousands of years people have associated their work with who they are, for example naming themselves after what they do to earn a living. For instance, in France, the name Pierre Boulanger literally means Pierre the baker. In Holland Bakker (baker) is also a common surname, as well as Visser (fisher) and Meijer/Meyer (land agent), whilst in Germany the name Schuhmacher (meaning shoemaker) and Zimmerman (meaning Carpenter) are also common names. Work has been, and still is, an important part of the way we live our lives in Europe. But our relationship to work is changing. Those who have precarious forms of work can 'lack a work-based identity' (Standing 2015: 20). No longer do we inherit the work our parents and grandparents once did – following in family tradition. Nor is it likely we will remain in one kind of employment for all of our lives. A Europe driven by neo-liberal economics and government policies is one in which work is characterised by instability and change. Far from work cementing our social status, the changing work patterns and insecurity have a tendency to produce 'status frustration' (ibid.: 16) with many people with a relatively high level of formal education having to accept jobs that have a status or income beneath what they believe is commensurate with their qualifications (Standing 2015).

Brian McDonough

6.3 Precarious work as a social problem

What is precarious work? Notions of poor quality, bad, insecure or precarious employment have been used in varying extents across Europe including France, Germany, Italy, Spain and the United Kingdom (EC 2004). For some countries the term 'precarious' is used in national debate, whilst in other countries the issues related to precarious work are reflected in discussions about the 'quality of employment' or 'quality in work' (ibid.). At the heart of the French debate is the idea of *statut* or 'status' (ibid.: 34). This refers to the social identity, personal security and sense of worth a job brings with it. Since employment is the very foundation of status, an erosion of it can be dangerous for society and social cohesion. In Germany, the debate revolves around the *Erosion der Normalarbeitsverhältnisse*, that is, the erosion of collectively regulated employment. Whilst in Spain, the debate is focused on *precariedad laboral*, that is, precarious labour (ibid.: 34), or on temporary employment (*trabajo temporal*). Unlike other European countries this appears to be a structural feature of the Spanish labour market. Other terms may also be used to describe this kind of employment including 'insecure employment'; 'unstable employment'; 'casual employment'; 'low wage work'; and 'dead-end jobs' (ibid.). Whatever term we choose to use, 'atypical', 'precarious employment' and other terms referring to this notion of employment describe employment categories that do not correspond to 'standard' and secure forms of employment.

To understand or measure precariousness of employment we can evaluate its instability, lack of protection, insecurity and social or economic vulnerability (EC 2004: 47). The European Foundation for the Improvement of the Living and Working Conditions equates 'precarious' employment with non-permanent contracts (fixed term and temporary contracts as well as self-employment and involuntary part-time employment). Even using this narrower definition of precarious employment we can see that precarious work is everywhere across Europe. From fast-food outlets to universities and hospitals, precarious forms of work occur everywhere we look. If we have not experienced precarious work directly in the past, we are likely to experience it in the future, or likely to know someone who is or has experienced precarious forms of work. Because of the widespread proliferation of precarious work across Europe we can understand it as a social problem.

What causes precarious employment? Precarious employment is the result of a kind of global economics we call neo-liberalism. In the pursuit of market efficiency, the labour markets of economies are opened up through deregulation. Everything becomes commodified, 'treating everything as a commodity to be bought and sold, subject to market forces, with prices set by demand and supply, without effective "agency" (a capacity to resist)' (Standing 2015: 44). Commodification makes the division of labour within organisations more fluid. If work activities can be carried out more cheaply in one location than another, they can be 'offshored (within firms) or "outsourced" (to partner firms or others)' (ibid.: 51). Standing (2015) argues that this fragments the labour process since internal job structures and 'careers' are disrupted due to uncertainty over whether jobs people might have expected to do will be offshored or outsourced.

Precarious employment is created as an intended side effect of neo-liberalist policies. But what is neo-liberalism? The economic theorist Milton Friedman wrote *Capitalism and Freedom* in 1962, and argued for freeing up markets and increasing privatisation, and advocated deregulation. Friedman was a major advisor of British Prime Minister Margaret Thatcher as well as US President Ronald Reagan. These ideas made Britain more closely aligned with economic policies of the US and less similar to the kind of policies augmented in other parts of Europe. But this type of economics has swept across the rest of Europe too. These economic ideas are rooted in a style known as 'laissez-faire', literally meaning 'let the market rip' or 'let the market do as it pleases'. They fiercely conflict with Keynesian style economics involving the interference of the state with labour market policies and protecting the jobs of workers (see the work of John Maynard Keynes 2013).

Precarious work should not be understood as something which is inevitable and unstoppable. On the contrary, precarious work is a result of the sorts of economics governments willingly adopt. And poor and unstable work conditions can be exacerbated by government policies and employment law. In 2014, for example, pressures on the French government to reform its unemployment benefit system sparked a debate. France's Prime Minister Manuel Valls wanted to reduce spending on what was deemed a costly unemployment benefit system. Proposals to implement labour market reforms included easing the 'hiring and firing' of people in the employment sector. Arguments seemed convincing – France's unemployment rate was above 10 per cent despite billions of euros spent to implement reform. But the decision angered both government officials and powerful trade union representatives because, although it increased the flexibility of the labour market, it also made workers more vulnerable to losing their jobs. Changing work contracts and restructuring the economy can serve to decrease unemployment statistics by allowing employers more flexibility – but it also has adverse effects on those in the labour market. Many governments in Europe are creating more part-time jobs which have poor contracts and are often only paying the legal minimum wage. Here precarious work is not just a consequence of economic forces but can be seen as a result of employment policies implemented by the state.

These concerns over precarious work have been most developed in Standing's (2015) work, *The Precariat: The New Dangerous Class*. The 'precariat' is a new social class formed by people suffering from precarity – a way of living without prediction or security. According to Standing (2015), the 'precariat' can be described as a neologism that combines an adjective 'precarious' and a related noun 'proletariat' (ibid.: 11). It can be thought of as a '*class-in-the-making*, if not yet a *class-for-itself*, in the Marxian sense of that term' (ibid.: 11, author's own emphasis). For Standing (2015) globalisation has fragmented existing national class structures and created a more fragmented global class structure. As inequalities have grown, and Europe moves towards a flexible open labour market, social class has not disappeared but altered. Using terms such as 'working

Brian McDonough

class', 'workers' and the 'proletariat' no longer works and people can no longer define themselves by the way they speak, dress and conduct themselves (ibid.). Standing (2015) identifies several new groups we can identify ourselves with, from 'the elite' (super rich global citizens), down to 'the precariat'. It is true that the precariat results from the neo-liberal economy that Europe is subject to. But it is not true to say that such conditions should be kept or ignored. Rather, such conditions are ways which surmount to gross inequalities that need to be challenged and re-balanced. Recognising the 'precariat' is one way of doing so.

6.4 Precarious employment across all sectors

Precarious work does not just affect those working in unskilled or manual occupations but affects all types of job categories and classifications. Medical doctors, nurses, university lecturers, electricians and plumbers can all suffer from precarious forms of employment. Their work is often characterised by casualisation, low pay, insecure contracts and poor benefits. For example, Rotenberg *et al.* (2008) studied the precarious employment of nurses in hospitals in Europe and found that the adverse effects of job insecurity can be harmful to health for both patients and workers. Fixed term or temporary contracts are common across a range of occupations in the health sector and can have a devastating impact on both the workers and health of the community alike.

One common example of precarious work across Europe is cleaning and maintenance jobs. Usually low paid with poor employment contracts, cleaners are often hired and fired depending on whether there is work available or not. In March 2014, the mainly Colombian and Ecuadorian cleaners of the School of Oriental and African Studies (SOAS), University of London, went on strike in protest for better pay and working conditions. Working on a contract for ISS, a transnational facility company with a global workforce of half a million, SOAS cleaners had to work unsociable hours, often beginning work as early as 4am and being part of a global class of billions living and working precariously with few rights, low wages and increased job insecurity. The poor working conditions can often be exacerbated by those who do not speak English, or speak English poorly. These employees can often be more exploited than others, as they lack the capacity to negotiate with their employers over their poor working conditions.

The zero-hours contract used in the UK and other parts of Europe has been referred to as the 'Burger King' contract. The multinational chain called Burger King is infamous for employing workers into low skill and low paid jobs using contracts with zero hours (often with employees earning little more than the minimum wage). This means that employees are not guaranteed a set number of hours each week – resulting in the pure casualisation of labour. This kind of contract is not unique to fast-food chains; it has also been implemented in universities, hospitals, schools and a plethora of private companies and multinational organisations. To describe these forms of work, some scholars have also used the term 'McJobs' to talk about the low-paying, low-prestige dead-end jobs often highly routinised and tightly controlled by management. The term was first thought to be coined by the sociologist Etzioni (1986) in an article in *The Washington Post* (US) entitled: 'The Fast-Food Factories: McJobs are Bad for Kids'. Etzioni (1986) argued that McJobs (jobs in fast-food outlets such as McDonalds) were not at all beneficial for the self-management, experience or personal development of employees. The disparaging term 'McJob' has however been criticised by some who see the benefits of working for fast-food chains. Gould's (2010) study of Australian McDonalds outlets showed that employees view their jobs as repeatedly doing a limited range of non-complex tasks. However, his research also showed that fast-food jobs offer human resource advantages, potential career opportunities and, for some, desirable forms of work organisation.

'McJobs' are not the only kind of employment embracing Europe. New forms of information and data management have created new kinds of employment in Europe. In June 2015, French taxi drivers brought Paris to a halt in protest against Uber – a taxi company which is largely controlled via an app that enables passengers to use their mobile phones to connect with a taxi, rideshare or private car. Uber is operating in several countries across the world, using technology as an easy means of reaching out to both employees and customers with little complication. Uber's multinational approach has been driven by a neo-liberalist tendency to accelerate privatisation, promote deregulation and to operate with minimalist interference from the state. Companies like Uber avoid government regulation. As a result, there are few legislative protections for workers and little chance to establish trade unions or other ways of generating the kind of social solidarity needed in order to challenge organisational injustice or inequalities, leaving those providing services without a host of workers' rights. This includes the right for employers to pay for social security, disability and unemployment insurance; the right to sick pay; the right to maternity or paternity paid leave; retirement benefits; profit sharing plans; and the right to offer protection from discrimination on the basis of race, ethnicity, religion, sex, age, sexuality or disability, or reports of sexual harassment or any other employer wrongdoing.

6.5 Unemployment in Europe

At the beginning of the year 2000 over 20 million people were reported unemployed in the EU-28 (the then twenty-eight countries that made up the European Union – including at that time, Britain). This equated to 9.1 per cent of the total labour force (Eurostat 2015). At the time employment figures were rising as the unemployment rate reduced to 8.6 per cent in 2001 – the number of unemployed was reduced to 19.4 million. In 2004, the unemployment figures would rise again, with 21.4 million recorded jobseekers and an unemployment rate of 9.2 per cent (ibid.). This increase of unemployment unsettled leaders of European countries and efforts were made to improve unemployment rates through large investment, changes in social policy and job creation. By working together leaders of European nations could maximise employment across the continent. For example, better integration through the free movement of goods, services, capital and workers would help boost economic growth, and could reduce unemployment levels in Europe. In the years that followed the rate of unemployment decreased. Between 2005 and 2008, European unemployment (the then EU-28) hit a low of 16.2 million, equivalent to an unemployment rate of 6.8 per cent (ibid.). Jobs in Europe seemed to be plentiful. However, the 2008 financial crisis, also known as the Global Financial Crisis, triggered unemployment levels across Europe. Between 2008 and 2010, unemployment would rise by more than 7 million, taking the rate up to 9.6 per cent. By 2013, the number of unemployed in Europe was at a record level of 26.6 million (10.9 per cent) and would only marginally decline in the years that followed (ibid.). In March 2015 it was estimated that over 23 million people were unemployed in the EU-28, of whom over 18 million were in the euro area (according to Eurostat 2015). But how does unemployment impact on the countries and people of Europe?

The 2008 financial crisis hit Europe hard but some countries were affected more than others. Among the member states, the lowest unemployment rate was reported in Germany, with just 4.7 per cent recorded as unemployed and the highest in Greece (25.7 per cent reported in January) and Spain (23 per cent reported). There is no question that the nations across Europe are economically connected. As we see unemployment rates go up in one country, it is often (though not always) the case that unemployment rates are rising across Europe. The countries across Europe are therefore interconnected by economic tides which come and go and impact upon individual nations.

Gendered marginalisation

One of the first major sources of information on unemployment in the European Union began in 1994, with the European Community Household Panel Study (ECHP). The study found that despite there being common features, the relative risks of unemployment of specific categories of the population differed considerably between different European nations (Gallie and Paugam 2010). The study found, for example, that women had a much higher risk of unemployment than men in several of the countries of Southern Europe, including Italy, Spain, Greece, Belgium and France. Although women are clearly still disadvantaged in other countries, there is quite considerably less difference in the relative unemployment risks of men and women in Denmark, Germany, Portugal and Ireland. In contrast, in the UK and Sweden it is men that are most affected. But there are several factors to consider when looking at unemployment statistics, such as, for example, the participation of women in the labour market or the considerable differences in the age composition of the unemployed. In terms of gender, women have been particularly disadvantaged across Europe in multifaceted ways. Until the latter part of the twentieth century, paid work in Europe was the responsibility of men who required a 'breadwinner's' wage to support the whole family. Women were marginalised because paid work in the public sphere was seen strictly as a man's domain. As a result, women remained in the private sphere and carried out domestic responsibilities such as cleaning, cooking and child-caring. But the twenty-first century has seen many changes. As more and more women have entered the labour market, there has been what is described as the 'feminisation' of work across Europe (Caraway 2007). With fewer people working in industrial manufacturing than in the twentieth century, most of the new jobs created are in service sector industries: offices; service centres; call centres and supermarkets. These job vacancies are often filled by women, not men. However, whilst the participation of women in the job market has increased across Europe and there is more recognition of the value of women's labour in the job market, it is still the case that the nature of women's employment remains significantly different to that of men. There is much criticism of the idea that women are now shattering the glass ceiling and achieving gender equality (Bolton and Muzio 2008). Far from it – women continue to be marginalised, downgraded and exploited in the workplace in a variety of ways (ibid.). There is still a gender pay-gap (across all European nations – though some worse than others) and occupational segregation, with women often engaged in part-time and low paid clerical, catering, cleaning and cashiering work. But these are not the only issues which disadvantage women. Women are more likely than men to occupy part-time employment. These jobs are usually associated with low pay, job insecurity and limited opportunities for promotion and career advancement (see previous section on precarious work). Women who step off a career ladder 'may end up more exploited, having to do much uncompensated work-for-labour outside their paid hours, and more self-exploited, having to do extra work in order to retain a niche of some sort' (Standing 2015: 26). And for women in the workplace, discrimination at work is still more common because of family and domestic responsibilities women are still (traditionally) tied to.

Young people

Young people are highly likely to experience insecure and precarious forms of work and are generally more vulnerable to being unemployed. Youth unemployment (those of working age under 25 years) is generally much higher and sometimes more than double unemployment rates for persons of all ages (ages 15–74, depending on the country). The overall youth unemployment rate in the then EU-28 (including Britain) declined sharply between 2005 and 2007, reaching its lowest value (15.1 per cent) in the first quarter of 2008 (Eurostat Labor Force Survey 2011–2013). Later in 2008, however, the effects of the financial and economic crisis severely hit young people across Europe. From the second quarter of 2008, the youth unemployment rate followed an upward path peaking at 23.6 per cent in the first quarter of 2013, before declining to 23.1 per cent by the final quarter of the same year (ibid.). The economic crisis severely impacted upon the job chances of young people in Europe and there are particular concerns over those who are not in education, employment or training (NEET, as some policy makers refer to it). In the UK for example, unemployment for youth became a particularly highlighted issue during the urban riots and looting in English cities in August 2011. In May 2011, the unemployment rate for young people in Britain (between the ages of 16 and 24) was 19.7 per cent (917,000 people), nearly three times higher than the overall employment rate in the UK (Darlington 2011). Across Europe, being young affects your life chances and opportunity to get a job, depending on your nationality and where you live. In Spain, for example, the youth unemployment figure is 55.5 per cent according to the Eurostat Labor Force Survey (2011–2013) and 58.3 per cent in Greece. France (24.8 per cent) seems to offer better job prospects for young people, whilst countries such as Germany (7.9 per cent) and Norway (9.1 per cent) clearly do not have significant youth unemployment problems, at least on the face of it – their youth unemployment rates are in line with overall unemployment patterns.

For young people across Europe the chances of being unemployed relate to the location and country in which one lives. Thus the country we live in dictates the chances of getting a job, doing particular kinds of work and living particular lifestyles (Russell and O'Connell 2001). The idea that society can limit or constrain our life chances (of getting a job) was laid out by the French social theorist Emile Durkheim in *The Rules of Sociological Method*. Here Durkheim (2006) argued that 'external constraints', as he called them, have the power to coerce individuals in how they think and act (ibid.: 51). Such constraints are societal and provide a set of powerful and influential structures which influence and limit the opportunities of individuals within any society. Durkheim argues that these external constraints are 'endued with a compelling and coercive power by virtue of which, whether [s]he wishes it to or not . . . impose themselves upon [her/]him' (ibid.: 51). A young 18-year-old man in Finland might experience trouble finding employment, but when nearly 1 in every 5 men in his country are out of work, this is an indication of a structural issue having to with job availability, economic stability and the wider social policies implemented by the state – rather than the skills or merits of the individual. From a Durkheimean perspective, it is the external constraints which limit and control the opportunities for finding employment, depending on social factors such as age, gender, ethnicity and social class.

Finland is a good example to note when understanding the social problem of unemployment. In 1994, the unemployment rate reached a staggering 18.4 per cent (Statistics Finland 1994: 1, 1996) with more than half a million unemployed. The economic recession affected all occupational groups and the number of unemployed far outstripped the number of open vacancies (Raito and Lahelma 2015). For example, the monthly average number of job vacancies in Finland in 1994 was 7,326, whereas the number of unemployed job seekers was 494,248 (Statistics Finland 1996: 344). It is not so much a question of how hard one tries to get a job, or even whether one has the necessary qualifications to find work (though this is important). Rather, it is more to do with our age and the kind of society we live in within Europe.

Migration and job insecurity

Most immigrant workers are subject to insecure and undependable forms of employment across Europe. Behtoui and Neergaard's (2010) study of immigrant groups working in Sweden shows that some immigrant groups and their children tend to be overrepresented in the lower echelons of the Swedish labour market, with lower wages, poorer working conditions and less employment security. This inferior position of immigrants in Sweden can be explained as a consequence of a human capital 'deficit' or of the cultural attributes of immigrants, but Behtoui and Neergaard (2010) argue that one further explanation is focused around the unequal opportunity for access to 'social capital'. The term social capital was developed in the work of Bourdieu (1986) and refers to the resources inherent in an individual's set of social ties and networks in a given society. Social capital, like other forms of capital, is synonymous with *power*, as Bourdieu (1986) argues. Thus, the social background (initial position) of an individual, his or her gender and 'ethnicity', in short, the *history* of the individual, play a crucial role in providing access to social capital. With a deficit in social capital, Behtoui and Neergaard (2010) found that immigrants in Sweden are more likely to have a substantial social capital deficit. They are likely to earn less and are less likely to achieve promotion within their organisation. Behtoui and Neergaard (2010) found that access to social capital is positively associated with higher educational levels, more work experience and higher parents' job status. But in-firm seniority is associated with less social capital (ibid.: 774). Regarding job rewards for employees in the firm, the average wages of immigrant workers are found to be lower than those of native-born workers and cannot be explained by educational achievements, general work experience or seniority.

The discrimination of immigrant workers is made worse by negative public perception fuelled by media scare-mongering and political discourse. When Romania joined the EU, many Romanian migrants travelled into Europe to find work. At a time when Britain was still part of the EU, many British politicians warned against a surge of Romanians who would 'invade' the UK to obtain free houses and benefits from the state. A British TV documentary series produced by Channel 4 called 'The Romanians Are Coming' (2015) told the tales of individuals and particular families who left Romania to settle in the UK. The programme showed the desperation of some Romanians (a small minority) who had tried to make a better life for their family. The documentary showed Romanian immigrants who would apply for British state welfare benefits among other things. But the programme received condemnation and sparked a diplomatic row between British and Romanian officials. Romanian ambassador Ion Jinga said that the programme incited 'hatred and discrimination' (*Daily Mail* 9th March 2015). Petitions to cancel the show received almost 10,000 signatures with hundreds protesting outside Channel 4 studios. Members of the Romanian parliament wrote to the British ambassador in Bucharest asking what kind of reaction would be given if Romanian film producers had made a programme about British people who are alcoholics and paedophiles. In a letter written, they reportedly said:

> We kindly ask you to consider what your reaction would be if TVR, the Romanian public television channel, would launch a campaign of denigration pointed towards the British citizens in our country, generalising

cases of alcoholism and paedophilia displayed by some British citizens (cases we are sure you are aware of), and turning them into the general image of all British citizens in Romania . . . This documentary broadcast by Channel 4 does the exact same thing.

(*The Guardian* 19th January 2015)

Romanian immigrants have been stigmatised by media campaigns and public and political discourses which have constructed Romanian people arriving into Britain as one of the biggest social problems. This conception has been highlighted by various politicians in the UK, most notably a Conservative government which was then led by David Cameron, and the UK Independence Party (UKIP) then led by Nigel Farage. Their portrayal of Romanians ruining the British way of living draws attention away from more important political agendas – issues to do with fair pay, the redistribution of wealth and the taxation of multinational corporations. Furthermore, their arguments could not be further from the truth. According to the Department for Work and Pensions (2015), there are only about 1,000 Romanians and 500 Bulgarians claiming job seekers allowance in Britain. These countries are way down the list in comparison to other nations. There are about 2,600 Irish nationals, 1,400 German nationals, 2,800 French nationals, 3,800 Spanish nationals and 3,500 Italian nationals living in Britain on job seekers allowance. And if we compare these figures to those British who are receiving unemployment benefits abroad, we see that the impact of Romanian immigrants claiming benefits is nothing out of the ordinary for any European country. In fact, there are 6,000 British living in Germany, 3,000 in France and 2,900 in Spain all claiming unemployment benefits. Based on the data provided, it is absurd to say that this is a surging problem. The social problem is clearly a social construction – a narrative created for feeding existing discourses about immigrants and problems of unemployment. Unemployed Britons in richer EU states outnumber claimants from those countries in the UK (*The Guardian* 19th January 2015). British people in other European countries are drawing much more in benefits and allowances in wealthier EU countries than their nationals are claiming in the UK. And yet, the British government argues that migrants are flocking into Britain to secure better welfare payments. The idea of 'benefits tourism' has been sensationalised by the media and has arguably created moral panic across the UK – undoubtedly a key factor in the British public's decision to exit the European Union.

6.6 The effects of precarious work and unemployment

So far in this chapter we have outlined the ways in which precarious work and unemployment has swept across Europe. But what are the effects of this? Precarious work and unemployment is detrimental to the lives and families of vulnerable employees and can also be costly to the wider community. In order to mitigate low wages, precariously employed workers must either work long hours or take on multiple jobs. But not all employees are in a position to do so. Seasonal agricultural workers, for instance, are often bound to an individual employer, and not allowed to circulate within the labour market. Many employees with precarious employment have little practical or perceived access to complaints procedures. They risk having their hours cut or losing their job altogether. Similarly, the lack of access to health care provision means that precarious workers in Europe are more susceptible to illness. They are less likely to have access to health benefits and paid sick days and are more likely to suffer from long-term illness as a consequence.

Unemployment impacts on the experiences of individuals and the level of participation in social life. A classic example is the work of Jahoda *et al.* (2009) who studied the impact of unemployment on social isolation in a small Austrian town called Marienthal after the closure of a local factory (during the Depression in Austria during the 1930s). Before the closure, there was wide participation in different clubs and associations. But afterwards, there was a total collapse of social links and networking according to the study. Jahoda *et al.* (2009) found that work was the basis of social integration and the foundation of all other social activities including culture, sport and theatre. Despite having 'more time' on their hands, the people of the small Austrian town of Marienthal became tired and disengaged from all other social activities in the community. Drawing on the work of Merton (1966) and Freud (2002), Jahoda *et al.* (2009) argue that although earning a living is the manifest function of employment, the institution of employment imposes latent functions on employees that contribute to their mental well-being. These functions relate to aspects of daily experience a paid job provides, such as enlarged social contacts; regular social interaction; participation in a collective purpose; and the regular activity involved in having a defined status and identity. The Jahoda *et al.* (2009) study is still relevant today. For example, Raito and Lahelma (2015) trace the lives of unemployed managers and journalists in Finland. They showed that the social contacts and networks individuals developed over the course of their career were of much more importance than the livelihood employment provided – such networks were the ones they continued to utilise when they became unemployed and were looking for work. They found that occupational identity was so profound that it was this that constituted the foundations on which journalists and managers based their choices and strategies for coping with the labour market in general and with long-term unemployment in particular (ibid. 2015).

Unemployment and stigma

When the social life of individuals depends primarily on their participation in the systems of economic production, there is a likelihood that unemployment will lead to the loss of social status, and a feeling of failure (Gallie and Paugam 2010). We saw the effects of precarious work on social status and identity earlier in this chapter. But these social problems are particularly true for those who find themselves in periods of long-term unemployment, like that during a recession.

Brian McDonough

Many of those who become unemployed are less likely to take part in the wider aspects of social life resulting in long-term anxiety or depression. When people do not work they can sometimes become stigmatised. The notion of 'stigma' is laid out most notably in Goffman's (1990) sociological classic *Stigma: Notes on a Spoiled Identity*. According to Goffman, society establishes the means of 'categorising persons and the complement of attributes felt to be ordinary and natural for members of each of these categories' (ibid.: 11). The routines of social intercourse in established settings allow us to deal with others without special attention or thought. But when the *actual social identity* of individuals who enter our presence do not fit in with the *virtual social identity* (the expectations we have of them) the situation results in stigma (ibid.). Goffman himself pointed out how unemployment can result in stigma. Goffman gives this example of a forty-three-year-old German man (a mason) who is unemployed during the Depression:

> How hard and humiliating it is to bear the name of an unemployed man. When I go out, I cast my eyes because I feel myself wholly inferior. When I go along the street, it seems to me that I can't be compared with an average citizen, that everybody is pointing at me with his finger. I instinctively avoid meeting anyone. Former acquaintances and friends of better times are no longer so cordial. They greet me indifferently when we meet. They no longer offer me a cigarette and their eyes seem to say, 'You are not worth it, you don't work.'
>
> (ibid.: 28)

Goffman's (1990) example has resonance with other studies of unemployment across Europe. It is not simply about not having a job, but more importantly about the social status having a job involves: social identity; sense of worth; self-respect; and being a provider for one's own family. But being unemployed is not the only form of stigmatisation linked to work. Whilst society sees employment as the key to social membership, the assumption that employees with disabilities are of less productive worth also leads to stigmatisation and discrimination (Fevre *et al.* 2013; Riach and Loretto, 2009). This assumption may have less to do with limitations arising from people's impairments than it has to do with the way in which people with disabilities are treated in the labour market and the workplace. If they are kept at the margins of the labour market because they are assumed to be less capable, their assumed lack of productive worth becomes a self-fulfilling prophecy (Fevre *et al.* 2013). If people with disabilities are ill-treated within the workplace, this will have a similar effect.

Flexible working and flexibility stigma

Flexible working arrangements are not only beneficial for employees and employers alike but can also be an intended government strategy aimed, for example, at keeping people in work during a recession. This was a strategy used by Germany and replicated by Denmark in 2009 after the 2007 recession – *arbejdsfordeling*, or work sharing, depends upon collective agreements in which employees agree to a reduction in working time (and thus wage costs) in exchange for a guarantee of continued employment (Jorgensen 2009; Lallement 2011). There has been much debate over recent initiatives by governments and employers across Europe to promote flexible working and work–life balance (Fleetwood 2007; Prowse and Prowse 2015). Whilst many policies can be seen to promote family-friendly practices and promote greater employee flexibility, critics of work–life balance policies argue that the practices of employers are in place to serve the needs of businesses and organisations only, and fail to provide the kinds of workplace equalities they appear to (Prowse and Prowse 2015; Sanchez-Vidal *et al.* 2012). One of the problems related to work–life balance policies in Europe is a so-called 'flexibility stigma' (Cech and Blair-Loy 2014; Prowse and Prowse 2015). Flexibility stigma describes employers' and employees' negative perceptions and treatment of co-workers who want flexible work arrangements. One example is women (or men) with parental responsibilities made to feel inadequate because they require flexible working arrangements. Another example can be those who have impairments (or disabilities) and also require flexible working hours. In both of these cases, those with flexible working patterns can be viewed as inferior to others in the organisation. What develops is a flexibility stigma, resulting in the marginalisation of employees, who are regarded as 'less committed to their job and which can lead to employer and co-worker resentment, along with reduced career opportunities' (Prowse and Prowse 2015: 758). The flexibility stigma will more likely affect the groups in society who require flexible working arrangements: women (or men) with parental responsibilities; those with impairments (or disabilities); and older workers or part-retired employees.

6.7 Conclusion

This chapter began by looking at precarious and insecure work and the various ways in which such employment could be defined. Precarious work related to types of contract we often call 'unstable employment'; 'casual employment'; 'low wage work'; and 'dead-end jobs' (EC 2004). Reports from the European Commission show that precarious work is increasing across Europe, leading to what Sennett (2006) calls an 'age of insecurity'. Despite the rise in precarious work, most countries (with the exception of Spain) still rely on permanent contracts as the main type of employment. But the precarious nature of work affects all types of job occupations, from unskilled and manual through to skilled and professional jobs. The precarious character of employment appears pervasive and not necessarily guided by social class. In Britain work contracts may deteriorate without the protection of European law and regulations – a consequence of Brexit (Britain's exit from the EU).

The notion of precariousness at work has been developed by Standing's (2015) idea of 'the precariat'. Using this idea helped us to understand the exploitative conditions of an emerging group across Europe as well as helping us to analyse the ways in which everything (including labour) becomes commodified within a neo-liberal economy. But this chapter argued that pre-carious work should not be understood as something which is inevitable and unstoppable. On the contrary, it was said that precarious work is a result of the sorts of economics governments willingly adopt.

This chapter also discussed unemployment across Europe and why certain social groups had unequal and unfavourable work opportunities due to factors such as gender (Bolton and Muzio 2008); age (Raito and Lahelma 2015; Riach and Loretto 2009); nationality (Behtoui and Neergaard 2010); and disability (Fevre *et al.* 2013; Riach and Loretto, 2009). It was argued that some work–life balance policies could result in a so-called 'flexibility stigma' for many employees with inferior contracts of employment (Cech and Blair-Loy 2014; Prowse and Prowse 2015). The chapter also showed that the consequences of unemployment can impact upon the health and well-being of individuals as well as the kinds of social status and sense of worth and belonging employment provides. Despite the unpredictability of neo-liberalism and the consequences of the financial crisis of 2008, this chapter claims that governments and organis-ations alike can make interventions to support the livelihoods of people and prevent gross inequalities across Europe.

Bibliography

Abendroth, A and Dulk, L (2011) Support for the work–life balance in Europe: The impact of state, workplace and family support on work–life balance satisfaction. *Work, Employment and Society* 25(2): 234–56.

Behtoui, A and Neergaard, A (2010) Social capital and wage disadvantages among immigrant workers. *Work, Employment and Society* 24(4): 761–79.

Bolton, S and Muzio, D (2008) The paradoxical processes of feminisation in the professions: the case of established, aspiring and semi-professions. *Work, Employment and Society* 22(2): 281–99.

Bourdieu, P (1986) The Forms of Capital. In Richardson, J (ed.) *Handbook of Theory and Research for the Sociology of Education*. New York: Greenwood, 241–58.

Caraway, TL (2007) *Assembling Women: The Feminization of Global Manufac-turing*. Ithaca, NY: Cornell University Press.

Cech, EA and Blair-Loy, M (2014) Consequences of flexibility stigma among academic scientists and engineers. *Work and Occupations* 41(1): 86–110.

Darlington, R (2011) *Report on Youth Unemployment*. London: Institute for Public Policy Research.

Department for Work and Pensions (2015) Published under the 2010–2015 coalition government. Research tracking the country of origin of benefit claimants in the UK. Available at: www.gov.uk/government/news/government-publishes-overseas-benefit-claimant-research [Accessed: 23 January 2017].

Durkheim, E (2006) *The Rules of Sociological Method*. London: Free Press.

Etzioni, A (1986) The fast-food factories: McJobs are bad for kids, *The Washington Post* (August 24).

European Commission Research (2004) *Precarious Employment in Europe: Comparative Study of Labour Market Related Risks in Flexible Economies*. ESOPE. Available at: https://cordis.europa.eu/pub/citizens/docs/kina21250ens_final_esope.pdf [Accessed: 23 January 2017].

Eurostat (2011–13) Labour Force Survey. Luxembourg: Office for Official Publications of the European Communities. Available at: http://ec.europa.eu/eurostat/web/microdata/european-union-labour-force-survey [Accessed: 23 January 2017].

Eurostat (2015) *Population and Social Conditions*. Luxembourg: Office for Official Publications of the European Communities.

Ferrie, JE (2001) Is job insecurity harmful to health? *Journal of the Royal Society of Medicine* 94(1): 71–6.

Fevre, R, Robinson, A, Lewis, D and Jones, T (2013) The ill treatment of employees with disabilities in British workplaces. *Work Employment and Society* 27(2): 288–307.

Fleetwood, S (2007) Why work–life balance now? *International Journal of Human Resource Management* 18(3): 387–400.

Freud, S (2002) *Civilisation and its Discontents*. London: Penguin.

Frone, MR (2003) Work–family balance. In Quick, JC and Tetrick, LE (eds) *Handbook of Occupational Health Psychology*. Washington, DC: APA, 143–62.

Gallie, D and Paugam, S (2010) *Welfare Regimes and the Experience of Unemployment in Europe*. Oxford: Oxford University Press.

Goffman, E (1990) *Stigma: Notes on a Spoiled Identity*. London: Penguin.

Gould, AM (2010) Working at McDonalds: Some redeeming features of McJobs. *Work, Employment and Society* 24(4): 780–802.

Jahoda, M, Lazarsfeld, PF and Zeisel, H (2009) *Marienthal: The Sociography of an Unemployed Community*. New Jersey, USA: Transaction Publishers.

Jorgensen, C (2009) Danemark: la crise économique conduit à un recours massif au partage du travail. *Grande Europe* 13(October): 52–9.

Keynes, J Maynard (2013) *The General Theory of Employment, Theory and Money*. London: Palgrave Macmillan.

Kirk, J and Wall, C (2010) *Work and Identity: Historical and Cultural Contexts*. London: Palgrave Macmillan.

Lallement, M (2011) Europe and the economic crisis: forms of labour market adjustment and varieties of capitalism. *Work, Employment and Society* 25(4): 627–41.

Merton, R (1966) *Social Theory and Social Structure*. New York: Free Press.

Mooney, G (ed.) (2004) *Work: Personal Lives and Social Policy*. Milton Keynes: The Open University.

Prowse, J and Prowse, P (2015) Flexible working and work–life balance: midwives' experiences and views. *Work, Employment and Society* 29(5): 757–74.

Raito, P and Lahelma, E (2015) Coping with unemployment among journalists and managers. *Work, Employment and Society* 29(5): 720–37.

Riach, K and Loretto, W (2009) Identity work and the 'unemployed' worker: age, disability and the lived experience of the older unemployed. *Work, Employment and Society* 23(1): 102–19.

Brian McDonough

Rotenberg, L, Harter-Griep, R, Fischer, FM, Fonseca, Mde J and Landsbergis, P (2008) *Working at Night and Work Ability among Nursing Personnel: When Precarious Employment Makes the Difference*. International Archives of Occupational and Environmental Health. New York: Springer.

Russell, H and O'Connell, PJ (2001) Getting a job in Europe: the transition from unemployment to work among young people in nine European countries. *Work, Employment and Society* 15(1): 1–24.

Sanchez-Vidal, ME, Cegarra-Leiva, D and Cegarra-Navarro, JG (2012) Gaps between managers' and employees' perceptions of work–life balance. *International Journal of Human Resource Management* 18(3): 374–86.

Sennett, R (2006) *The Culture of New Capitalism*. New Haven, CT: Yale University Press.

Standing, G (2015) *The Precariat: A New Dangerous Class*. London: Bloomsbury.

Statistics Finland (1994) *Labour Statistics Annual Report*. Helsinki: Tilastokeskus.

Statistics Finland (1996) *Annual Report*. Helsinki: Tilastokeskus.

Warhurst, C, Eikhof, DR and Haunschild, A (2008) *Work Less, Live More? Critical Analysis of the Work–Life Boundary*. Houndsmills and New York: Palgrave Macmillan.

chapter 7

Health

Jennifer Newton

7.1 Introduction: the four 'd's: diabetes, depression, dementia and death

In a text book on social problems, one might ask why there is a chapter on health. In answer to this, I will cite our editor, who in *Social Problems in the UK*, argued that issues affecting large numbers of the population in one way or another become identified as 'social problems' 'for a variety of reasons. But underlying the concern is usually the perception of a threat to our social structures' (Isaacs, 2014: 12). This chapter will focus on four 'd's: diabetes, depression, dementia and death, the first three of which are increasingly discussed as threats: diabetes to the sustainability of affordable health services; depression to the efficiency of the workforce and the quality of family life; and dementia to the social care infrastructure, both formal and informal, and cost to the State.

Regular readers of the news will have been following each of these stories, and be familiar with the tendency in political responses and media coverage to focus on the individual and their family. In the case of diabetes, the emphasis has been on individual blame. For instance, the link between obesity and diabetes has led to a bizarre and highly stigmatising suggestion by the current UK government to review benefit payments to anyone who has health problems related to obesity and who refuses treatment. 'It is not fair to ask hardworking taxpayers to fund the benefits of people who refuse to accept the support and treatment that could help them get back to a life of work' (BBC News, 2015). Similar proposals were considered in 2010 and 2012 in relation to people with drug or alcohol addictions who refused treatment. Note the assumption that the people concerned are all claiming state benefits, adding to the negative stereotype. Diabetes, dementia and depression are all highly stigmatised conditions, which is linked to their perceived threat to our social structures.

But there is another reason why these are social problems. There is indeed a link with social disadvantage, a correlation with social class, and no doubt this has helped to feed the negative stereotyping. More poor people than wealthy people have diabetes, and the same is true of depression. There is not a link with poverty and the onset of dementia, but the cost of care is of course greatest for those with no savings or property to fund their care. And each of these conditions arises, at least in part, out of the social context of our everyday lives – diabetes increasing in line with our changing eating and exercise patterns; depression linked with stressful life events, childhood maltreatment, supportive (or rather – unsupportive) relationships; and dementia as well as depression more often identified and labelled as a medical condition than in the past. Individual pathology from biological causes is a part of the story in each case, but by no means the most important.

Evidence relating to behaviour, life circumstances and labels associated with a diagnosis emerges from research questions arising from what is commonly described as a *medical model*. That is, the researcher starts from an assumption that there is a real disease or disorder which can be defined, identified and measured, which has causes that might be discovered, and for which treatment or prevention strategies can then be planned. However, it is too often then framed in terms of an analysis of what may change at the individual level. At worst, the focus on lifestyle factors may suggest that if we each made better choices in life, we would all be much healthier. It is the patients fault. Statistics prove this. Countries with high rates of smoking have high rates of lung cancer.

A serious consequence of this type of thinking is the stigma that is then associated with having some types of ill-health, arising from the way these conditions are socially constructed. These are conditions which not only threaten our health services, economic efficiency, family life and more, but it seems that the individuals who experience them might be at least partly to blame. Clearly this perspective can then complicate the treatment and recovery of those affected in a way that is altogether different for those with a broken arm (assuming it was an accident) or arthritis. There are negative social consequences of receiving the label once diagnosed, both for themselves and for close others.

Some of the people who live with disabilities, such as Michael Oliver (e.g. Oliver, 1990) have helped us re-conceptualise ill-health and disability, by arguing that the 'problem' lies less with the fact that the individual may have an impairment or health condition and more in the failure of appropriate adaptations of their environment to minimise the impact of the condition on the activities of the individual. The individual is not at fault, the problem lies with society. This is the *social model*. In relation to the *causes* of ill-health, the social model focus would emphasise the role of housing, unemployment or the food industry, rather than individual behaviour.

While the concepts linked to the social model have been extremely important in politicising the disability movement, and in their campaigning, its very success has more recently been seen to be a weakness (Shakespeare and Watson, 2002). The terms medical and social are arguably now too politicised and divisive, so that the challenges are argued from one side or the other – as an either/or, black or white. All activists must share the social model, and those who draw on a medical perspective are part of the problem – the oppressors. Yet the reality is that both perspectives are essential.

health   113

But first – to death – which one might assume is not so much of a social problem, except in so far as for Europeans it now usually comes after nearly eight decades of life, when it can sometimes be preceded by a period of very costly care. Most countries in the West have completed their 'epidemiological transition', which is the phrase given for the time when, after advances in nutrition, income, medicine and the availability of health care as countries developed, causes of death for the majority of the population changed from nutritional disorders and communicable diseases (such as malaria, TB, diarrhoea, measles or pneumonia) to chronic and degenerative disorders (such as heart disease and cancer). This means that death rates among children and young adults moved from high to low, and life expectancy increased. This transition also brings marked reductions in birth rates over a period following falls in death rates. So after a period of rapid population growth, population size in most high income developed countries has now levelled off or is declining.

This brings us to another social problem. Not a serious one in the UK as yet, given birth rates are 1.9 at the last count and immigration is strong. But the average woman needs to have 2.1 babies in her lifetime in order for the population to remain stable in size without immigration. Much more than this and populations will be growing rapidly, as in most sub-Saharan African nations, much less than this, as in most of Europe, and populations will be shrinking. In terms of the future of the planet, population decline would be welcome of course. But for the economy of individual countries, this imbalance in the numbers of young compared to old poses a problem. Who is going to care for, and who is going to pay for, the growing numbers of people over retirement age when they are in poor health? How are companies to remain competitive?

Japan is the country most often discussed in this context, but it is a threat now for most of Europe, where the average birth rate, according to the US Population Reference Bureau data (PRB, 2014), has dropped from 2.3 in 1970 to 1.6 in 2013. The implications of changing demography are discussed further in Chapter 2. This is an economic problem, with which social problems are likely to be associated given the speed of change needed in so many of the European nations. Retirement ages will rise, or have already risen, pension income will be delayed, more support and some change in attitudes to facilitate combining motherhood or other family caring responsibilities with employment is needed, and immigration needs to be supported. Population profiles will become more diverse, more multi-cultural.

So most Europeans now live well into old age, 8 out of 10 dying after they reach the age of 65, to on average almost 80 years old. The most common cause of death is from one of the cardiovascular diseases, which account for at least 4 in every 10 deaths, with cancer in second place killing about another 1.6. Communicable, neonatal, nutritional and maternal causes explain over 60 per cent of deaths in sub-Saharan Africa, (showing they have not yet completed an 'epidemiological transition') compared to just over 6 per cent in Europe (where they have) (WHO, 2014a).

For wealthy countries in the West, there are choices to be made for end of life care for the terminally ill, about how far and how best to intervene to prolong

Jennifer Newton

life. The cost of end of life care can be high, but can sometimes decrease rather than increase quality of life for the weeks or months remaining. Hence there are increasing efforts to promote 'palliative care', and to encourage older people to make a will both for their financial assets and also one stating their end of life care preferences, and to appoint a relative or friend to the role of attorney (able to make decisions on their behalf if necessary). Discussing and planning for one's own death remains a taboo subject, and the majority of people have no plans in place, despite the fact that public attitude surveys say most of us claim to be comfortable discussing death (NEoLCIN, 2013).

Many of us in good physical and mental health, who have not lived through long periods with a condition that seriously impacts on everyday life, tend to take good health for granted. For us, illness is usually a trivial matter, typically a minor infection from which we'll recover after a few days, perhaps with the help of a visit to the doctor and some medication. We assume that more serious or long-lasting ill-health will come with old age and, unless unlucky, or involved in an accident, it is not an issue of concern for those in youth, early adult life or mid-life. But while mortality rates largely support this view, there remains a considerable 'disease burden' which is not revealed by statistics that focus on death rates, of those non-communicable disorders experienced throughout life. The cost associated with these long-term conditions rises with rising life expectancy, and shrinking proportions of tax payers and carers. Hence this chapter starting with a focus on age of death.

WHO (the World Health Organisation) and other international organisations measuring 'disease burden' have often utilised a measure known as DALYs – disability adjusted life years – a calculation of the number of years lost due to premature death or disability from serious conditions. The main sources of disease burden not surprisingly include many disorders that are not so high among causes of death. The three listed in the opening paragraph are not only a current threat but also one which is increasing. All three have strong implications for social structures and social policy; social factors are linked to the onset, labelling and course of all three; furthermore, some of the social factors are the same ones – hence each affects the others.

Taking diabetes first, this has a strong association with lifestyle, but lifestyle is framed by the socio-cultural and structural environment, and wealth. Media discussion, however, tends to focus on the actions of the individual, and coverage sometimes demonises those whose lifestyle puts them at increased risk. In the case of diabetes, the risk is associated with growing rates of obesity.

7.2 Diabetes and obesity

According to Gatineau and colleagues (2014) 90 per cent of adults with type 2 diabetes in England are overweight or obese. The prevalence of diabetes is increasing in Europe, along with the rise in obesity, with 1.8 per cent of DALYs associated with diabetes in 2000 and 2.2 per cent in 2012 (WHO, 2014b). Diabetes brings an increased risk of many other chronic health conditions including cardiovascular disease, blindness, amputation, kidney disease and depression. . . . Diabetes leads to a two-fold excess risk for cardiovascular disease, and diabetic retinopathy is the leading cause of preventable sight loss among people of working age in England and Wales.

(Gatineau *et al.*, 2014: 5)

In other words, the medical costs associated with diabetes are not primarily the care of the condition itself but the cost of treating the many health complications arising. The overall treatment costs, and the costs due to lost productivity and informal care needs, are substantial, with prescription costs alone for people with diabetes already almost 10 per cent of total prescribing costs in England in 2012–13, and all predictions are for all these costs to continue to rise dramatically. The prevalence of, and therefore the costs associated with, type 2 diabetes is about ten times as high as type 1. The latter is an auto-immune condition where the body's immune system attacks its own source of insulin. It often starts in childhood, and requires lifelong injections of insulin, whereas risk of type 2 increases with increasing age. The picture is similar elsewhere, with an OECD/ European Union (2010) publication writing in terms that help explain the headlines of panic in the press (such as 'Diabetes threatens to "bankrupt" NHS within a generation', in *The Guardian* newspaper in 2012 [Campbell 2012], and again in many media sources in 2015).

Diabetes is increasing rapidly in every part of the world, to the extent that it has now assumed epidemic proportions. Estimates suggest that more than 6% of the population aged 20–79 years in EU countries, or 33 million people, have diabetes in 2010. Almost half of diabetic adults are aged less than 60 years. If left unchecked, the number of people with diabetes in EU countries will reach more than 37 million in less than 20 years.

(OECD 2010, drawing on data from IDF, 2006)

While this may seem almost melodramatic, the updates paint a worse picture, with data from the IDF atlas for 2013 estimating the European rate as 8.5 per cent – 56 million people (Tamayo *et al.*, 2014).

Social causes and social consequences

While family history, through our genetic inheritance primarily, is the most important risk factor for either type 1 or type 2 diabetes (the answer to the 'who' question), lifestyle and environment also play a role, particularly in type 2 diabetes. These determine the 'how many' question. The dramatic rise is being attributed to the type of food we now eat, our increasing weight (and rapid weight gain in childhood is implicated in type 1 diabetes) and our sedentary lifestyles. Findings cited by Tamayo and colleagues (2014) suggest that one-third of European citizens report being seldom or never physically active, with people in Nordic countries and the Netherlands more active than those in southern European states. People who smoke, eat a good deal of red meat and who drink

Jennifer Newton

sweetened beverages have a raised risk, while those who drink tea and eat a Mediterranean diet, plenty of fruit and vegetables, fermented dairy products and oily fish have a reduced risk (ibid.).

Differences in diet may in part explain the differing rates between countries, with more than 8 per cent of adults in Turkey, Cyprus and Germany having diabetes in 2010 as compared to less than 4 per cent in Iceland, Norway and the UK (OECD/European Union, 2010). However, the story is reversed when rates of type 1 are considered in children, with Norway and the UK close to the top of the list. Hence there is as much emphasis in UK policy on risk of diabetes in children as in adults. That healthier diet and more exercise will reduce risk has been demonstrated by intervention studies; hence this has been taken up strongly in health policy. But other factors are also implicated – stress, depression, educational level, job strain and the wealth of the population. Pollution too has been studied, and low vitamin D (Tamayo *et al.*, 2014). These of course are interactive factors – it is hard to separate out the effects of one from another. In fact, if a broader consideration of chronic ill-health of all kinds is taken, it becomes clear how often this constellation of factors surfaces: chronic stress, social status and the powerful influences that shape both these and the choices we make. Might these in fact be the causes of the causes?

Rose (1985) brought the distinction between sick individuals and sick populations back to the forefront of public health thinking 30 years ago, describing the relative importance of addressing *causes of population rates* as often likely to be more effective than a focus just on *causes of cases*. In a subsequent and equally thoughtful paper (Rose and Day, 1990), he challenged us to reflect on the extent to which the average, 'normal' behaviour predicts the number of 'deviants' (see also the discussion in Newton, 2013). Weight, as well as calories consumed, and amount of fruit, red meat or tea consumed is likely to have a distribution which is hat shaped in a graph – perhaps not quite a 'normal distribution', but one with a peak in the middle representing the body weight and consumption of the average person. But move this peak very slightly along the x axis and the whole distribution (the hat) moves too, markedly increasing or decreasing the numbers of the 'deviants', i.e. those at the rim of the hat or, in statistical language, those in the tail of the distribution. In the case of body weight – depending on the direction up or down the x axis – the obese are at one end, the extremely underweight at the other.

Looking for causes of cases is what is described as the medical model. Why does this individual get this illness at this time? Looking for causes of population rates requires a universal approach – considering why the whole population engages as they do with the risk factors concerned; why the rate in country X is double the rate in country Y; why does this community have much higher rates than that one? Furthermore, how much exercise we get, how stressful our jobs are, how well educated we are, how much sun we get and even what we eat are by no means fully within the control of the individual. In relation to the food we consume, much of the sugar, salt and fat is added to processed food before it becomes available to the consumer. The multi-national food companies and fast food outlets arguably play a far greater role in the nation's health than the individual buying from them.

And consider too the fairly obvious disadvantages of an approach which scapegoats the 'deviants', as in the clip from the Express newspaper in the UK in 2014 following the release of another study on diabetes and obesity.

Express

War on diabetes: Doctors told to snitch on patients piling on pounds.

Published: 20:17, Fri, December 26, 2014.

Family GPs are to be told to identify patients who are putting on weight under the new national programme to fight obesity. Companies will also be asked to reward staff who lose weight with shopping vouchers and prizes.

The move comes after latest figures show that Britain is the second fattest country in Europe – behind only Hungary in official European Commission obesity ratings.

It is unlikely that Talcott Parsons, who has famously described the key role of the family doctor in gatekeeping the 'sick role' in order to protect the efficiency of the economy (Parsons, 1951), had envisaged such an assertive approach.

The ideal environmental conditions for diabetes are where people tend to be physically inactive and to have easy access to high calorie foods and sweet drinks. The association with wealth is not a simple one. In high income countries it is more often the poorer sections of the population that have the less healthy diets, and get less exercise, while in poorer countries it may be those with more money who have the most inactive lifestyle and unhealthy, high calorie diet. Transnational food companies have a stake in all these communities and arguably the most influence on population diet and weight. In the global market for profit, adding sugar and salt adds taste. Reduction of these ingredients by one company would lose them market share. Legislation is what has made the most difference to smoking rates, and is what is needed across a whole range of policies in numerous sectors.

The multinationals, of course, can bring enormous political pressure to protect their interests, or they can collaborate to change practice together. The sugar lobby has resisted attempts by policy makers to discourage consumption for decades, policies urged previously by those concerned for dental health. But the balance in favour of action has now changed since the links with diabetes have become clearer, and the multinationals themselves are beginning to respond to the new priorities. Public Health England is now advocating a policy pathway similar to that followed to reduce tobacco consumption – tighter controls on advertising, discouraging incentives for purchasers with multi-packs and special offers, clear labelling on products, increase taxes on sugary foods and soft drinks, and encourage suppliers to reduce portion sizes, so that the social norm is moved (Tedstone *et al.*, 2014). These efforts may move the average consumption a little,

Jennifer Newton

and therefore reduce the numbers at the extreme end of the tail far more effectively than addressing the 'deviant' behaviour of those at the extremes. As Rose and Day (1990) said so clearly – the population must take responsibility for the tail of its own distribution. The obese person, and the heavy drinker, should not be condemned by the average person who is considered 'normal' despite normal being overweight and a moderate alcohol drinker.

Seeing people who occupy the extremes of the spectrum as different from 'us', brings stigma, raised rates of depression, prejudice and bullying. This is as much a problem in mental health.

7.3 Depression

In the league table of conditions with the highest global burden of disability, or YLDs (years lived with disability), depression is now close to the top of the list, and is one of the leading sources of days lost to disability in all the regions of the world as found in this now astonishingly extensive study, involving 188 countries in the 2010 and 2013 analyses (GBD, 2013, 2015).

> Major depressive disorder was a crucial contributor in developed and developing countries alike: it is the leading cause of YLDs in 56 countries, the second leading cause in 56 countries, and the third in 34 countries.
>
> (GBD, 2015: 45)

As with diabetes, the associated costs are bringing this condition far more attention in health policy than in the recent past. Again, the financial cost is not just medical treatment but also state benefits for those out of work, cost to industry of those on sick leave and cost to industry for those whose work is impaired by low energy, low motivation and poor concentration. The latter has been termed 'presenteeism' and has been estimated to cost substantially more than absenteeism (SCMH, 2007). The personal cost to relationships, to families and to individual quality of life is also substantial. Mental health problems in general markedly impair opportunity, as employers are more reluctant to take on those who declare a mental ill-health history than those who have physical disabilities or ill-health (Sayce, 2015).

Depression is nearly twice as common in women as in men, with somewhere between 1 in 6 and 1 in 4 of the population living in urban areas in Europe in any 12 month period experiencing one of the 'common mental disorders', of which a mixture of anxiety and depression is the most common of all (see Newton, 2013). It can be acute – i.e. arise quite suddenly in the context of a very stressful experience, and resolve quite rapidly too, and/or it can be chronic, lasting a year, sometimes many years.

Social causes and social consequences

Depression is more common among people who are separated or divorced, live alone or are single parents. People living with a longstanding physical health

condition, living in social housing, in an urban area, and without paid work are also over-represented among those with chronic depression (Singleton *et al.*, 2001; Brown and Moran, 1994). There is a substantial social class variation, with working class mothers of young children experiencing particularly high rates. But this is not just about wealth, or the lack of it, but about the experiences that are more likely to occur in poor households. Some of the most detailed studies of the social factors at play in depression have been undertaken by the team led by George Brown and Tirril Harris in London. Their book *Social Origins of Depression* in 1978 marked the beginning of a major shift in thinking in psychiatry, which had hitherto seen mental illness as primarily determined by biology. So entrenched was this view that early papers by Brown and colleagues were declined by major medical journals, who argued that the suggestion that the condition was largely a result of social factors was too 'far-fetched' an idea (Harris, 2000).

Their research, now widely supported by epidemiological studies since, shows that depression usually follows an event which carries a major long-term threat. Threat that is interpreted by the person as conveying both a sense of humiliation, and of entrapment – no way of avoiding this – is particularly damaging to self esteem. Those who are more likely to become depressed following such life events or difficulties are people who currently lack a strongly supportive close relationship and/or have experienced a period of a year or more during childhood without this kind of support. In particular, damaging childhood experience or maltreatment is that experienced through relationships which were abusive, neglectful, or rejecting (see Brown *et al.*, 2008, reviewed in Newton, 2013).

Childhood experiences of parenting are of course linked to problems in relationships between the adults sharing the parenting role. That is, child maltreatment is more likely to occur when there is marked discord between the adults. Tracing the social problems back further, financial hardship is one of the factors making family discord more likely. But these difficulties are not uni-directional either. The challenges of parenting a child with emotional, behavioural or even physical health problems or disability are associated with higher rates of depression in mothers, as much as a mother's depression can further challenge her capacity to manage problematic child behaviour. Causes and consequences are thus difficult to disentangle. Numerous social factors linked to wealth and status (income, education, housing and unemployment, for instance) correlate with childhood mental ill-health. But when their associations with each other are removed through careful statistical analyses, many disappear (ONS, 2003; Newton, 2013). The associations which remain for childhood mental health, however, are those between child mental health, special educational need and long-term mental ill-health in the mother. In other words, the links with wealth for the child arise indirectly through the links between health and wealth for the parents.

But while social policy to strengthen child protection services, reduce domestic violence, support parents with children with special educational needs, or to consider how those facing life events and difficulties might be better supported,

Jennifer Newton

this is still, in Rose's words, a focus on the causes of cases – a medical model. What we need to understand better is why some marked population differences in rates of such causes of cases occur, and how policy might affect these. For instance, children and adults living in inner cities have much higher rates of depression than those in rural areas, and we have seen that this is largely explained by the higher rates of life events, family breakdown, teacher and pupil turnover in schools and other social disadvantages in cities. The prevalence of humiliating experience together with a sense of being powerless to change events explains the 'how many' question. But what we do not know is why these problems arise more frequently in cities, nor how to change this.

Similarly, teenagers in the UK are sexually active at an earlier age than those in most other European countries, and many more of them, as compared to sexually active young women in most other European countries, give birth (UNICEF, 2007). In this comparison of the lives of children and young people in 21 of the OECD countries, the best environment for child wellbeing is achieved by the Netherlands and Sweden. Italy and Ireland are halfway down this league table, while the UK lies at the bottom. Again, these are population differences associated with societal norms. The UK may need to explore how the Netherlands and Sweden provide a more supportive environment for families, and a sense of security and of feeling well supported.

One might speculate on the potential role of social integration and status, particularly in rural areas. Brown (2002) reports comparative results from studies using their measures which showed that Basque speaking women in the Basque region of Spain had significantly lower rates of depression than Spanish speaking women in the same area, while for women in the inner cities higher social class appears to be a more important feature contributing to a protective environment (ibid.).

7.4 Dementia

Dementia is a condition which is strongly age related. However, despite the commonly encountered assumption that most older people will have some level of dementia eventually, this is a long way from accurate. It is not a natural part of aging, and the majority of older people at any age do not develop this organic disease. From a meta-analysis of 65 studies, The Dementia Report 2015 (ADI, 2015) calculates the prevalence among people in Western Europe as 1.6 per cent of 60–64 year olds. The rate then doubles every 6 years or so, so that for 80–84 year olds the prevalence is 12.3 per cent, and at age 85–89 it is just over 20 per cent, rising to nearly 40 per cent of those who live 90 years or more. However, for those unlucky enough to be affected, it can damage multiple aspects of brain function, including memory, language, comprehension, judgement and learning capacity. There can also be an effect on emotional control and social skills, and for the few who live through to the most advanced stages, it can eventually reduce physical and mental capacity to that of an infant. Most people will die from other conditions before this, however. The diagnosis most familiar to the general public is Alzheimer's Disease, which is not surprising, given that this accounts for roughly two-thirds of all dementia 'cases' (ibid.). But there are numerous different types of dementia, with vascular dementia the second most common (associated with interruptions in, or reduced supply of, blood to the brain, such as resulting from repeated small strokes or infarcts) and Lewy Body Dementia the third most prevalent. The growing proportion of the population of Europe over the age of 65 is inevitably reflected in growing rates of dementia. With so many more of the population living until they are over 80 years of age, the numbers with dementia will increase proportionately.

It is this concern that has ensured dementia is widely identified as a *social problem* and fostered assumptions, including by those with the condition, that older people are a 'burden'. The bio-medical explanations of the condition, as described above, help to keep the condition in a special place among our fears of getting old, and fuel the perception of older people as senile. Those of us past middle age are truly terrified to think, when we cannot remember where we parked the car, or left the keys, or we realise we have just retold a story, that this might be the first sign of this dreaded condition: a condition which will render us dependent, in which our mental capacity will mean others take decisions for us and profoundly threaten our sense of who we are. Until greater progress has been made towards treatment or cure, the wisdom of the call for early diagnosis might be questioned.

This is particularly so because of the damaging effect of the label on the attitudes and behaviour of others towards the person with dementia and their family and friends. Sympathy for the family may veer towards pity; and the individual themselves, after a lifetime of being treated with respect, may find others speaking to them as if they are of very low intelligence and are aged under 5 years. In fact, the brain damage is different for each person, and will mean that differing functions are affected. And having a poor memory does not necessarily mean the person cannot give an informed view of an issue being discussed, or make choices about events in their lives. Yet the understanding of dementia as a disease associated with old age, and which progressively diminishes brain capacity, has led the person with Alzheimer's to be to a large extent, re-constructed as a 'non-person'. This is not the case in all societies, and some fascinating anthropological studies of the status of older people, sense of selfhood and kinship relations, show that there are less negative views of dementia where greater weight is given to non-medical explanations (Hashmi, 2009).

Dementia in the early stages need not affect daily life too seriously. A deterioration in memory – mainly recent events – a greater difficulty in concentration and in ability to think flexibly might be noticed, but not unduly troublesome. The diagnosis of dementia is often given as one of three severity levels: mild, as just described; moderate – when memory problems may mean the person does not know what day, time or month of the year it is, or they have difficulty finding the right words, and get easily confused, agitated or anxious; or severe. It is this latter group for whom round the clock supervision and support will be needed, as their memory loss may mean the person no longer recognises their own family members, or their environment, with speech, co-ordination and movement also badly affected.

Jennifer Newton

Social causes and social consequences

The social consequences of moderate and severe dementia are all too clear. Families and close friends will need to provide support, and the demands on their time, social and economic circumstances and their own health can be substantial. Depression is a particularly common health consequence for carers (Schneider *et al.*, 1999). It becomes increasingly difficult, as the disease progresses, for one relative to manage this alone. Help in the home or, where this is not possible, a move to specialist residential provision becomes essential. In providing the care required to the numbers that now require it, all European countries have needed to revisit the balance of responsibilities between the family, the market and the State.

For many countries and cultures, family duty has been the bedrock of all expectation about who *should* care. Gender has also framed this, with many cultures more likely to expect women to 'care for' while men might 'care about', but arrange for others to do the 'caring for' (Dalley, 1996). Those societies with strong welfare states have shifted the social norm to some extent towards an assumption that the State should be the main provider. However, the perceived threat to the economy linked to the rising age of the population is fast reversing this move, or at least governments are aiming to do so, and cast the State as a fall-back – not a main provider. The phrase 'rolling back the State' was a well worn short-hand for this in the UK Thatcher administration. Hospital, nursing home and residential care are expensive. Supporting the family and other informal carers can help to reduce the need for this.

While countries across Europe rely on informal carers as the main providers of long-term care, most do not have a process in place to systematically identify them and assess their needs for support. This is made more difficult due to the expectation of the carers – many of whom do not view themselves in this way, but rather as dutiful, loving partners, parents, children. The most common type of help provided is financial, followed by respite care and training (Courtin *et al.*, 2014). The financial support sought by informal carers includes flexible working arrangements and pension protection, and this is also in the interests of the State, so that as many people as possible remain in the workforce and contribute tax to the Treasury at the same time as supporting their family members or friends (ibid.).

The majority of family carers are of working age, though often in the later stages of their working lives; Carers UK (2015) calculates that at least 1 in 5 people over the age of 50 have a caring role. But some of the changing family and gender relationships throughout Europe are impacting on the availability of traditional sources of informal care. The proportion of households where older adult children and their parents live together has declined; a higher proportion of women are in paid employment; divorce or separation is more common. Among working age adults, it is still the case that more carers are female than male, according to UK census data, but the difference is not as great as some may assume – 1 in 4 women, 1 in 6 men at age 50–65 – but this reverses in later life, so that after the age of 85 nearly 60 per cent of carers in the UK are male, usually caring for their partner.

The financial, emotional, physical, social and health related demands increase with increased hours of care, of course. Those caring for more than 20 hours a week, and particularly those living in the same household, are often doing more personal care, longer hours and are less likely to be in paid employment. Those caring at a distance will be more likely to have other caring responsibilities, perhaps combining care for a young family with care for older relatives, and perhaps also paid employment. Carers UK (2015) describes those caring for two families as the 'sandwich generation' who are increasing in number as the average age for having children continues to rise, alongside the numbers of older people needing care. The organisation has commissioned numerous surveys on the lives of carers, and document clearly the drop in income frequently associated with taking on a caring role, as carers pass up progression opportunities associated with higher work commitment, reduce their hours, or give up work completely, and the consequent economies required for heating and food.

Social class and level of education show some small association with rates of dementia but, on the whole, the social factors most well understood as implicated in the development of dementia are the lifestyles linked to heart disease risk – diet and exercise. What is good for the heart is good for the brain, it seems. Once the disease is established, then social factors like the level of family support are implicated in survival times.

To support people trying to combine caring and paid employment, policy to ensure paid or unpaid care leave and flexible working arrangements is in place in 15 European countries. A similar number offer some kind of pension credit. Courtin's team interviewed experts in 27 European countries during 2012 to explore the extent of services targeting informal carers directly, and national policies and legal entitlements, including help received via the eligibility of the cared for person. Other than financial supports, they found a wide variation in the availability of support. Respite care was provided in 21 European countries, training and information in 17, counselling in 12 and 4 countries were providing no support of these types at all. Many services are provided nationally by NGOs rather than the State.

In the last 30 years, community care strategy has become far more focussed on the needs and wishes of the individual with dementia, not just the needs of the carer and the State. 'Needs led' thinking of the 1990s (rather than service driven planning of the 1980s) has become 'personalisation' in the 2000s, and given rise to cash-for-care schemes. These approaches aim to give individuals the choice of whom they employ to provide support, and what type of support they commission, often via a 'personal or individual budget'. In France, this has enabled informal carers to move towards a care co-ordination role, while more of the personal care is provided by professional carers employed out of the personal budget (Courtin et al., 2014). However, some of the concerns about the rights and protection of the unpaid informal carer can then surface in relation to the professional carers employed directly by the individual. How best are their employment and social rights protected?

Only nine European countries provide a carers allowance, and it is generally low. Far more common is an 'attendance allowance' payable directly to the cared for person, although take-up is often low. In fact only England, Malta

Jennifer Newton

and Sweden have national policy allowing identification and assessment of the needs of carers independently of the assessment of the cared for person (Courtin *et al.*, 2014).

7.5 Conclusion

Diabetes, depression and dementia are social problems in the sense that they can be construed as a threat to social structures: the affordability of health service provision; the efficiency of the workforce; the quality of family life; and the social care infrastructure, both formal and informal. The onset, or progression or consequences or all of these are affected by wealth, social class and status. Those affected are stigmatised by the label, and seen as burdensome. This stigma further contributes to the chronic stress in the lives of those so labelled. For instance, those revealing a mental ill-health history will experience discrimination in the labour market. Social disadvantage and chronic stress contribute to many types of chronic ill-health, particularly to the common mental health conditions like depression and anxiety, and to obesity and diabetes. But casting the individual as the social problem – their choice of diet, being overweight, lack of work, relationship problems or stressful lives – will do little to reduce the population rates of depression, diabetes or dementia. Structural factors and social norms play the major role in individual lifestyle choice, and in the availability of support. The more important consideration is the norm, and how it might be moved.

Social and economic policy plays a key role to the extent to which it helps us to feel safe, valued and supported (Newton, 2013), clearly carrying implications for housing, education, employment and crime control. More specifically, it will be beneficial if it is made less acceptable for partners to abuse and control; if people with mental health histories can find work; if corporal punishment is less acceptable; and if the norm is moved too in relation to child sexual exploitation, gender equality, consumption rates of sugar, alcohol, fat and red meat, attitudes to older people, and to support for informal care of all types. That is, we need policy to change the behaviour of the average person rather than a focus on the 'deviant'.

References

ADI (Alzheimer's Disease International) (2015) *World Alzheimer Report 2015 The Global Impact of Dementia: An Analysis of Prevalence, Incidence, Cost and Trends*, London: Alzheimer's Disease International.

BBC News (14 February 2015) Obese could lose benefits if they refuse treatment – PM www.bbc.co.uk/news/uk-31464897 (last accessed 30 April 2016).

Brown, G.W. (2002) Social roles, context and evolution in the origins of depression *Journal of Health and Social Behavior*, 43(3): 255–76.

Brown, G.W. and Harris, T.O. (1978) *Social Origins of Depression*, London: Routledge.

Brown, G.W. and Moran, P. (1994) Clinical and psychosocial origins of chronic depressive episodes. 1: a community survey *British Journal of Psychiatry*, 165(4): 447–56.

Brown, G.W., Craig, T.J.K. and Harris, T.O. (2008) Parental maltreatment and proximal risk factors using the Childhood Experience of Care and Abuse (CECA) instrument: a life-course study of adult chronic depression - 5 *Journal of Affective Disorders*, 110(3): 222–33.

Campbell, D. (2012) Diabetes threatens to 'bankrupt' NHS within a generation, *The Guardian*, 25 April 2012 www.theguardian.com/society/2012/apr/25/diabetes-treatment-bankrupt-nhs-generation (last accessed 22 January 2017).

Carers UK (2015) *Facts about Carers*, London: Carers UK.

Courtin, E., Jemiai, N. and Mossialos, E. (2014) Mapping support policies for informal carers across the European Union *Health Policy*, 118(1): 84–94.

Dalley, G. (1996) *Ideologies of Caring: Rethinking Community and Collectivism*, second edition. London: CPA.

Gatineau, M., Hancock, C., Holman, N., Outhwaite, H., Oldridge, L., Christie, A. and Ells, L. (2014) *Adult Obesity and Type 2 Diabetes*, London: Public Health England.

GBD 2010 Country Collaboration (2013) GBD 2010 country results: a global public good *The Lancet*, 381(9871): 965–70.

GBD (Global Burden of Disease Study 2013 Collaborators) (2015) Years lived with disability (YLDs) for 1160 sequelae of 289 diseases and injuries 1990–2010: a systematic analysis for the Global Burden of Disease Study 2010 www.thelancet.com Published online 8 June 2015 http://dx.doi.org/10.1016/S0140-6736(15)60692-4 (last accessed 20 June 2016).

Harris, T. (ed.) (2000) *Where Inner and Outer Worlds Meet: Psychological Research in the Tradition of George W. Brown*, London: Routledge.

Hashmi, M. (2009) Dementia: an anthropological perspective *International Journal of Geriatric Psychiatry*, 24(2): 207–12.

IDF (International Diabetes Federation) (2006) *Diabetes Atlas*, 3rd edition, Brussels: IDF.

Isaacs, S. (ed.) (2014) *Social Problems in the UK: An Introduction*, London: Routledge.

NEoLCIN (2013) *What We Know Now 2013. New Information Collated by the National End of Life Care Intelligence Network*, London: Public Health England.

Newton, J. (2013) *Preventing Mental Ill-health: Informing Public Health Planning and Mental Health Practice*, London: Routledge.

OECD/European Union (2010) Diabetes prevalence and incidence, in *Health at a Glance: Europe 2010*, Paris: OECD Publishing. http://dx.doi.org/10.1787/9789264090316-19-en (last accessed 20 June 2016).

Oliver, M. (1990) *The Politics of Disablement*, Basingstoke: Macmillan.

ONS (Meltzer, H., Gatward, R., Corbin, T., Goodman, R. and Ford, T.) (2003) *Persistence, Onset, Risk Factors and Outcomes of Childhood Mental Disorders*, London: TSO.

Parsons, T. (1951) *The Social System*, London: Routledge.

PRB (Population Reference Bureau) (2014) 2014 World population data sheet www.prb.org/Publications/Datasheets/2014/2014-world-population-data-sheet/data-sheet.aspx (last accessed 3 January 2015).

Rose, G. (1985) Sick individuals and sick populations *International Journal of Epidemiology*, 14(1): 32–8.

Rose, G. and Day, S. (1990) For debate: the population mean predicts the number of deviant individuals *British Medical Journal*, 301(6759): 1031–4.

Sayce, L. (2015) *From Psychiatric Patient to Citizen Revisited*, London: Palgrave Macmillan.

Schneider, J., Murray, J., Banerjee, S. and Mann, A. (1999) EUROCARE: A cross-national study of co-resident spouse carers for people with Alzheimer's Disease: factors associated with carer burden *International Journal of Geriatric Psychiatry*, 14(8): 651–61.

SCMH (Sainsbury Centre for Mental Health) (2007) *Mental Health and Employment. Briefing No. 33*, London: Centre for Mental Health.

Shakespeare, T. and Watson, N. (2002) The social model of disability: an outdated ideology? *Research in Social Science and Disability* 2: 9–28 http://disability-studies.leeds.ac.uk/files/library/Shakespeare-social-model-of-disability.pdf (last accessed 10 May 2016).

Singleton, N., Bumpstead, R., O'Brien, M., Lee, A. and Meltzer, H. (2001) *Psychiatric Morbidity among Adults Living in Private Households 2000*, London: Stationery Office.

Tamayo, T., Rosenbauer, J., Wild, S.H., Spijkerman, A.M.W., Baan, C., Forouhi, N.G., Herder, C. and Rathmann, W. (2014) Diabetes in Europe: an update *Diabetes Research and Clinical Practice* 103(2): 206–17. DOI: http://dx.doi.org/10.1016/j.diabres.2013.11.007 (last accessed 20 June 2016).

Tedstone, A., Anderson, S., Allen, R. and staff at PHE (2014) *Sugar Reduction: Responding to the Challenge*, London: Public Health England.

UNICEF (2007) Child poverty in perspective: an overview of child well-being in rich countries *Innocenti Report Card No. 7*, Florence: UNICEF Innocenti Research Centre, Florence www.unicef.org/media/files/ChildPovertyReport.pdf (last accessed 21 January 2017).

WHO (2014a) *Global Health Estimates Summary Tables: Deaths by Cause, Age and Sex, by World Bank Income Category and WHO Region, 2000–2012*, Geneva: World Health Organisation.

WHO (2014b) *Global Health Estimates Summary Tables: DALY by Cause, Age and Sex, by World Bank Income Category and WHO Region, 2000–2012*, Geneva: World Health Organisation.

part III

Education

chapter 8

European ideals, schooling and modern childhood

David Blundell and Sandra Abegglen

8.1 Introduction

> [C]hildren and youth are often perceived through opposition to adulthood and as 'people in the process of becoming rather than being'. . . . Here, children and youth appear as pre-social and passive recipients of experience. They are portrayed as dependent, immature, and incapable of assuming responsibility, properly confined to the protection of home and school . . . This concept developed amongst the middle class in Europe and North America and has been universalized in such a way that youngsters who do not follow this path are considered either to be at risk or to pose a risk to society.
>
> (Honwana and De Boeck 2005, p. 12)

It is an unremarkable observation that children matter; a simple audit of the resources devoted to children and the pursuit of a 'good childhood' quickly confirms that 'small human beings' occupy a central place in the imagination, culture and institutions of the societies to which they belong. However, it is not always clear in what sense they 'matter'. This chapter argues that European modernity, armed with the sort of middle-class fantasies to which Honwana and De Boeck (2005) refer, has never seen the education and care of children as simply or solely a matter of concern for the particular children in question – the notion of a 'good childhood' is always intercut by the European Enlightenment's political project to achieve moral, social and economic progress through the education of 'the young'. However, if, as the Swiss childhood theorist Jean Piaget (1934) said, 'Only education is capable of saving our societies from possible collapse, whether violent, or gradual', this begs not only immediate questions about what might be meant by education and whether its role is to sustain society or make collapse more likely but also whether what could be seen as Eurocentric ways of seeing children and addressing childhood are tenable when children's lives are increasingly marked by globalised circumstances and inter-cultural encounters.

8.2 The construction of European childhood

A clear focus for current European legislation and policy concerning children and childhood is early years education and welfare; this is because the phenomenon constructed under the headline 'Early Childhood Education and Care' (ECEC) is seen as the 'essential foundation for successful lifelong learning, social integration, personal development and later employability' (European Commission 2011). This developmental view on children implies not only that the first years are crucial in a child's development but also that children are born with a very basic 'mental structure' requiring constant attention and monitoring by adults and the adult-world if cognitive and physical growth are to keep step with one another and normative outcomes are to be secured. This instantiates Honwana and De Boeck's (2005, p. 12) claim that Eurocentric modern childhood portrays children 'as dependent, immature, and incapable of assuming responsibility, properly confined to the protection of home and school'.

Support for the developmental view on children has conventionally come from the psychologically focused theorisation of developmentalists and retains heavy reliance on the work of the Swiss natural historian, philosopher and social scientist Jean Piaget (1964, 1952). Piaget undertook a number of iconic experiments with children to ascertain how they constructed knowledge and understanding of the world; these experiments appeared to suggest that a child's cognitive capabilities and, hence, capacity to learn unfold through a series of successive and qualitatively distinct developmental stages. Educationists, amongst others, have inferred from his work that children cannot undertake certain cognitive tasks such as engaging in abstract reasoning, understanding another's point of view or being able to imagine phenomena in the absence of concrete experience until their mental apparatus is appropriately mature. Quoting MacKay (1973, p. 28), James and Prout (1997, p. 13) reveal how this account proceeds on an assumption of fundamental differences, whereby 'children are regarded as "immature, irrational, incompetent, asocial [and] acultural" with adults being "mature, rational, competent, social and autonomous" . . . They are, in effect, two different instances of the species'.

The view that children have a less-developed mental structure than adults is underlined by the brain research informing a summative and comparative review by Gabriela Arias de Sanchez *et al.* (2012) of early childhood curriculum documents produced by 17 countries between 1996 and 2011; these included

David Blundell and Sandra Abegglen

documents from Finland, Norway, Sweden, Ireland and Scotland. The authors noted that 'Brain malleability and plasticity during the first years of life were emphasized in the majority of these documents as the reason for developing and assuring quality early childhood learning experiences' (ibid., p. 39). This leads to the largely unquestioned view that:

> What happens during the first months and years of life matters a lot, not because this period of development provides an indelible blueprint for adult well-being, but because it sets either a sturdy or fragile stage for what follows.
>
> (Shonkoff and Phillips 2000, p. 5)

The authors go on to point out the links between these ways of thinking about children and the priorities shaping educational systems:

> These developments appear to be driven by common beliefs and ideals regarding early childhood such as the value of the early years as the most dynamic period of brain development, the role of formal early childhood education as the primary stage in the lifelong learning continuum, and the belief that investing in early years is a worthwhile investment of society's resources.
>
> (Arias de Sanchez *et al.* 2012, p. 43)

Furthermore, in discussing their multinational review of early childhood policy documents, Arias de Sanchez *et al.* (2012) suggest that the essentialism at the heart of mainstream developmentalist thinking retains a tenacious grip on policy-makers' imagination so that, despite globalisation with its transnational encounters and increasing social diversity across national, social and cultural contexts, developmentalist ways of seeing approach a universal conviction. They found that:

> Even though the documents are grounded in cultural difference and demonstrate respect and support of different socio-cultural backgrounds, the similarities among the majority of these frameworks/curricula are remarkable . . . [and] . . . a pervasive sense of 'one size fits all' does exist.
>
> (ibid., p. 43)

The relegation of sociologically rooted differences of class, ethnicity, gender, (dis)ability, sexuality, etc. in favour of more psychologically oriented theories of children's developmental growth found in the 'one size fits all' approach underlines the proposition that 'the child' represents an objectified Weberian 'ideal type' providing a *template* form around which proper provision for children can be identified, arranged and justified (James and Prout 2014, 1997).

The template child, assembled largely through rationalistic scientific methodologies – with brain science the latest contributor – serves as both model and justification for the idea that children need to be placed in separate, goal-directed institutions such as schools, nurseries, children's centres, youth clubs and junior sports clubs that seek to address their needs and assure normative growth. At a time when outcomes from research into the quality of children's lives reveal wide variations across Europe (UNICEF 2014, 2007; Blundell 2015) it seems timely to ask whether the installation of this late eighteenth-century template child requires re-evaluation. Furthermore, the pressing challenges of large-scale human migration, including large numbers of refugees seeking asylum in Europe, question whether conceptions of education and schooling based on one-dimensional developmentalist assumptions represent the best way to approach uncertain futures faced by children who simultaneously identify with national, European and global communities.

8.3 Children and children's lives: childhood as a social construction

Over the past 30 or so years sociologists, anthropologists, human geographers, educationists, critical psychologists, cultural theorists and historians have made common cause in challenging developmentalism and the belief that the facts of biology/psychology are sufficient to inform how we should arrange and provide for young people's lives. Allison James and Alan Prout consolidated this multi-disciplinary effort by publishing their 'New Paradigm for the Sociology of Childhood' in 1990 (republished in 1997, 2014) through which they sought to define and catalyse a research agenda for the broad, interdisciplinary field that has become the New Social Studies of Childhood. This work has laid stress on the proposition that childhood is a social construction with a quite specific historical provenance, i.e. a way that particular cultures and societies make sense of bio-logical facts of immaturity, and that there are many ways that this immaturity intersects with other sociological variables, including class, ethnicity, gender, disability, sexuality, etc.

This social constructionist view of childhood champions children as agentic social actors constructing their worlds and challenges the idea that they are passively driven by developmental forces that place them on a one-directional 'up-escalator' towards adulthood. Thus, James and Prout (1997) set about tackling the claims to naturalness and universality found in the developmentalist assumptions of modern childhood along with the belief that developmental maturity is identified by the achievement of a particular sort of rationality. They wrote:

> This dominant developmental approach to childhood, provided by psychology, is based on the idea of natural growth . . . It is a self-sustaining model whose features can be crudely delineated as follows: rationality is the universal mark of adulthood with childhood representing the period of apprenticeship for its development. Childhood is therefore important to study as a pre-social period of difference, a biologically determined stage on the path to full human status i.e., adulthood. The naturalness of children

David Blundell and Sandra Abegglen

both governs and is governed by their universality. It is essentially an evolutionary model: the child developing into an adult represents a progression from simplicity to complexity of thought, from irrational to rational behaviour.

(ibid., p. 10)

Feminist commentators such as Valerie Walkerdine (1984), Donna Haraway (1991) and Erica Burman (1994) emphasise essentialist assumptions lodged at the heart of the developmentalist narrative for human becoming and suggest that its normative rationality is far from natural or universal but represents a particularly masculine form of consciousness.

There is a central ambivalence here about the relation between the natural and the nurtured that mirrors the tension between scientific objectivity and social application structuring psychological research: it seems that the natural course of development has to be carefully monitored, supported and even corrected in order to emerge appropriately. That which is designated natural or spontaneously arising is in fact constructed or even forced.

(Burman 1994, p. 19)

For exponents of this critical social constructionist position, 'modern childhood' is a historically and culturally specific product of the European Enlightenment and offered one approach to *les philosophes'* concern to establish a clear understanding of human nature in an increasingly secular world where religious authority was no longer the unquestioned source for knowledge and understanding in such matters (see Gay 1969). Philosophers, notably the Englishman John Locke and the Swiss Jean-Jacques Rousseau, saw opportunities in children's fresh, new-minted qualities to glimpse humans' original nature and thereby offer a starting point for a philosophical and political project to improve people and society. Thus in the late-seventeenth and early-eighteenth century we see the philosopher John Locke writing extensively on the upbringing of children followed by Rousseau's 'Emile: ou de l'education' published in 1762 (see Blundell 2012). Although Locke and Rousseau represent markedly different approaches to understanding children, what unites them is a sense that childhood has a purpose and should be understood in relation to adulthood and society.

Rousseau used Emile to argue for an approach to children's education that is in harmony with their nature and protects them from the corrupting expectations and demands of society for as long as possible; he believed this would allow a healthy and confident form of self-regard – identified by him as '*amour de soi meme*' – to flourish, rather than the neurotically harmful '*amour propre*' and its concern with status in relation to others.

Hold childhood in reverence, and do not be in any hurry to judge it for good or ill. . . . Give nature time to work before you take over her business, lest you interfere with her dealings. You assert that you know the value of time and are afraid to waste it. You fail to perceive that it is a greater waste of time to use it ill than to do nothing, and that a child ill taught is further from virtue than a child who has learnt nothing at all. You are afraid to see him spending his early years doing nothing. What! is it nothing to be happy, nothing to run and jump all day? He will never be so busy again all his life long.

(Rousseau 1762 reprinted 2013, p. 84)

Amongst Rousseau's followers was the great Swiss educator Johann Pestalozzi; we can discern Rousseau's influence in Pestalozzi's injunction to all who would educate children as well as an assumption that natural growth and learning are inextricably braided with one another:

I wish to wrest education from the outworn order of doddering old teaching hacks as well as from the new-fangled order of cheap, artificial teaching tricks, and entrust it to the eternal powers of nature herself, to the light which God has kindled and kept alive in the hearts of fathers and mothers, to the interests of parents who desire their children grow up in favour with God and with men.

(Pestalozzi quoted in Silber 1965, p. 134)

These ideas took root in the circumstances of the German Enlightenment through the work of Johann Friedrich Froebel. Froebel promotes the child as a philosophical avatar through which not only the relationship between childhood, education and nature can be explored and discussed but also German aspirations to political nationhood can be realised. Froebel was working in the particular circumstances that saw the rise of German nationalism through the first half of the nineteenth century and a growing demand to see Germany unified as a single nation state. Following exile in England his aristocratic supporters, including Baroness Marenholtz von Bulow and an educationist named Bertha Ronge, promoted his ideas through writing and training colleges where women students could acquire the Froebelians' pedagogic methods. These methods were rooted in the idea of natural growth, whereby childhood represented a graduated, stage-by-stage progress towards adulthood that is also found in Rousseau, Pestalozzi and Rudolf Steiner.

These intuitive insights regarding children and their education seemed to be confirmed by the experimental work of Jean Piaget, the Swiss genetic epistemologist with a particular interest in children and how they acquire knowledge of the world. However, despite the claims to universality and naturalness underpinning Piaget's rationally conceived staged schema for children's development there lurks a distinctly Eurocentric conception of human progress. Piaget (1964, 1952), as mentioned earlier, suggests to us that children's cognitive processes develop from birth via a series of stages; each stage represents a step towards the attainment of what he terms 'formal operational' cognitive function that is marked by a capacity for abstract reasoning. Piaget's assertion that the stages preceding the attainment of formal operational rationality are marked by qualitatively different modes of cognition can be traced to his enthusiasm for the

David Blundell and Sandra Abegglen

work of a French anthropologist and philosopher named Lucien Levy-Bruhl and thence into recesses of nineteenth-century European intellectual endeavour in the Social Sciences that are now widely swept under the carpet.

Levy-Bruhl (1922, 1910) had worked in French colonies of sub-Saharan Africa with indigenous populations and proposed that black African peoples' cognition was qualitatively different from that of white Europeans. For Levy-Bruhl not only were African and European ways of thinking different but, in an echo of Hegel, he believed that European intellectual culture represented the pinnacle of human evolution thus far and, by extension, argued that Africans exhibited what he called a 'primitive mind'. This relied on racist hierarchical assumptions that were a typical feature of European academic social and human science at the time; Levy-Bruhl translated a particular reading of evolutionary theory expressed in the aphorism that '*ontogenesis recapitulates phylogenesis*'. From this he constructed an account for human development based on the proposition that the developmental path followed by an individual member of a species recaps each of the evolutionary stages passed through by that species over its complete and much longer evolution. Levy-Bruhl deployed evolutionary theory to naturalise and explain the imperialist ascendancy of Europeans, justifying it as a necessary outcome from evolutionary forces, thereby side-stepping other accounts based on a more honest political and economic understanding of power relations.

The developmental study of children has apparently been shorn of this racist aspect, not least by its claims to universality and naturalness; however Sadaf Shallwani (2010, p. 238) suggests that its presence abides in a common 'yearning for White civility' inscribed not only within the developmentalism of theorists, such as Piaget, concerned with the production of human capital but also in deterministic theories of development concerned with economic capital:

> the notion of 'development' as 'progress' implies a linear and progressive path from 'the primitive' to 'the civilized' . . . and is thus tied up with moral and cultural ideas of White civilized superiority . . . Whether the discourse is about countries or humans, it is implied that there is one path to 'development', and all entities can be ranked on this continuum (e.g. under-developed, developing, developed) . . . Progress and improvement are thus conceived as the pathway from racialized and gendered Other – signified by 'the under-developed/developing', 'the primitive', 'the child' – to the White man – signified by 'the developed', 'the civilized', and 'the adult'

The philosophical and moral currency of Eurocentric and even racist developmentalist constructions of the child and childhood is further challenged by the bald fact that the overwhelming majority of the world's children do not live in Euro-America, or what is increasingly known as the 'minority world' (Wells 2009). Nine out of every ten children live within the 'majority world' (UNICEF 2011) – and although developmentalism informs the assumptions and practices of the institutionalised education that increasingly shapes their lives, it cannot be assumed that their cultural worlds and lives as social actors are congruent with these assumptions and practices.

Some of these commonalities between child- and economic-development are explored by Anne Trine Kjørholt (2007) in research examining children's lives in both majority and minority world situations. Kjørholt describes the experience of Norwegian children taking part in a government-sponsored initiative entitled 'Try Yourself'. This initiative aimed to promote children's engagement in civil society through a number of self-initiated projects, such as repairing cars or baking bread. Kjørholt shows how although these projects seek to model real life enterprises, they are always a form of play and, therefore, will always be a simulation of real life. This simulation reinforces the developmentalist norms that shape institutional life for children where *being* at a stage is understood as preparation to *become* a particular sort of adult. It is also founded upon the assumption that children as 'adults in the making' will always need supervision, direction and regulation.

By contrast, Kjørholt (2007) points to the very real and painful conflicts felt by Mary, a young girl from The Philippines, who struggles to combine backbreaking work to support her family with her passion for learning at school. However, when Mary was invited to address an international conference on child labour hosted by the UN, she movingly told of the real and unavoidable conflicts between hard labour, its abolition and attending school. Campaigns to abolish child labour would reduce her family's income and make school attendance almost impossible so that she can have work without school, but not education without work. Mary's testimony reveals that attempts to impose a version of childhood based on the template child without recognition of her circumstances as a complete social actor could, therefore, be anything but liberatory for her.

Mary and the Norwegian children have very different lived experiences, but both face constraints on their agency as social actors and find themselves firmly under the discipline of adult-world imperatives. For Mary the experience is brutal and hard, and this should not be diminished, but the assumption that the Norwegian children's experience is implicitly benign should not lead us to conclude that this is how children see it. Shallwani and Kjørholt (both cited earlier) each underline the point that the template child bequeathed to us by modernity has never solely been about children and their interests, but recruits them to achieve a raft of social, political and economic goals. The examples below suggest that this can lead to acute conflicts within established social and institutional contexts, especially as demands grow for acknowledgement of social and cultural diversity across Europe's nation states.

This chapter now goes on to explore ways that the template child is applied in three areas of educational and social policy. These are: (1) UNICEF reports by the Innocenti organisation on children and young people's well-being; (2) Eurostat data concerning the size and structure of Europe's population of children and young people; and, (3) The case of Programme for International Student Assessment (PISA) tests and the growing influence of the Organisation for Economic Cooperation and Development (OECD) in debates about standards and educational attainment.

David Blundell and Sandra Abegglen

8.4 Policy and the template child: case studies

The following case studies are selected because they have direct implications for policy-making, and particular relevance and purchase within a European context. However, more than this, the case studies also point to the importance of the template child as a *Eurocentric* concept and the contribution its developmentalist ideas make to the processes of framing, implementing and evaluating policy interventions on a global scale.

UNICEF reports

The promotion of modern, European childhood to global status as an ideal type was lent considerable impetus by the appearance of the United Nations Convention on the Rights of the Child (UNCRC) in 1989. The convention universalises and normalises standards for children's lives on a global scale through its 45 articles defining rights that surround questions of education, consultation, life, health, welfare, relationships, safety, discrimination, exploitation, justice and work. It followed that the propositions found in the UNCRC encouraged and enabled interest in international comparisons of the quality of childhoods. At the forefront of international comparisons has been a series of reports produced for UNICEF by the Innocenti organisation. The most recent were published in 2008 and 2013, and presented findings from surveys undertaken in 29 wealthy countries that were all members of the OECD – and all but two were in Europe. The most recent survey published in 2013 (Adamson 2013) – but relying on statistics gathered in 2009–10 before the Eurozone crisis hit – looked at the condition of childhood under five dimensions: material well-being, health and safety, education, behaviours and risks, and housing and environment. Well-being was principally evaluated using a range of statistical indicators for each of these dimensions along with 11-, 13- and 15-year-old children's own assessments; this enabled the construction of a 'life satisfaction league table'. The research found that the Netherlands headed the table followed by Iceland, Spain, Finland and Greece all with scores over 90 per cent life satisfaction. The lowest scores were recorded in Romania with 77 per cent life satisfaction and Poland, Lithuania, Hungary and Slovakia were just above them. The UK was placed squarely in mid-table on 86 per cent – above Italy, Austria, France and Germany but below all of the Nordic countries as well as Spain, Greece, Switzerland and Ireland. Children's evaluation of their well-being was based on how they felt about key relationships in their lives, including those with their mothers, fathers and peers. Again, children in The Netherlands and Nordic countries were most positive about these relationships. The data suggested that relationships with mothers scored most positively, followed by peers – but the findings suggested that fathers were least easy to talk with in all cases.

Broad statistics like these not only invite curiosity about the meanings that lie behind the findings, but also invite closer examination of the constructions of children and childhood with which they operate and that form their foundational assumptions. It is axiomatic for the survey that age (as a proxy for biological, intellectual and emotional immaturity) is sufficient both to qualify as a respondent and to identify who is and who is not a child. This not only obviates national institutional differences of meaning and interpretation but also overlooks how young people are located as social actors within diverse cultural and social formations based on class, ethnicity, gender, disability and sexuality within national boundaries. These aspects of children's social worlds represent what James and Prout (1997, p. 4) called 'facts of culture' and are vital to understanding socially constructed ways of seeing biological immaturity; furthermore, they frequently mean that an appeal to age alone is insufficient to understand the lives of children and young people. What do children mean when they say they have a 'good relationship' with their mother? Why should it be assumed that having a good relationship with mothers, or fathers, in particular, is vital to well-being?

The Innocenti research operates with assumptions not only about the meaning of childhood and families, but also an atomised *template child* that marginalises social structures, networks and relationships; in this it proceeds upon the dominant assumptions of childhood as a universal and natural condition. An example drawn from the work of Sue Welch (2008, p. 18) illustrates how 'real' children's lives are frequently at odds with these assumptions of incompetence and irrationality, and demonstrates not only the resilience some children are required to develop due to the challenges they face as social actors but also how they rise to the task; consider Jason and how his situation might be important in understanding the meaning of responses he might make to UNICEF about his well-being:

> Jason is 10 years old and lives with his mother and younger brother. His mother suffers from depression and often relies on Jason to get himself and his brother up and ready for school. He also shops, prepares meals for them all in the evenings, goes to the launderette and keeps the house clean and tidy. Jason takes these responsibilities very seriously and both boys appear well cared for. His mother is able to keep going because of the support Jason gives her in these ways and because he is sensitive to her difficulties. He is concerned that if he tells anyone what is happening his mother may be blamed.

The relationship between Jason and his mother is not only a clear inversion of the normative assumptions underlying the UNICEF research that are rooted in the template European childhood but also challenges the discourse of the 'upstream intervention' that is found within its rationale:

> the need to promote the well-being of children is widely accepted. As a pragmatic imperative, it is equally deserving of priority; failure to protect and promote the well-being of children is associated with increased risk across a wide range of later-life outcomes.
>
> (Adamson 2013, p. 4)

David Blundell and Sandra Abegglen

Clearly there are arguments to support Jason, as for anyone whose burden becomes unbearable, but it should not be assumed that taking away his obvious sense of responsibility and agency in the name of restoring a 'proper childhood' would represent a priority for him nor would it comply with how he sees the risks he faces.

Eurostat

Similar to the reports produced by the Innocenti organisation, Eurostat, the leading provider of statistics on Europe, tries, amongst many other things, to provide insight into the quality of children's lives in Europe. One of the most interesting and relevant Eurostat datasets on children and young people in the European Union can be found in the 'Being Young in Europe Today' report (2015 Edition) (Eurostat 2015). The report aims to shed light on what it means 'to be young in Europe today' in relation to the 'Youth Strategy 2010–2018' set up by the European Union in 2009 and the Recommendation 'Investing in Children: Breaking the Cycle of Disadvantage' published by the European Commission (EC) in February 2013. The report is based on the data available on the Eurostat website, the official portal of the statistical office of the European Union. It is divided into seven chapters covering population; family and society; health; education; access and participation to the labour market; living conditions; and the digital world.

The 2015 report shows that the share of children and young people aged between 0 and 14 years in the population of the European Union (EU) has been decreasing continuously over recent years. 'In 2014, the EU population stood at 507 million people, of whom only 169 million (or 33.3%) were children or young people (aged under 30)' (Eurostat 2015, p. 10), although there are some disparities between individual EU Member States. As outlined in the report, 'The share of households with children has generally declined in the EU over the last few years' (ibid., p. 10). The EU's demographic challenges are predicted to be replicated across the continent. This means not only that there are fewer and fewer children but also that these children carry a greater responsibility towards the older generation.

> If we add up the share of young people and old-age people who will depend on the working population, today's generation of children are facing an increased burden in relation to supporting the remainder of the population as they move into work.
>
> (ibid., p. 39)

In addition, it is predicted that the falling number of children and young people in the total population could result in labour market shortages, which, in turn, could prevent sustainable economic growth (Eurostat 2015). This means, today's youth carries an enormous social and economic responsibility not only for their families but also for the future of their nation state. Hence, strategies to tackle the demographic challenges provoked by low birth rates and the increased longevity, not only in the EU but across Europe's population, are highly debated, for example in the European Demography Forum.

Equally debated amongst the EU Member States and others is the 'well-being' of children and young people. Although most children in the EU grow up in favourable conditions, the 'Being Young in Europe Today' report shows that 3 out of 10 children are at risk of poverty and social exclusion, with children in certain EU Member States worse affected than in others (Eurostat 2015). In this regard, 'monetary poverty' poses the highest 'risk' to children:

> Households with children are usually financially worse off when compared with households without children, as the former face more expenditure linked to the cost of bringing up children.
>
> (ibid., p. 168)

This means each child in a family reduces the average income per family member and, as such, increases the risk of poverty for the child and its family. This seems ironic: children posing a risk to their own welfare – especially when considering the wealth of policies in place to tackle child poverty (see Isaacs *et al.* 2015).

Most of the policies in place to tackle child poverty echo the belief found in the UNCRC that just as a child should not be held responsible for the beliefs and actions of their parents, their life-chances should not be pre-determined by the characteristics of the family into which they are born. For example, the '2010 to 2015 Government Policy: Education of Disadvantaged Children' published under the 2010 to 2015 Conservative and Liberal Democrat coalition government in the UK states: 'We believe it is unacceptable for children's success to be determined by their social circumstances' (Department for Education 2015). However, these policies are not only based on the idea of 'equal opportunity' but also that a 'successful childhood' leads to a 'successful adulthood' and, vice versa, issues in the early years lead to problems in later life. As stated by the European Commission (2015) in relation to social protection and social inclusion:

> Children that grow up in poverty are more likely to suffer from social exclusion and health problems in the future, and also less likely to develop to their full potential later in life.

Hence, early intervention is seen as key. As outlined by the 'Statutory Framework for the Early Years Foundation Stage' in the United Kingdom (Department for Education 2014, p. 5):

> Good parenting and high quality early learning together provide the foundation children need to make the most of their abilities and talents as they grow up.

All this supports a developmental view on children and childhood. As outlined in section 8.2, this is problematic not only because children are seen as in

David Blundell and Sandra Abegglen

need of constant support and guidance but also because it helps to 'cement' the idea of a 'template child' that conforms to particular ideas and ideals:

> Assessment plays an important part in helping parents, carers and practitioners to recognise children's progress, understand their needs, and to plan activities and support. Ongoing assessment (also known as formative assessment) is an integral part of the learning and development process. It involves practitioners observing children to understand their level of achievement, interests and learning styles, and to then shape learning experiences for each child reflecting those observations.
>
> (Department for Education 2014, p. 13)

However, when looking more closely at the data in the Eurostat reports, it is difficult to find evidence for much resemblance between the actuality of children's lives and the norms inscribed in the template child or childhood. For example, the data on the living conditions of children and young people shows that 'Generally, life satisfaction within the EU population decreased as a function of age' (Eurostat 2015, p. 58); meaning that a '*happy childhood*' does not necessarily need to lead to a '*successful adulthood*'. Equally, data shows that more and more children do not live in the country in which they were born and that family structures are changing, with the number of children born outside marriage increasing:

> The share of children born outside marriage rose from 20% in the early 1990s to reach almost 30% by 2002, before continuing to increase during the most recent decade for which data are available, reaching almost 40% by 2011.
>
> (ibid., p. 50)

This means children's lived experiences vary greatly. Considering further that there are fewer and fewer children born, the theoretical and practical separation of children and adults seems questionable, especially when considering the current social, political and economical challenges faced on a national and international level. Despite this, the idea of modern, European childhood is not only celebrated within Europe and European policy and legislation but also projected onto a global scale.

PISA, OECD and normalising educational attainment

Whilst the UNCRC continues to exert global influence in discussions concerning children's lives, other more closely targeted initiatives seek to 'standardise' children's lives. An example of this is PISA introduced by the OECD to encourage international comparisons between educational systems and thus a closer synchronisation of outcomes across participating states as well as those aspiring to participate.

The OECD was established in 1962 by the USA and its Western partners with a mission to liberalise trade and facilitate greater flexibility in the global movement of capital (Scholte 2005) and has become closely identified with the strategic extension of neo-liberal free-market economic activity. Since 2000 the organisation has invested heavily in educational performance by overseeing the administration of tests for 15 and 16 year olds in core curricular areas every three years (Carvalho and Costa 2014). The 2012 PISA tests were taken by a sample of 510,000 students in 65 countries whose GDP together accounted for 80 per cent of the global economy (OECD 2014); tests were set in reading, mathematics, science and financial literacy. The results facilitated the construction of comparative tables of national performance that have established the OECD as an increasingly significant *eminence grise* in shaping education policy in the UK, across Europe and beyond (Martens and Niemann 2013).

Although concerned with the performance of young people towards the end of formal schooling, the PISA effect is widely felt as many nations seek to improve or sustain their rank position. So that whilst several authors (Aydin *et al.* 2011; Martens and Niemann 2013; Carvalho and Costa 2014) explore differences in the ways that nations respond to their league position, there is limited discussion of whether a league table can represent educational achievement or what a particular league position means. By publishing PISA league tables the OECD appears to have grasped the global educational agenda, thereby diminishing discussion of difference and diversity in favour of the metaphors of 'catching up', 'extending leads' and 'moving up' that implicitly validate the idea of national educational development resembling childhood developmentalism as uni-directional and ladder-like (see Shallwani, 2010).

Supporters of the project see PISA as a source of educational hope and point to its rootedness in the Universalist Enlightenment values of neutral expert *science* and the possibilities for *progress*, thus:

> PISA provides optimism about the possibility of reform and creates confidence in national policy actors . . . Moreover, PISA brings the comfort of legitimizing policy problems and solutions with the blessing of putative universal, independent, expert knowledge. And it is perhaps this combination of universalism and scientism that makes PISA an 'obligatory passage point' . . . for many debates about education today.
>
> (Carvalho and Costa 2014, p. 7)

Hence, the OECD's PISA programme not only promotes the idea that it is desirable to make international comparisons but also that it is possible to do so because a 'standard global pupil' exists and can be tested meaningfully. However, this relegates cultural and social differences to the margins or as a 'bolt-on' feature, but leaves intact the underlying universal child rooted in the 'scientism' of biology and psychology.

David Blundell and Sandra Abegglen

8.5 Conclusion: children of 'commonworlds'

Earlier we saw how Arias de Sanchez *et al.* (2012) criticised the 'one-size-fits-all' tendency they found in early childhood curriculum documents drawn from across the globe, and we have similarly pointed to the deployment of what we have called a 'template child' through which institutions, practices and policies can be framed and children's lives can be governed. As has been suggested by those who deploy this template themselves (namely OECD), these deployments are underpinned and authorised by reference to science or, more accurately, *scientism* and its largely unreflective assumption of universality. As we have seen, the idea of 'natural development' underpins those constructions of childhood emanating from the Enlightenment and lends them an almost unassailable legitimacy – to establish that something is 'natural' is to assign it the power of a 'knock-down punch' in matters of dispute and renders questions of judgement or political dispute otiose (Latour 2004). By contrast, the cultural relativism of the social constructionist position appears to circumvent the silencing effects of natural development on debate and to be more in tune with the diversity of possibilities for childhoods found when encountering children's lives. This position seems, in consequence, more able to respond to the experience of globalisation where differences found in inter-cultural encounters are commonplace.

However, exponents of the social constructionist position, including Alan Prout in 'The Future of Childhood' (2005), have expressed concerns that whilst it appears to be able to deconstruct the claims of the developmentalists, it seems merely to reproduce and entrench a dualistic distinction between nature and culture – more familiarly expressed in the lore of childhood studies as 'nature v. nurture'. If developmentalist claims are rooted in science and nature then social constructionists stand by culture and there is a state of impasse that is reflected in curricula, curtailing efforts to understand and accommodate real children and their lived experience. In response, some theorists suggest that debates about whether we are the product of nature or culture – and/or how the proportions work out – miss the point, because they both rely on a set of unquestioned assumptions; in each case, our language leads us to assume that both are 'real things' that can be separated out and identified. Indeed, the idea of *culture* as a thing is as Eurocentric in its conception as is modernity's conception of *nature* as a thing. Hence, Alan Prout proposes a more fluid and entangled view of what it is to be human; reference to historical perspectives found in the work of Deleuze and Guattari suggests that nature and culture are unstable categories catalysed by technological change to be in a constantly shifting state of modification. His examples include debates about developments in genetics and possibilities for so called 'designer babies' as well as psycho-active performance-enhancing drugs; suggesting that each renders questions about whether nature can be separated from culture meaningless. Thus, Prout (2005) prefers to speak of childhoods as 'nature-culture-technological assemblages'.

Recent declarations that the Earth is now so dominated by human activity and agency that it has entered a new geological epoch called the Anthropocene – or age of the humans – where there is no pristine, virginal or untouched nature to be found (see Crutzen and Müller 1989, Lovelock 2000, Pearce 2007, Sagan

1994) seem to support these arguments and suggest that modernity's 'nature' in general and Rousseau's distinction between natural childhood and socialised adulthood, in particular, is now meaningless and in urgent need of revision.

An Australian geographer and childhood theorist named Affrica Taylor (2013) takes things further in order to propose ways to understood children's lives by embracing the entanglements of hybrid nature-cultures. Taylor has spent many years working as an educator with children and communities of native Australians – groups with an ancient way of life that has been marginalised and supplanted by the very recent invasion of European settlers. Taylor proposes that the lives of the children she works with can be understand by recognising how they inhabit what she calls 'commonworlds' (after Latour 2004) comprising close bonds and affiliations between themselves, their family, pets, stock and wild animals, buildings, rocks, lumps of metal, plants, landscapes and anything else that is part of reflexively constructed entangled and ever-changing life-worlds of meaning for them. Reflection suggests that this way of seeing describes ways that we all live – in relation to others and the world of things – and that agency is not the private property of individuals but shared and relational. It also invites closer and more respectful interest in children and their lives, and obviates attempts to impose the narrow rationalities found in template childhoods upon them – especially when considering that many children now live global lives.

References

Adamson, P. (2013). *Child Well-being in Rich Countries: A Comparative Overview*. Innocenti Report Card 11. Available online: www.unicef-irc.org/publications/683 [Accessed 25.01.16].

Arias de Sanchez, G., Doiron, R. and Gabriel, M. (2012). An International Examination of Early Childhood Curricula from 17 Countries, *Canadian Children*, 37(2), pp. 29–47.

Aydin, A., Erdag, C. and Tas, N. (2011). A Comparative Evaluation of PISA 2003–2006 Results in Reading Literacy Skills: An Example of Top-Five OECD Countries and Turkey. *Kuram ve Uygulamada Egitim Bilimleri*, 11(2), pp. 665–73.

Blundell, D. (2012). *Education and Constructions of Childhood: Contemporary Issues in Education Studies*. London and New York: Continuum.

Blundell, D. (2015). Childhood and Education. In Isaacs, S., Blundell, D., Foley, A., Ginsburg, N., McDonough, B., Silverstone, D. and Young, T. *Social Problems in the UK: An Introduction*. London: Routledge, pp. 117–39.

Burman, E. (1994). *Deconstructing Developmental Psychology*. London: Routledge.

Carvalho, L. M. and Costa, E. (2014). Seeing Education with One's own Eyes and through the PISA Lenses: Considerations of the Reception of PISA in European Countries. *Discourse: Studies in Cultural Politics of Education*, 36(5), pp. 638–46.

Crutzen, P. J. and Müller, M. (1989). *Das Ende des blauen Planeten? Der Klimakollaps: Gefahren und Auswege*. München: Beck.

Department for Education (2014). *Statutory Framework for the Early Years Foundation Stage: Setting the Standards for Learning, Development and Care for Children from Birth to Five*. Statutory Framework. Available at: www.gov.uk/government/uploads/system/uploads/attachment_data/file/335504/EYFS_framework_from_1_September_2014__with_clarification_note.pdf [Accessed 01.11.15].

Department for Education (2015). *2010 to 2015 Government Policy: Education of Disadvantaged Children*. Policy Paper. Available at: www.gov.uk/government/publications/2010-to-2015-government-policy-education-of-disadvantaged-children/2010-to-2015-government-policy-education-of-disadvantaged-children [Accessed 01.11.15].

European Commission (2011). *Early Childhood Education and Care: Providing all our Children with the Best Start for the World of Tomorrow*. Communication from the Commission, 17 February 2011. Available at: http://eur-lex.europa.eu/legal-content/EN/ALL/?uri=CELEX:52011DC0066 [Accessed 01.11.15].

European Commission (2015). *Social Protection and Social Inclusion: Investing in Children*. Polices and Activities. Available at: http://ec.europa.eu/social/main.jsp?catId=1060&langId=en [Accessed 01.11.15].

Eurostat (2015). *Being Young in Europe Today – 2015 Edition*. Luxembourg: Publications Office of the European Union. Available at: http://ec.europa.eu/eurostat/web/products-statistical-books/-/KS-05-14-031 [Accessed 25.01.16].

Gay, P. (1969). *The Enlightenment. An Interpretation. Vol. 2: The Science of Freedom*. New York: Norton.

Haraway, D. (1991). *Simians, Cyborgs and Women: The Reinvention of Nature*. New York: Routledge.

Honwana, A. and De Boeck, F. (2005). *Makers and Breakers: Children and Youth in Postcolonial Africa*. Oxford: James Currey.

Isaacs, S., Blundell, D., Foley, A., Ginsburg, N., McDonough, B., Silverstone, D. and Young, T. (2015). *Social Problems in the UK: An Introduction*. Oxon and New York: Routledge.

James, A. and Prout, A., ed. (2014, 1997, 1990). *Constructing and Reconstructing Childhood: Contemporary Issues in the Sociological Study of Childhood*. London: Routledge Falmer.

Kjørholt, A. T. (2007). Childhood as Symbolic Space: Searching for Authentic Voices in the Era of Globalisation, *Children's Geographies*, 5(1–2), pp. 29–42.

Latour, B. (2004). *The Politics of Nature: How to Bring the Sciences into Democracy*. Cambridge, MA: Harvard University Press.

Levy-Bruhl, L. (1910). *Les fonctions mentales dans les sociétés inférieures*. Paris: Alcan.

Levy-Bruhl, L. (1922). *La mentalité primitive*. Paris: Alcan.

Lovelock, J. (2000). *Gaia: A New Look at Life on Earth*. Oxford: Open University Press.

MacKay, R. (1973). Conceptions of children and models of socialization. In Dreitzel, H. P. (ed.) *Childhood and Socialization*. London: Collier-MacMillan, pp. 27–43.

Martens, K. and Niemann, D. (2013). When Do Numbers Count? The Differential Impact of Ratings and Rankings on National Education Policy in Germany and the US. *German Politics*, 22(3), pp. 314–32.

OECD (2014). *PISA 2012 Results: What Students Know and Can Do – Student Performance in Mathematics Reading and Science*. Volume 1, Revised Edition. Paris: PISA, OECD Publishing. Available at: www.oecd.org/pisa/keyfindings/pisa-2012-results-volume-i.htm [Accessed 25.01.16].

Pearce, F. (2007). *The Last Generation: How Nature Will Take Her Revenge for Climate Change*. London: Eden Project Books.

Piaget, J. (1934). Rapport du Directeur: Cinquième Réunion du Conseil, in *Le Bureau International d'Éducation en 1933–1934*. Genève: BIE, pp. 3–31.

Piaget, J. (1952). *The Origins of Intelligence in Children*. New York: International University Press.

Piaget, J. (1964). *The Early Growth of Logic in the Child*. London: Routledge.

Prout, A. (2005). *The Future of Childhood*. London: Routledge.

Rousseau, J. J. (2013). *Emile*. Mineola and New York: Dover.

Sagan, C. (1994). *Pale Blue Dot: A Vision of the Human Future in Space*. New York: Random House.

Scholte, J. A. (2005). *Globalization: A Critical Introduction*. 2nd edn. Basingstoke: Palgrave Macmillan.

Shallwani, S. (2010). Racism and Imperialism in the Child Development Discourse. In Cannella, G. S. and Soto, L. D. (ed.) *Childhoods: A Handbook*. New York: Peter Lang, pp. 231–44.

Shonkoff, J. P. and Phillips, D. A., ed. (2000). *From Neurons to Neighborhoods: The Science of Early Childhood Development*. Washington, DC: National Academy Press.

Silber, K. (1965). *Pestalozzi: The Man and his Work*. 2nd edn. London: Routledge & Kegan Paul.

Taylor, A. (2013). *Reconfiguring the Natures of Childhood*. Oxon and New York: Routledge.

UNICEF (2007). *Child Poverty in Perspective: An Overview of Child Well-Being in Rich Countries*. Innocenti Report Card 7. Available online: www.unicef-irc.org/publications/pdf/rc7_eng.pdf [Accessed 25.01.16].

UNICEF (2011). *The State of the World's Children 2011: Adolescence – An Age of Opportunity*. Report. Available at: www.unicef.org/publications/index_57468.html [Accessed 25.01.16].

UNICEF (2014). *Subjective Impact of the Economic Crisis on Households with Children in 17 European Countries*. Innocenti Working Papers 2014–09. Available online: www.unicef-irc.org/publications/725 [Accessed 25.01.16].

Walkerdine, V. (1984). Developmental Psychology and the Child-Centred Pedagogy: The Insertion of Piaget into Early Education. In Henriques, J., Hollway, W., Urwin, C., Venn, C. and Walkerdine, V. (ed.) *Changing the Subject: Psychology, Social Regulation and Subjectivity*. London: Routledge, pp. 153–202.

Welch, S. (2008). Childhood: Rights and Realities. In Jones, P., Moss, D., Tomlinson, P. and Welch, S. (ed.) *Childhood: Services and Provision for Children*. London: Routledge, pp. 7–21.

Wells, K. (2009). *Childhood in Global Perspective*. Cambridge: Polity Press.

David Blundell and Sandra Abegglen

chapter 9

The digital divide
Neoliberal imperatives and education

Jessie Bustillos

9.1 Introduction

We live in a time of rapid technological and digital development, with information communication technologies (ICTs) permeating everyday life, socially, economically and educationally. The rise of information societies in Europe, characterised by increased use of ICT and the Internet has produced an increasing social concern around the digital divide between European states, which has quickly become an indicator of social exclusion (Facer and Furlong, 2001). In this chapter, we shall explore the European digital divide within the proposition that it has become one of Europe's social problems. Significantly, the new information poverty posited by the digital divide, and its implications for individuals and the economy, has been taken up in political discourse, policy-making in Europe and it has also become a vital part of the European Union's political agenda. Some of this is evidenced by the attention dedicated to the digital divide in European policy texts such as the World Summit on the Information Society (WSIS) in 2003, the European Commission's report, *A Digital Agenda for Europe*, presented in Brussels in 2010 and the communication from the Commission to the European Parliament, *Opening up Education: Innovative Teaching and Learning for All Through New Technologies and Open Educational Resources* (2013).

With reference to European information societies, this chapter seeks to address some of the existing insufficiencies in understanding the digital divide, which may limit the treatment of the issues as needing to be framed through the 'proposing of simple, dichotomous models, building on the classic 'haves vs have nots' distinction' (Comunello, 2013: 631). This chapter will also build theoretically harnessed implications for education; formal systems of education are envisaged as sites where, as a society, we continuously seek to address society's pressing social problems. This chapter explores different characteristics of the digital divide in Europe, including the different types of divide (such as the user type divide), the divide which cuts across the different European countries and the invisibility of the digital divide. It is also argued, by drawing upon Foucault and others, that Europe is characterised by a new sort of education fuelled by neoliberalism. This chapter will situate these ideas by looking at the notions of the cyber-learner and cyber-citizen as a new form of citizenship in a digitally divided Europe. On the one hand, the chapter approaches the issues presented sociologically: with a socio-cultural analysis, accounting for the national digital divides in Europe and for how the digital divide has shifted in recent years. Another part of the analysis focuses intermittently on education and outlines some of the entanglements between the new enterprise culture affecting European education and the focus on developing neoliberal subjectivities as expressed by recent legislations and policies in Europe. On the other hand, it uses the notions of neoliberal subjectivity (Rose, 1996) and power and governmentality (Foucault, 1994) to critique the cultivation of neoliberal imperatives – autonomy, fulfilment, responsibility and choice – through the apparently equality-seeking policies addressing the digital divide in Europe, which have been produced by the European Commission, leading to the Europe 2020 strategy.

9.2 The digital divide as part of changing European societies

Having located this chapter within an initial theoretical and argument-led structure, the next section starts to ground definitions and describe geographical nuances and indicators that have traditionally pointed to the existence of a digital divide in Europe. Keeping this goal in mind, it is important to remind ourselves that debates concerning issues of social justice, such as the digital divide, need to be understood as axiomatic with the nature of changing societies. European societies have undergone a huge transformation in the last thirty years, entering a phase of rapid technological advancement, which has made the world of the digital a necessary knowledge for modern living in these new digitalised information societies. Lack of know-how of technological and digital innovation affects individuals' opportunities in the world of work, education and everyday life, as well as becoming a new aspect of social exclusion (Scheuch and Sciulli, 2000). The gap in skills, usage levels, access and everyday utility associated with the digital divide have a direct impact on the lives of individuals, thus transforming these new inequalities into a modern social problem in Europe. Some of the key challenges faced by European states in the new millennium were seen to be the steady transformation of European societies into societies 'where everyone can create, access, utilize and share information and knowledge' (WSIS, 2003: 9). European states find themselves under various pressures, which exceed those of a national environment to a global environment, thrust upon them by the dynamics of the European Union (EU). To this effect, the EU has released the Europe 2020 strategy, 'which seeks to exit the crisis and prepare the EU economy for the challenges of the next decade' (European Commission, 2010a: 42). Yet, in Europe these challenges are closely aligned with political discourses, juxtaposing economic growth, a need for a technologically informed population and profound changes to systems of education. In the UK, the harnessing between digital advancements, economic growth and education have been repeatedly articulated by politicians, perhaps better illustrated by PM Tony Blair's comments:

> To thrive in the global knowledge economy it is going to be important to change the whole educational system to ensure a wide base of knowledge workers who understand and use new information technologies . . . It is important that there be an army of skilled technical experts who understand and can apply technical knowledge. These workers are the underpinnings of the knowledge economy.
>
> (PM Tony Blair cited in Ball, 2008: 16)

With these various motions of policy enactment in Europe and political discourses, it seems evident that information and communication technologies have a central role in the needed growth and socio-economic development that needs to take place if Europe is to realise the goals of the Europe 2020 strategy. The profound changes in the political, legislative, economic and growth-oriented landscape in the EU have also had a huge effect on the everyday social life of people living in Europe: a social reality which requires an increasingly digital and technological immersion and skill, and which needs to be reflected in government practices and administrative processes, pervading the experiences and minutiae of everyday life of individuals. Before we take a step towards our further analysis, it is important to assess the term digital divide and to outline some of the attempts to measure it in Europe.

9.3 Understanding the digital divide in Europe

The digital divide as a phenomenon has been examined through various disciplines; this has produced an intersectionality about the term. For instance, in political science the digital divide is investigated in terms of aspects of governance and democracy; in communications there is an emphasis on the digital divide debate as a wider debate for social inclusion; and in economics and business it has been observed as a challenge to desired e-business and e-commerce activities (Lengsfeld, 2011). Whilst there have been various convincing attempts at defining and measuring the digital divide, and attempts to consider its implications for labour markets and other economic and technological aspects in Europe (Ramos and Ballell, 2009; Lengsfeld, 2011; Cruz-Jesus et al. 2012; Armas Quintá and

Macía Arce, 2013), there is often an overlook of any socio-cultural dimensions linked to the digital divide in Europe. This chapter offers a study of the digital divide in Europe which considers the sociological, educational and wider socio-economic implications, not just as one of Europe's social problems but also as a process of 'neoliberal becoming', which occurs differently in the various European states.

With reference to the emergence and importance of the digital divide in research, and later in aspects of governance within the EU, it is significant to point out that in the last fifteen years there have been around '852 journal articles and books published . . . with more than 26,000 citations using the term "digital divide" as keyword' (Cruz-Jesus et al., 2012: 279). The numerous scholarly articles on the digital divide, coupled with the attention world leaders give to the term, puts this phenomenon at the centre of the digital agenda for political change in Europe. This is partly because digital development is seen as a driver in the creation, progression and maintenance of information societies.

The Organisation for Economic Co-Operation and Development (OECD) defines the term: 'digital divide refers to the gap between individuals, household, businesses and geographic areas at different socio-economic levels with regard both to their opportunities to access ICT and to their use of the internet for a wide variety of activities' (OECD, 2001: 32). This is an important definition because it speaks of the term with reference to two dimensions, access and use, but it also uncovers geographical aspects and socio-economic aspects that might characterise this dimension of inequality in Europe. There has been a definite move from understanding the digital divide as to do with the 'haves and have nots' to a wider view involving patterns of access, usage, socio-economic factors and geographical differences in Europe.

Recent studies like the one conducted by Cruz-Jesus et al. (2012) have provided a comprehensive picture of what the digital divide looks like in Europe. Their study proposes that the European digital divide can be currently explained:

> by two latent dimensions. . . . The ICT infrastructure and adoption by population . . . This dimension includes the internet and broadband penetration rates, the usage of mobile devices to access the internet, the availability of e-government services by the supply (public) side, the adoption of e-government services by the users' (population) side, as well as the nature and intensity of Internet use. The second dimension is related to the commercial use of the ICT . . . and is therefore named e-business and Internet access costs . . . related to the diffusion of e-business, including the diffusion of e-commerce.

> (ibid.: 283)

Based on these two dimensions the analysis by Cruz-Jesus et al. (2012) shows that Bulgaria and Romania have the lowest levels in relation to the average on the two previously mentioned dimensions. The countries setting the average in Europe without particularly high levels of ICT infrastructure, or ICT adoption by population, but still considered 'relatively digitally developed, with balanced levels on both dimensions', are Austria, Belgium, Germany, Ireland, Malta, Poland, Portugal, Slovakia, Spain and the United Kingdom (ibid.: 284). There are other countries which have 'highly unbalanced digital development and which have been called, the individual-side focused', because of their emphasis on population usage and access, which does not convert to balanced levels in e-business; these countries are Estonia, France, Hungary, Latvia and Slovenia (ibid.: 284). Finally, the groups leading digital development and presenting less disparities in their own national digital divides are Denmark, Finland, Luxembourg, the Netherlands and Sweden. This study is useful in understanding the asymmetries between European countries; however, it does not account very clearly for the reasons why these digital divides might exist. Interestingly, the study does provide an outline of how many EU countries, which are considered to be developed economies, for instance France, have such uneven disparities between ICT adoption and usage by population and the proliferation of e-business and e-commerce.

9.4 Different aspects of the digital divide: shifting to differences in usage?

Having made sense of some of the initial differences in technological and digital activity and engagement in Europe, it is important to understand the digital divide more holistically. In recent years there have been new ways in which the digital divide in Europe has been studied. These have led to a re-conceptualisation of the digital divide, which problematises trends in Internet usage, rather than just demarcating issues of access. These new perspectives are also useful in helping us understand why there are developed countries in Europe with uneven uptakes of ICT usage and adoption.

These disparities could be partly understood by considering economic inequalities in different EU states. To this effect, Hsieh *et al.* (2008) have shown that economically advantaged and disadvantaged people have very different post-implementation behaviour and use of ICT; they argued that 'economically advantaged people have a higher tendency to respond to network exposure' (Hsieh *et al.*, 2008: 97). Similarly, the digital divide in Europe might be connected to other demographic factors; links have been traced between this new dimension of inequality and how it affects individuals from lower income families, those belonging to ethnic minorities, those with disabilities or those with low educational attainment. Recent studies have pointed to how the digital divide between European states is:

> mainly a consequence of economic inequalities between countries. The term information rich and information poor have appeared to classify countries in terms of their digital development. Besides economic development, countries with lower educational attainment also tend to present lower rates in the use and adoption of ICT.
>
> (Cruz-Jesus *et al.*, 2012: 280)

As pointed out above, education is also understood as a wider characteristic that can be explored to explain why the digital divide is how it is in Europe. In terms of education, studies have considered the influence of aspects of education on the digital divide, such as school attendance, levels of educational attainment and use of ICT in schools and universities (Sims *et al.*, 2008; Youssef and Ragni, 2008; Warschauer *et al.*, 2004). These factors, arguably, have a strong effect on how individuals learn to be digitally literate, and how they envisage their own digital use in everyday life.

There are other important distinctions regarding ICT and Internet access and usage. Contrary to what people might think, there are various cases in Europe where people from poorer backgrounds and people with low educational levels have high levels of ICT and Internet access and usage. With reference to this factor, Van Deursen and Van Dijk (2013) report on how people with low levels of education in the Netherlands use the Internet for more hours a day, in comparison to their more educated counterparts. Moreover, they also found that disabled people use the Internet for more hours a day than their employed counterparts. This is an interesting result, since it challenges a lot of the research on the digital divide in Europe. Additionally, the case of the Netherlands is interesting, since the country, as explored above, has high and balanced levels of ICT usage, adoption by individuals, and government and e-business implementations. Van Deursen and Van Dijk (ibid.: 507–8) claim that, 'in the first three decades of its history, the Internet was completely dominated by people with a high or medium level of education, both inside and outside of work and school'. Therefore, these observations around people with low levels of education surpassing Internet usage levels, when compared to others who have higher levels of education, may suggest that the digital divide may finally be closing. Yet, they seem to suggest something different in relation to the digital divide – that it is changing, and that the nature of Internet use emerges as a more critical issue (ibid.; Brandtzæg *et al.*, 2010).

The emerging issue here is that the digital divide literature had discounted the role of ICT and digital development in relation to the sustenance of knowledge-based societies and the knowledge economies in Europe. This points to how in Europe the digital divide has shifted from simple inequalities of access or adoption of technologies to differences in usage. Van Deursen and Van Dijk (2013) argue that this new distinction can be founded on the theoretical relevance of the 'knowledge gap and the usage gap hypothesis'. The knowledge gap theory suggests that, with the instilling of mass media information into social systems of everyday life, the groups in society with higher socio-economic (and educational) levels tend to appropriate this information more rapidly than other groups in society. The use of traditional mass media, on which the knowledge gap focuses, is relatively straightforward and uniform if it were to be compared to Internet use (Bonfadelli, 2002). Namely, the functionality of media, such as radio, television and print media, and the Internet is significantly different; the 'latter requires a broad range of skills enabling navigation through a vast amount of information rather than simply reading newspapers or watching television' (Van Deursen and Van Dijk, 2013: 509). Consequently, the Internet creates a

Jessie Bustillos

usage gap that is different from the knowledge gap, since the knowledge gap is about the possible drawing of knowledge from traditional media, whereas the usage gap is more relevant to the information-rich societies in Europe. The usage gap implies that there is a normative account as to what is valuable and worthwhile Internet use, and that there are some activities that are more desirable for people to engage in, which should enable them to benefit from living in information-rich, knowledge economies, like many European societies (Hargittai and Hinnant, 2008; DiMaggio et al., 2004).

Similarly, Brandtzæg et al. (2010) have also conducted some research which claims a shift in the traditional digital divide. In their research, Internet usage patterns in Europe allowed them to cluster users into five categories: Non-users; Sporadic users; Entertainment users; Instrumental users; and Advanced users. Some of their findings suggest that a total of 60 per cent of their sample was reported to be falling within the clusters of Non-users and Sporadic users, which points to how 'most citizens still lack the higher level of usage patterns for digital participation. This situation indicates that the digital divide is still a large scale problem in Europe' (ibid.: 132). With reference to previous studies conducted between 2004 and 2006, Brandtzæg et al. (2010) found that there had been a decline in the digital divide of only 2 per cent; they found this surprising, since the countries researched are well developed countries, with healthy economies, and with high Gross Domestic product (GDP).

Importantly, the study by Brandtzæg et al. (2010) found an increase in Entertainment users in Europe; however, these variations seemed to have little effect on the overall digital participation desired from citizens in Europe. There seems to be a clear shift in the ways the digital divide is understood in Europe. Whilst issues of access seem to be useful in explaining why there are more instrumental users in countries such as 'Austria, Spain, and Norway', it does not help explain Instrumental users in 'Sweden and UK', where there are high levels of Internet and Broadband access (ibid.: 133). It is evident from Brandtzæg et al.'s findings that the Internet usage divide is the key feature of the new digital divide among European countries with considerably high access to both PC and Internet technologies. All of the different clusters of Internet use represent a different form of online participation and 'a digital divide that goes beyond "the haves" and the "have nots". The results rather suggest a "user type divide", where unequal Internet usage or online participation is the key to understand the new digital divide' (ibid.: 135).

Subsequently, the growing concern around the digital divide as referring to gaps in access to computers (Van Deursen and Van Dijk, 2010) has been diffused among a more critical dimension which problematises issues of digital equality in Europe. Arguably, the new digital divide encompasses not just the access divide, but also 'the misconception that all users are equal and equally creative, particularly in relation to the so-called Web 2.0 culture in which everyone is defined as being a participant in the new internet services' (Brandtzæg et al., 2010: 123). The world of the Internet and the culture of the Internet mean different things to different people; differential uses and personal appropriations of the Internet in Europe might be widening the gap within this new perspective on the digital divide. As we have explored, there are various indications pointing to education and more specifically schooling as the site where digital inequalities can be addressed. Nevertheless it is not sufficient to account for the way in which the digital divide has shifted. The new digital divide is therefore marked by an intrinsic desirable set of Internet practices and, of course, a less desirable set of Internet practices. The desirability of these Internet practices is then constructed around the needs of the economy, dominant political discourses and neoliberal imperatives.

Crucially, it is not the case that countries with marked disparities in their national digital divides have poor systems of education; rather, it might be suggested that it is a consequence of how these economies are pervaded by neoliberalism (which will be explained in more detail later in the chapter) and wider economic inequalities (Rose, 1996), which we have been discussing. The new digital divide as concerns Internet usage activities suggests that:

> Some activities offer users more chances and resources in moving forward in their career, work, education and societal position than others that are mainly consumptive or entertaining . . . In terms of capital and resources theory, inspired by Bourdieu (1984), one could also say that users build more economic, social and cultural capital and resources.
>
> (Van Deursen and Van Dijk, 2013: 509)

This passage explains how the expected use of the Internet needs to involve people digitising themselves in ways that benefit the competitive economic realities of Europe. Both in the policies of the European Commission (2010a, 2010b) on the digital divide and in political discourse, citizens need to use digital technologies and the Internet to further their careers, to secure a stable and financially independent existence and to have a better chance at improving their social mobility. These are important characteristics of the type of neoliberalism present in Europe and which demarcates the digital agenda for the EU.

9.5 The digital divide and the case for European education

The digital divide, unlike more pragmatic inequalities in housing, welfare, health or educational attainment, has tended to remain invisible within calls for social justice in Europe. Crucially, the existing calls for modernisation in education in Europe seek to undo the invisibility of digital inequalities, and articulate a clear need for addressing aspects of the digital divide in Europe. Established systems of education are entangled with the digital formidability needed to keep up with global economies marked by competition and technological innovations. To this effect, there have been several communications to the European Parliament indicating 'the need for more advanced EU education', as it is seen as 'failing to keep pace with the digital society and economy' (European Commission, 2013: 2). Similarly, concerns surrounding social justice in European education are perceived to be challengeable through the systematic incorporation and uses

Jessie Bustillos

of technologies to improve students' experience of education. Policy-makers within the European Union are preoccupied with how the 'EU also risks lagging behind other regions of the world', when 'technology provides the opportunity to increase efficiency and equity in education' (European Commission, 2013: 2/3); this, in turn, has further entangled improvements to education with technological advancements. Therefore, the future of European education is embedded within the wider plane and promise of access and expert use of information, communication and digital technologies.

These entanglements discussed above, traversing systems of education, concerns with social justice, economic imperatives of competition and digital and technological innovations make up the socio-cultural landscape in which the digital divide exists now. Importantly, these aspects influence the way in which the purposes of education are understood, the roles of students and teachers within education systems, ideas of learning as not bounded by space, but they also conflate digital and technological advancements with what students want and need to thrive in education in Europe:

> Today's learners expect more personalization, collaboration and better links between formal and informal learning, much of it being possible through digital-supported learning. However, between 50% and 80% of students in the EU never use digital textbooks, exercise software, broadcasts/podcasts, simulations or learning games. The EU lacks a critical mass of good quality educational content and applications in specific subjects and multiple languages as well as connected devices for all students and teachers. A new digital divide in the EU, between those who have access to innovative, technology-based education and those who do not, is on the rise as a consequence of this fragmentation of approaches and of markets.
>
> (European Commission, 2013: 2)

At policy level we see that Europe is preoccupied with not just providing a digitally advanced technology-based education but also with the creation of digital content of a particular educational value. The value still appears to be dictated by wider economic pressures and the market in which education happens. Therefore, students are constructed as needing and wanting to experience an education marked by digital and technological advancements at different levels. However, these assumptions are also evidence of how 'young people, like technologies, are constructed within current popular discourse as the natural inheritors of future societies' (Facer and Furlong, 2001: 452); as such, trajectories in education need to change to supply the demands that this construction of young learners requires. It is then not surprising that the new envisaging of the modern learner and the young in our society is closely associated with the mastery of digital technologies. In Europe, these entanglements are characterised by the need to remain a global, competitive economy, in which the digital divide is a pressing threat, since the 'easy appropriation of technological expertise is . . . associated with the acquisition of cultural capital in a technology-rich economy' (Facer and Furlong, 2001: 452).

At the heart of the calls to understand, measure and address the digital divide in Europe is also an awareness of other global competitors and their innovations. This is coupled with the need for digitality and technological development in education, as it is seen as crucial to maximise issues of inequality of access and inequality of outcome:

> The EU also risks lagging behind other regions of the world. The USA and some Asian countries are investing in ICT-based strategies to reshape education and training. They are transforming, modernizing and inter-nationalising education systems with tangible effects in schools and universities on access to and cost of education, on teaching practices and their worldwide reputation or branding. A case in point is that much of the supply of digital content comes from players outside Europe, including from educational institutions offering their courses globally through Massive Open Online Courses (MOOCs). . . . and yet technology provides the opportunity to increase efficiency and equity in education.
>
> (European Commission, 2013: 3)

Interestingly, in Europe there has been a gradual equation of higher levels of social justice with the creation and provision of technology-based education. Much of this understanding has been arrived at through a process of societal and political development and change, which saw the emergence of new information societies in Europe, re-defining social life as becoming technology-led, open to global digital content and needing a new digital generation to decode the future. This new digital generation has been written about as the 'Net generation', the 'Digital Natives', or, the age-specific term, the 'Cyberkids' (Facer and Furlong, 2001: 463). These constructions are also suggesting something very specific about learning, and the rise of the new information age and the knowledges it produces. More specifically, that technology-based education provides the conditions for understanding the fluidity of knowledge, the malleability and availability of information and the power of digital collaboration and digital content within the social justice ideal of education for all:

> The potential benefits of the digital revolution in education are multiple: individuals can easily seek and acquire knowledge from sources other than their teachers and institutions often for free; new groups of learners can be reached because learning is no longer confined to specific classroom timetables or methods and can be personalised; new education providers emerge; teachers may easily share and create content with colleagues and learners from different countries; and a much wider range of educational resources can be accessed. Open technologies allow All individuals to learn, Anywhere, Anytime, through Any device, with the support of Anyone.
>
> (European Commission, 2013: 3)

It is evident that in Europe there is a current move to open education up, not just to the digital revolution but also to a more globalised understanding of knowledges;

however, this is still bounded by the needs of the knowledge economy. Open technologies are seen as enabling and generating a new response-ability to both students and educators: to create spaces of learning attentive to global circumstances and digital content that can make learning accessible and open to all.

Nevertheless, these recent calls and modernisations often essentialise the effects of non-participation by students in this almost inevitable digital culture. There has been an overlooking of these effects, even when there is extensive evidence that the digital divide exists, that it is changing to differences in usage and that it has a long-lasting impact on individuals' lives. These debates are problematic and the phenomenon of needing to be digitally aware and participating, as expressed by the term 'cyberkid', unravels very differently for young people involved in education in Europe. In this digital age, the idea of being 'successfully young' is embedded within the features of being technologically skilled and digitally participating; the young people excluded from the information revolution through lack of expertise or access to technology explicitly distance themselves from the values of the digital age in an attempt to save face. This distancing process is further mapped out in research by Facer and Furlong (2001) when interviewing a teenager residing in a rural area of southwest England:

> It's like because if you can't do it . . . if you think about it right, if you can't play football you think it's rubbish, if you can't do like computers you think it's rubbish . . . because if you're not that good at it, well, you don't like it do you? You don't want to do something you don't like.
>
> (463)

Yet, there is a further aspect of exclusion that arises if students do not engage in participatory practices that characterise education in the age of the digital revolution. Students who do not engage in technology-based education and who do not digitally blend their learning are not seen as engaging in the new formations of knowledge and knowing about the world that the new information age requires. These students are seen as failing to develop the digital and technological capital needed to navigate through the new information-rich and knowledge-based economies. Whether this is as a consequence of the effects of the digital divide or through personal circumstances becomes irrelevant, since, within education, the new identity of the ideal learner is constructed upon the notion of the cyber-student: a student who accesses global information, and digital content, whilst creating, sharing and manipulating tangible digital content, which evidences his learning and his positioning as a successful student within a new digitised reality in European education.

9.6 The development of new digital selves: neoliberalism and subjectivities

As we have explored throughout this chapter, the digital divide in Europe has shifted from its emergence as the existing gaps in access to ICTs and the Internet to the various differences in Internet use by individuals. In the context of the European Union, there seems to be a central preoccupation with developing and maintaining Internet practices that allow individuals to participate in social environments imbued with digital and technological advancements:

> where everyone can create, access, utilize and share information and knowledge, enabling individuals, communities and peoples to achieve their full potential in promoting their sustainable development and improving their quality of life.
>
> (WSIS 2003: 9)

Within this shift of the digital divide, civic and active social participation becomes increasingly reliant on technological and digital prowess and know-how. As with many other perceived social problems in Europe, education has been used to address many of the perceived inequalities. As a result of this, it is important to point out that calls to address the digital divide in Europe through changes to systems of education has led to new ideas about learning and the learner in Europe: first, ideas about learning as becoming increasingly shared and global and de-centralising the power of the teacher as a bearer of knowledge, and knowledge as becoming more autonomous through information technologies; and, second, ideas about the learner as wanting and needing this perceived autonomy that the Internet and ICTs afford, which have successively constructed students as the 'Net Generation', idealising students as cyber-learners who should use digital technologies to further their education and to self-instruct.

Yet, an important part of these new understandings and the shifts in the digital divide indicate that these new ideal constructs of the 'cyber-learner', or the 'cyber-citizen', who has the required digital awareness to navigate life in technologically advanced societies, are impinged by the logics of neoliberalism. Within this context neoliberalism is understood as 'an enterprise culture accorded a vital political value to a certain image of the human being', the 'image of an enterprising self' (Rose, 1996: 151): a self that works on itself, that reflects and improves his/her quality of life, that has response-abilities, which, as an expert, it understands and uses to act upon his/her 'self'. As explored in the initial quote above, these neoliberal selves are to self-develop in a digital environment, using technologies in a way that allows them 'to achieve their full potential in promoting their sustainable development and improving their quality of life' (WSIS 2003: 9). Here is some of the political value that Rose (1996) points to, a value that denotes the power governments exert over subjects through legislations and policies.

In the case of the European Union and the digital divide, it is interesting to see how there is an emphasis on digital skills and Internet use to translate into commercial uses of ICT that lead to increased e-business and e-commerce (Cruz-Jesus et al., 2012: 283), again pointing to the desirability and undesirability of certain Internet practices and uses in Europe. This presupposes that the individual is to become a digital self that can act in correlation with desired political values which promote capitalist enterprise, entrepreneurship, economic independence

Jessie Bustillos

and autonomous citizenship. This in turn favours the new economic targets of governments in Europe currently reforming and reducing social welfare and public services. This is the enterprise culture, so important to the creation of neoliberal subjectivity, which has been 'associated in particular with the regimes of Margaret Thatcher in the United Kingdom . . . and now proving so attractive to politicians in the many former welfarist polities in Scandinavia, Australia, New Zealand and elsewhere' (Rose, 1996: 150).

As explored in previous parts of this chapter, the usage gap that characterises the new digital divide suggests that there is a normative and desirable set of Internet practices that individuals should engage in. These Internet practices are important contributors to the development of neoliberal subjectivities that are perceived to thrive in information-rich societies, like most of the societies of European states. Van Deursen and Van Dijk (2013) argued that the new shifts in the digital divide in Europe create a new usage gap, which goes beyond the original access gap. Crucially, this usage gap is also underpinned by neoliberal imperatives seeking to develop subjectivities (that is, people who think of themselves and *on* themselves) that value economic independence, entrepreneurship, autonomy and self-promotion in the new knowledge economies of the twenty-first century. As Rose (1996: 151) argues, these neoliberal subjectivities envisage the individual as:

> a subjective being, it is to aspire to autonomy, it is to strive for personal fulfilment in its earthly life, it is to interpret its reality and destiny as a matter of individual responsibility, it is to find meaning in existence by shaping its life through acts of choice. These ways of thinking about humans as selves, and these ways of judging them, are linked to certain ways of acting upon such selves.

Of course notions of subjectivity and personhood vary greatly from country to country, from society to society. These variations can be explained by examining the ways in which *being a person* might become connected to religious, legal, economic or other practices which bear upon people at a particular time and in a particular social, economic and political climate. However, this notion of neoliberal subjectivity allows us to uncover some of the enterprise culture which has swept across Europe in recent times. The ways in which the digital divide has been presented, defined, studied and repositioned has allowed us to see the various forms of political and governmental power which filtrate down through to our-*selves* through various aspects of social life, such as education and work. Michel Foucault's work on power is very illustrative here, since in his writings Foucault (1994) concentrated on rejecting the traditional ways in which power is made sense of, as restraining, constraining and repressive. Instead, Foucault presents us with an account of the study of forms of power which 'analyzes power not as a negation of the vitality and capacities of individuals, but as the creation, shaping, and utilisation of human beings as subjects' (Rose, 1996: 151). Therefore, power is not an abstraction or concept, nor a set of rules; power works through people and not against people.

Similarly, another way to explore power relations as argued by Foucault is through the notion of 'governmentality': a notion explaining the various mentalities of government which produce specific practices, regulations, policies, political strategies and tactics which influence social institutions (or the authorities) to seek desirable states in human lives, such as, wealth, health and economic independence. These desirable states reflect the particular 'governmentality' of nation states. In the case of Europe, it can be argued that the mentality of government seeks to act upon the lives of people by nurturing and rewarding the neoliberal economic imperatives of economic independence, self-efficacy, accountability through the promotion of choice and a sense of responsibility for one's own well-being. We can explore how this form of power works, following a Foucauldian perspective, through the emphasis placed on using the Internet for e-commerce and e-business in Europe; this has become a strong indicator of the new digital divide among European states (Cruz-Jesus *et al.*, 2012). As indicated by Van Deursen and Van Dijk (2013) in their study of the Netherlands, the unemployed, the disabled and the less educated use the Internet and various ICTs for longer hours than other sections of society. Yet, there is a marked difference in Internet use, which points to a usage gap, whereby people in employment and in formal education are more likely to use the Internet and ICTs for self-promotion online, improving work statuses and business start-ups, whilst their less educated and unemployed counterparts use the Internet and other ICTs for gaming, online entertainment or to access basic public services. This latter group are constructed as 'failing' to engage in the meaningful and constructive digital activities which allow them to benefit from living in information-rich societies (Hargittai and Hinnant, 2008; DiMaggio *et al.*, 2004), but only because there is an accepted and desirable use of the Internet and ICTs marked by neoliberalism and pursued by current governments in Europe. There is an envisaged 'enterprising digital self' in the legislations and policies produced by the EU on the need for developing digitally advanced societies which can meet the 2020 economic targets. The term enterprising here 'designates an array of rules for the conduct of one's everyday existence: energy, initiative, ambition, calculation, and personal responsibility' (Rose, 1996: 154). The enterprising digital self is that who seeks to make the most of its technological and digital engagements, to make the most of business opportunities online, to present itself as a credible candidate on social media, to showcase itself as a project online through calculated Internet engagements which help it shape itself into that which it wishes to become. The described ways in which we are expected to engage with the Internet and ICTs in Europe, in order to address the current digital divide, is to ascertain a neoliberal reality, to think of our-*selves* as neoliberal subjectivities in the world of education, in the world of work and even in our private lives.

9.7 Conclusion

For a better understanding of the digital divide in Europe there is a need to recognise that the original digital divide, which described the gap between people who have and do not have access to the Internet and computers, has shifted and produced a new digital divide. The new concerns around the digital divide seem to suggest that there is a growing gap in terms of Internet usage and digital skills. Through exploring the various communications by the European Commission (2010a, 2010b, 2013) it is evident that developing digital and Internet skills across the EU nation states is an important priority for Europe – a priority which has been extensively addressed through systems of formal education. There are clear calls to modernisation within debates around the future of European education. The proposed changes suggest that increased digitality and technological advancements in education are paramount to give students a truly global education. Similarly, there are claims that technologies help achieve issues of social justice in education. This is in direct opposition to the findings by recent studies discussed in this chapter on the digital divide, which suggest that increased access to the Internet and computers opens up a second, more inscrutable, divide around Internet usage differences.

Having explored various policies and texts by the European Parliament, there is consensus that they are pursuing solutions to the current digital divide. Nevertheless, the way in which Internet use and technological development have been envisaged in policy is also against the backdrop of neoliberalism. There is an inherent political agenda which asks of individuals particular types of Internet use: to self-promote, to do business online, to use the Internet to develop their own lives as an enterprise. This has been argued in the chapter with the help of the notion of neoliberal subjectivity. Developing measures to address digital inequality espousing the logics of neoliberalism in private, personal spheres, that is, in people's everyday lives, might aggravate social inequalities in Europe. The focus on using the Internet and developing digital skills to allow us to wield a neoliberal subjectivity which is autonomous, competitive, entrepreneurial and self-efficient becomes a new dimension of social exclusion, and a very difficult one to challenge. If people with low levels of Internet skills struggle to find information online in an age when an increasing amount of information is going online, they become disadvantaged through their own gap in skills, or lack of physical resources. These disadvantages could be addressed by upskilling the population and making physical resources, such as PCs and fast Broadband connections, available. But if they then are expected to use the Internet and other technologies in particular ways that suit political agendas, they become ideologically and structurally excluded.

References

Armas Quintá, F. and Macía Arce, J. (2013) The Information Society in Europe: Policies to Stem the Digital Divide, *Quaestiones Geographicae*, 32: 2, 25–38.

Ball, S. J. (2008) *The Education Debate*. London: Routledge.

Bonfadelli, H. (2002) The Internet and Knowledge Gaps: A Theoretical and Empirical Investigation, *European Journal of Communication*, 17: 1, 65–84.

Bourdieu, P. (1984) *Distinction: A Social Critique of the Judgement of Taste*. London: Routledge & Kegan Paul.

Brandtzæg, P., Heim, J. and Karahasanović, A. (2010) Understanding the New Digital Divide: A Typology of Internet Users in Europe, *International Journal of Human-Computer Studies*, 69: 3, 123–38.

Comunello, F. (2013) Digital Divides in Europe: Culture, Politics, and the Western–Southern Divide, *Information, Communication & Society*, 16: 4, 631–3.

Cruz-Jesus, F., Oliveira, T. and Bacao, F. (2012) Digital Divide Across the European Union, *Information and Management*, 49: 6, 278–91.

DiMaggio, P., Hargittai, E. and Celeste C. (2004) From Unequal Access to Differentiated Use: A Literature Review and Agenda for Research on Digital Inequality. In: Neckerman, K. *Social Inequality*. New York: Russell Sage Foundation, 355–400.

European Commission (2010a) *A Strategy for Smart, Sustainable and Inclusive Growth*. Brussels: European Commission.

European Commission (2010b) *A Digital Agenda for Europe*. Brussels: European Commission.

European Commission (2013) *Opening up Education: Innovative Teaching and Learning for All through New Technologies and Open Educational Resources*. Brussels: European Commission.

Facer, K. and Furlong, R. (2001) Beyond the Myth of the 'Cyberkid': Young People at the Margins of the Information Revolution, *Journal of Youth Studies*, 4: 4, 451–69.

Foucault, M. (1994) *Power: The Essential Works of Michel Foucault 1954–1984: v. 3*. London: Penguin Books.

Hargittai, E. and Hinnant, A. (2008) Digital Inequality: Differences in Young Adults' Use of the Internet, *Communication Research*, 35: 5, 602–21.

Hsieh, J. J. P., Rai, A. and Keil, M. (2008) Understanding Digital Inequality: Comparing Continued Use Behavioural Models of the Social-Economically Advantaged and Disadvantaged, *MIS Quarterly*, 32: 1, 97–126.

Lengsfeld, J. (2011) An Econometric Analysis of the Sociodemographic Topology of the Digital Divide in Europe, *The Information Society*, 27: 3, 141–57.

OECD (2001) *Understanding the Digital Divide*. Paris: OECD Publications.

Ramos, J. and Ballell, P. (2009) Globalisation, New Technologies (ICTs) and Labour Markets: The Case of Europe, *Journal of Information, Communication & Ethics in Society*, 7: 4, 258–79.

Rose, N. (1996) *Inventing Our Selves: Psychology, Power and Personhood*. Cambridge: Cambridge University Press.

Scheuch, E. and Sciulli, D. (2000) *Societies, Corporations and the Nation State*. Leiden: Brill.

Sims, J., Vidgen, R. and Powell, P. (2008) E-Learning and the Digital Divide: Perpetuating Cultural and Socio-Economic Elitism, *Higher Education, Communications of the Association for Information Systems*, 22: 23, 429–42.

Van Deursen, A. and Van Dijk, J. (2010) Internet Skills and the Digital Divide, *New Media & Society*, 13: 6, 893–911.

Van Deursen, A. and Van Dijk, J. (2013) The Digital Divide Shifts to Differences in Usage, *New Media & Society*, 16: 3, 507–26.

Warschauer, M., Knobel, M. and Stone, L. (2004) Technology and Equity in Schooling: Deconstructing the Digital Divide, *Educational Policy*, 18: 4, 562–88.

WSIS (2003) *World Summit on the Information Society: Declaration of Principles*. Geneva: World Summit on the Information Society.

Youssef, A. B. and Ragni, L. (2008) Uses of Information and Communication Technologies, *Europe's Higher Education Institution: From Digital Divides to Digital Trajectories*, RUSC, 5: 1, 72–84.

chapter 10

Eurovisions

'European values', rites of passage and scripting the curriculum

David Blundell and Peter Cunningham

10.1 Introduction

This chapter is concerned with children and young peoples' formal learning about their citizenship in Europe in the light of growing popular discourse surrounding putative European values. Impetus for this focus has been given by a recent European Union declaration on 'Promoting citizenship and the common values of freedom, tolerance and non-discrimination through education' (EU, 2015) that builds on an earlier Council of Europe Charter. Such initiatives argue that a primary purpose of education is not only to develop knowledge, skills, competences and attitudes and to embed fundamental values but also to help young people to become active, responsible, open-minded members of society. While we endorse the need for education that promotes active, democratic citizenship, the chapter uses the concept of the rite of passage to problematise taken-for-granted assumptions underpinning current initiatives to embed these so-called 'European values' in national curricula. In doing so we draw on a number of helpful concepts found in cultural geography to view Europe as a discursive space in and through which images of Europe and European-ness are constructed; furthermore, we see the curriculum as a tool that helps to 'script' these images. We utilise the spatial metaphor of 'Europe as a container' to examine ideas and to argue that the lived experience of young people as citizens with identities rooted in their membership of local, national, European, transnational and global communities may make an appeal to 'European values' difficult to sustain. Our approach relies upon a holistic understanding of the term 'curriculum' as embracing aims, structures, processes, content and pedagogic practices found in schooling as an institution.

10.2 Europe, European-ness and Eurocentric childhoods

Open any world atlas and the status of Europe as a named geographical space comprising a cluster of peninsulas and archipelagos north of the African land mass and to the west of continental Asia seems confirmed. However, the labelled territory we encounter in the atlas is not solely informed by the physical geography of these peculiarly disparate pieces of land and sea but also by convictions that it is coterminous with a unifying and distinctive human geography, not only with historically rooted cultural and social commonalities but also more problematically with racial and ethnic commonalities; in short, that the facts of geography authorise meaningful talk not only of Europe but also of being European and an imagined or ideological quality of European-ness. Indeed, following more than 500 years of colonial expansion that has left no continent untouched, much that can be said to be European in this ideological sense can be found beyond the rather confined limits of what on a global scale is amongst the smaller continental landmasses. Therefore, it is helpful to think of Europe as what geographers refer to as a 'discursive space' (Teather, 1999, p. 3); that is, as a space whose referent may be physical and material, but whose meaning is constructed, reproduced and affirmed in terms of discourses of European-ness. These discourses and the discursive space that serves to legitimate them produce Europe as a socially constructed phenomenon through which social policy can be framed and, in this case, educational curricula can be designed for European children and young people. There is an obvious sense in which social constructionist arguments calling on the concept of discourse are circular, because as Foucault suggests they are 'practices which form the objects of which they speak' (Foucault, 1972, p. 49 in Burr, 2003, p. 64). However, while this may suggest a closed or settled circuit of meaning, historical and more recent evidence suggests that neither the boundaries to Europe as a discursive space nor European-ness as an ideological basis for identity can be regarded as settled or beyond controversy. A globalising world presents insistent challenges as shifts in economic power, ongoing conflicts at Europe's margins and the resultant crises for refugees as well as the demands for post-colonial restorative justice (that might be said to include economic migration) threaten to shred the delicate fabric of its political institutions along with settled notions of European-ness. These globalising factors and their complex relation to European identities were certainly given an airing during the recent referendum campaign in the UK, when, despite a slim majority in favour of leaving the European Union, few, if any, presented this as a denial of European-ness.

Therefore, although a conception of European-ness may be seen as definitive for a quite specific geographical and material space, as an imagined geography it may be far from unitary or simply congruent with that space. This brings into question not just what children and young people as persons with particular identities and embodiments learn about their society and where they are positioned within it, but, more acutely, whether current initiatives to embed fundamental European values within the curriculum are sustainable. Our approach to exploring these questions will draw on the work of social and cultural geographers because we believe that a spatialised approach can reveal not only an understanding of Europe as a material or geographical entity but also what it means to be European as an imagined condition and the territorial boundaries, overlaps and intersections that bring these things into relation with one another. Our approach is to suggest that our language and thinking makes an implicit appeal to the metaphor of Europe as a container within whose discrete and distinctive spatial confines policies, practices and institutions have jurisdiction. This way of seeing people and territory has served the European political imagination since the Treaty of Westphalia that brought the Thirty Years' War to an end in the mid seventeenth century; moreover, it suggests that seeing Europe as a discursive space can reveal the relationship between European-ness, as that which is assumed to be held in common, and boundaries beyond whose threshold lies 'the Other'.

This macroscopic conception of Europe as container serves in scaled-down form as template for its educational institutions – whether conceived materially as school buildings or in ideological terms as curricula – and their role in reproducing populations possessing authentic national or transnational European consciousness. Seen this way, curricula operate as institutionalised simulacra that contain and separate children and young people from everyday life – ironically in order to prepare them for lives in the everyday world (see Kjørholt, 2007, and in Chapter 8). This separation owes something to educational traditions based upon the rule of the Church and its monastic orders, but also to distinctly Eurocentric humanistic philosophical convictions about the nature of children and childhood. Driven by a confidence in Cartesian reason and Newtonian science the Enlightenment sought to transform the prospects of humankind – or by and large the white European section of it – through the exploitation of nature and the rational reproduction and governance of populations through properly ordered childhoods. Thus the form and processes of a properly ordered childhood becomes a legitimate field of philosophical interest, with John Locke and Jean-Jacques Rousseau as early contributors to discussions about the character of 'the child' as an ideal type informing the practices of institutions within which individuals and populations are reproduced. Despite starting with fundamentally different convictions about children's moral and intellectual status, Locke and Rousseau see childhood as a naturally ordained, preparatory yet separate condition from the rest of humankind, whereby passage through a series of developmental stages delivers children from domination by nature's

David Blundell and Peter Cunningham

instinctual drives to the light of mature adult reason (Prout and James, 1997, 2014, p. 13; Blundell, 2012, p. 6).

Guided by a Foucauldian perspective, Nikolas Rose is clear about the impact of these institutionalised containers for childhood on children's lives and the separation from everyday life they effect; he says:

> Childhood is the most intensively governed sector of personal existence.
> . . . The modern child has become the focus of innumerable projects that purport to safeguard it from physical, sexual, or moral danger, to ensure its 'normal' development, to actively promote certain capacities of attributes such as intelligence, educability, and emotional stability.
>
> (Rose, 1997, p. 124)

This containerisation of children based on the idea that they are a distinct and separable sort of human has been challenged by the educational sociologist Berry Mayall (2007; see also Qvortrup, 2001) especially because of the way that it seems inexorably to subordinate their lives to formal education. Echoing Rose's assertion that childhood is subject to intensive and extraordinary levels of governance, Mayall identifies this as an increasing 'scholarisation' of childhood; that is, a growing articulation of children's lives and the meaning of their biological immaturity in terms of the institutional rhythms, spaces, values and practices of schooling. Thus, they argue, education and its curricula increasingly occupy centre-stage in shaping properly appointed childhoods and organising children's lives through the regulation of space and time, thereby diminishing effective acknowledgement of their agency as social actors.

10.3 Curricula for nation, subjects and citizens

To assert an association between schooling and national interests appears commonplace and even a truism in the early twenty-first century where most European states operate some form of national curriculum and recent decades have seen a concerted drive towards the adoption of Common Core Standards. Indeed, if we accept Benedict Anderson's view of the nation as an imagined community then the ideational responsibility of education to reproduce a common imagination for that community that will underpin collective affili-ation to it becomes clear. Thus schooling is charged with the task of: high-lighting symbolic events in history deemed significant to the nation; endorsing iconic symbols of nationality (maps, flags, anthems, etc.); and, encouraging assimilation into a national language, literature and culture.

The importance attaching to education and schooling in the construction of the modern nation state and securing its sustainability is confirmed by historical evidence. The political movement that sought German unification during the first half of the nineteenth century was infused with the concept of *bildung* – a term defying easy translation into English – in which concepts of education, nation, people and culture cohere. The importance of *bildung* for German national consciousness is manifest in the work of Friedrich Fröbel (1782–1852).

Despite becoming hugely influential as an educational innovator and thinker in England and North America after his death, Fröbel made explicit connections between young children's education and the political movement seeking German unification as a single political entity during the first half of the nineteenth century (Adelman, 2000, p. 112; Blundell, 2012, p. 42). The *kindergarten* may have become a popular synonym for nursery education in general, but in Fröbel's original conception it was a distinctly ideological institution that implicated very young children in the reproduction of German consciousness. Similarly, the *Volkschule* promoted by Fröbel's disciple Friedrich Wilhelm Wander (1803–79) was intended to serve patriotic purposes; according to Hahn (1998, p. 25) it was

> [p]rimarily an attempt to unite teachers from every sort of school, but – in the spirit of the new German patriotism – also the desire to create a comprehensive education system, from nursery school to university . . . As a consequence, the term Volkschule refers to a national school for all the people.

This is not to say that there was a universal acceptance of these institutions and their conception of nation and people; indeed, the quasi-spiritual terms of the Fröbelian conception of land and people was viewed with huge suspicion by the state authorities in Prussia, so that the kindergarten as the institutionalised expression of his life's work was subject to a banning order during Fröbel's lifetime that was, somewhat tragically, only rescinded just after his death.

This is not say that the Prussians were without an interest in popular education and did not grasp its relation to national prosperity and growth; indeed, the landmark 1870 Elementary Education Act that paved the way for universal popular education in England and Wales was framed and passed against a background of intense economic and territorial rivalry with the recent and politically invigorated Germany. In introducing the Bill to the UK Parliament in 1869, W.E. Forster explicitly invokes the threat to Britain's colonial and economic dominance posed by Germany with the perceived excellence of its system of education explicitly implicated in it. This influence extended beyond being a matter of political rivalry and economic competition to become one of open emulation as Edward Robert Robson and his assistant T. J. Bailey, inaugural chief architects for the London School Board, drew extensively on what they identified as the Prussian system of education when establishing a template for the design of the rash of new Board Schools that followed the passage of the 1870 Act. This was nakedly in preference to more familiar systems and methods of British educationists such as Joseph Lancaster and the Reverend Andrew Bell. So although these schools adopted a patriotic English decorative vocabulary found in the popular Queen Anne Revival style, the grammar underlying their forms and systems was distinctly Prussian. Indeed, these forms and systems continue to set the spatial and temporal rhythms of children's schooling and with them their experience of childhood across England and Wales.

History shows that the rivalry between Germany and Britain, along with other European powers, did not confine itself to the educational sphere but led to huge loss of life in a series of wars starting with the Franco–Prussian war of 1870–1 and included the global cataclysm that was the First World War. Amongst the outcomes from the latter conflict was an attempt by the British Government to extend and enhance the relationship between nation state and schooling through the introduction of the 1918 Education Act, also known as The Fisher Act after its originator, the academic and President of the Board of Education, H.A.L. Fisher. In introducing the Bill to Parliament, Fisher invokes connections between the war, economic rivalry, nation and education in ways that make an appeal to history but seem distinctly parsimonious when it comes to the geographical facts of Britain's location at the centre of a huge global Empire! Thus, he says:

> We have reached a point in our history when we must take long views. We are a comparatively small country, we have incurred the hostility of a nation with a larger population and with a greater extent of concentrated territory and with a more powerful organization of its resources. We cannot flatter ourselves with the comfortable notion, I wish we could, that after this War the fierce rivalry of Germany will disappear and hostile feeling altogether die down. That in itself constitutes a reason for giving the youth of our country the best preparation that ingenuity can suggest.
>
> (from MacLure, 1986)

When Fisher goes on to suggest that what he calls 'the civic spirit' of the population has been vital to the prosecution of the war with Germany, there is not only a clear appeal to the idea that there are indeed common and unifying spiritual bonds within the nation but also that the task of recognising, affirming and preserving this will entail the education of its children and young people:

> we are making a greater demand than ever before upon the civic spirit of the ordinary man and woman . . . and how can we expect an intelligent response to the demands which the community propose to make upon the instructed judgement of its men and women unless we are prepared to make some further sacrifices in order to form and fashion the minds of the young . . . education is one of the good things of life which should be more widely shared than has hitherto been the case, amongst the children and young persons of this country . . . We assume that education should be the education of the whole man, spiritually, intellectually, and physically, and it is not beyond the resources of civilization to devise a scheme of education, possessing certain common qualities, but admitting at the same time large variation from which the whole youth of the country, male and female, may derive benefit.
>
> (from MacLure, 1986 and Blundell, 2012 pp. 116–7)

Despite their idealistic tone and his liberal-humanist appeal, Fisher's sentiments have roots in rather more pragmatic interests that concerned Britain's
legislators in the decade before the First World War and were driven by a sense of
national emergency. The shattering impact of a series of battlefield humiliations
during the South African Wars of 1899–1902, wherein the British army struggled
to vanquish well-organised but lightly provisioned and armed Boer settler
insurgents, caused consternation at home in the imperial heartland, with the poor
health and physical fitness of its youthful recruits cited as a major contributory
factor (Judd and Surridge, 2002, p. 60). In response the UK government passed a
raft of social welfare legislation aimed at improving the health of the young that
included the provision of meals at school and regular health inspections. These
measures are widely regarded as the precursor to the emergence of the Welfare
State following the Second World War and were a response to perceived
inadequacy of Victorian Poor Law institutions that arguably emphasised punishment for being poor over the alleviation of poverty. The point here is that
whether conceived as beneficent or self-interested, the state's active interest in
young people's welfare consolidated both the idea that these were the nation's
children and the potential of public schooling, with its near-universal reach, in
making such interventions possible (Foley, 2001, p. 12–14). This interest in
physical welfare was accompanied by a desire to use schooling to reproduce a
sense of British exceptionalism and entitlement amongst the youthful subjects
who found themselves at the heart of the largest land Empire that had ever
existed. Thus, attempts to inculcate the 'right values' figured large across the
rudimentary curriculum offered to the subjects of Empire and, not least, in what
children learned about history and geography. Rex Walford writes of the way
that from the late nineteenth century suitable imperial lessons found their way
into the classrooms of the new Board Schools. Once again, a sense of German
nationalism, accompanied by a snipe at the French, animates British educators,
as in a report from 1886 entitled 'The Royal Geographical Society and the
Germans' J. Scott Keltie writes:

> The Royal Colonial Institute is again calling the attention of headmasters to
> the importance of colonial geography and history as subjects of instruction
> in schools. It certainly does seem odd that so little should be done in British
> schools to give boys and girls an adequate idea of the development and
> resources of the various parts of the Empire. If the French or the Germans
> had an Empire of equal extent and splendour, then we may be sure that they
> would take good care that justice was done to it in their national system of
> education.

Furthermore, Keltie is sure that children would not only identify with the
topics but that the content would prove its value in later life so that teaching
would not be arduous:

> Properly taught, the leading facts relating to India and the colonies would
> greatly interest young people and in many cases the knowledge obtained at

David Blundell and Peter Cunningham

school would be of practical service in later life. Moreover the study could not fail to encourage the growth of wholesome patriotism.

(from Walford, 2001, p. 53)

Thus children in the new elementary schools were presented with geography 'readers' wherein the lives of 'native' populations were contrasted with the exploits of white imperial adventurers, missionaries and entrepreneurs. These were not simply calculated to inspire the foot-soldiers of Empire but also, despite their own grinding poverty, to inculcate a sense of their privileged status at the heartland of the British Empire and in relation to European rivals.

Our point is that the responsibility placed on schools and their curricula to accomplish a set of ideological tasks and to serve as an instrument for the interests of the nation state is manifest as we examine this material and comes with a long pedigree; so how might this help us to understand the recruitment of school curricula as tools for the cultivation of European identity and consciousness?

10.4 European (re)construction and scripting the curriculum

Go back just over 70 years and Europe was a continent devastated by ten years of war, if the Spanish Civil War of 1936–9 is concatenated with the Second World War. Statistics are difficult but, if the USSR is excluded, estimates suggest that around 20 million of Europe's population were killed during these conflicts through direct military action, civilian bombing or the planned industrial-scale genocide of the Holocaust. Besides this breath-taking death toll, many of the continent's finest and most industrially productive cities had been severely damaged by strategic aerial bombardment, the moral and social fabric of many countries had been damaged by years of brutal occupation or dictatorship, a vast refugee army swilled around Europe in the wake of liberation and pretensions to a return to pre-war imperial dominance by the European powers looked distinctly shaky. There was an obvious sense in which Europe was in need of extensive economic, political, moral and social rebuilding and that a new political geography was emerging as the victorious Western and Soviet allies sought territorial jurisdiction and dominance. Division along ideological lines was reinforced, ironically through a measure initially intended to avoid such outcomes. In the face of the desperate need for rebuilding, the Americans devised and financed a plan formally entitled the European Recovery Programme (generally known as The Marshall Plan) with the intention of restoring the shattered European economic order through what at their insistence should be a transnational organisation to distribute investment and ensure that goals were achieved (Blacksell, 1981, pp. 34–56). The resultant Organisation for European Economic Cooperation (OEEC) provided stimulus to the movements that were to establish the European Economic Community (EEC) in 1957 that became the European Union via the Maastricht Treaty in 1992 and, following the collapse of the Soviet Union in 1991, has seen the accession of many former eastern-bloc states to become a union of 28 sovereign states with the accession of Croatia in 2013. Other states have sought to join the EU; notably, although Turkey first applied in 1987, it has yet to meet entry criteria, including in relation to human rights. In June 2016, the UK held a referendum in which a majority voted to leave the EU. At the time of writing, no official request had been made by the UK government for the UK to leave the Union, but it is likely to do so. No doubt new arrangements will be made with the EU with regard to labour, trade and services (including education) but we suspect it will make little difference to the detail of the national curriculum.

Accompanying these more direct initiatives to achieve the economic and political reconstruction of Europe in the wake of the Second World War there was recognition of the role that education could and should play as an ideological agent in the construction of a liberal democratic order. The intentions of the Allies were set out in 1945 at the Potsdam Conference just after victory in Europe had been secured, and at the heart of their resolution they expressed the need for a process of de-Nazification, thus: 'German education shall be so controlled as completely to eliminate Nazi and militaristic doctrines and to make possible the successful development of democratic ideas' (Hahn, 1998, p. 96); in this way the curriculum was given a central role in helping to script a transformed national consciousness. Similarly, the establishment of the Council of Europe in 1949 embraced a vision for the continent through its promotion of legal standards, human rights, democratic development, the rule of law and cultural cooperation. The Council now has 47 member countries, including all those in the European Union along with the Russian Federation, Ukraine, Georgia and others. In recent years their work, together with that of the European Union, has played an increasing role in informing the development of policy and practice across Europe. This has embraced initiatives in a number of social and economic areas in order to script a common understanding of a particular European vision and, as in post-war Germany, the curriculum has been central to achieving this.

Established in 1987, the COMETT programme was the first EU initiative designed to support training in advanced technology and link research to business with the goal of improving European industrial competitiveness. This was followed by a number of initiatives (including education and training programmes for schools, universities and higher education along with vocational education and training for young people and adults) that promoted institutional cooperation, exchange of practice and student and staff mobility schemes. Alongside these programmes a European Education policy was developed following the Lisbon Summit (EU, 2000) as part of a broader strategy to address stagnant economic growth, with educational policy feeding into what was conceived as 'a learning economy'. Policy initiatives adopted a twin-track approach via a process of 'harmonisation' on the one hand and through the principle of 'mutual recognition' on the other. In higher education policy, for example, the Bologna Process sought to combine harmonisation and mutual recognition by framing a European qualifications' framework 'against which

David Blundell and Peter Cunningham

individual national frameworks could articulate with due regard to the institutional, historical and national context' (Bologna Group, 2003).

Of specific importance to discussion in this chapter is the European Ministers of Education agreement to the Council of Europe's Charter on Education for Democratic Citizenship and Human Rights Education (formally adopted in 2010 with preambular paragraphs that cite how the Charter builds on agreements dating back to the early 1990s). The Council's Charter emphasised four main purposes of education: preparation for sustainable employment; preparation for life as active citizens in democratic societies; personal development; and, the development and maintenance, through teaching, learning and research, of a broad, advanced knowledge base. Additionally, these purposes were underpinned by a declaration of respect for human rights, democracy and the rule of law as shared values. European Union member states went on to adopt the Charter and endorse those same 'European' values, seeing them as key to deeper political and economic integration. Having done this, the European Commission has elaborated on them through various strategy documents designed to support national initiatives and address common challenges. For example, the Strategic Framework for Education and Training (ET2020), sets out four common objectives that EU countries are expected to address by 2020: Strategic objective 1 – Making lifelong learning and mobility a reality; Strategic objective 2 – Improving the quality and efficiency of education and training; Strategic objective 3 – Promoting equity, social cohesion and active citizenship; and, Strategic objective 4 – Enhancing creativity and innovation, including entrepreneurship, at all levels of education and training. Strategic objective 3 has particular salience for this chapter because of its concern to promote equity, social cohesion and active citizenship; the Strategic Framework elaborated it thus:

> Education and training policy should enable all citizens, irrespective of their personal, social or economic circumstances, to acquire, update and develop over a lifetime both job-specific skills and the key competences needed for their employability and to foster further learning, active citizenship and intercultural dialogue. Education and training systems should aim to ensure that all learners — including those from disadvantaged backgrounds, those with special needs and migrants — complete their education, including, where appropriate, through second-chance education and the provision of more personalised learning. Education should promote intercultural competences, democratic values and respect for fundamental rights.
>
> (EU, 2009)

However, in response to global financial and economic crises, the role of education in relation to the economy was given primacy:

> The broad mission of education and training encompasses objectives such as active citizenship, personal development and well-being. While these go hand-in-hand with the need to upgrade skills for employability, against the backdrop of sluggish economic growth and a shrinking workforce due to

demographic ageing, the most pressing challenges for Member States are to address the needs of the economy.

(European Commission, 2012)

Nevertheless, despite this explicit emphasis on economic purposes of education, social and political aims were not entirely forgotten, as witnessed in comments from Androulla Vassiliou, Commissioner responsible for Education, Culture, Multilingualism and Youth. In stressing the Council of Europe's Charter on Education for Democratic Citizenship and Human Rights Education, she wrote:

European countries need citizens to be engaged in social and political life not only to ensure that basic democratic values flourish but also to foster social cohesion at a time of increasing social and cultural diversity. In order to increase engagement and participation, people must be equipped with the right knowledge, skills and attitudes. Civic competences can enable individuals to participate fully in civic life but they must be based on sound knowledge of social values and political concepts and structures, as well as a commitment to active democratic participation in society.

(Eurydice, 2012)

Such responses to changing economic and social conditions help illustrate that the curriculum is rarely if ever a monolith erected to foster one ideological mindset (Longstreet and Shane, 1993); rather, it can be seen as a discursive space, with contestation not only over content, assessment and pedagogy but also subject to various contextual influences that include systems and institutions operating in the broader social milieu. Contestation and the interactive accomplishment of the curriculum can be seen at all scales, from the individual – where, for example, teachers may make a professional stand against curricula policy or practice in order to best fit the need of their students – to the transnational European level with swings in emphasis scripted by response to perceived crises. However, in viewing the curriculum as being interactively accomplished and as merely a best fit response to social and economic conditions, there is danger in underplaying the form that these pressures can take, for example the rather less direct anxieties surrounding comparative international performance induced by the PISA tables (OECD, 2014).

More recently and in response to terrorist attacks in Denmark and Paris there has been an attempt to script a vision of Europe and the meaning of being European that, we argue, may bring its own imposed pressures to bear in unhelpful ways. At an informal meeting of European Union Education Ministers (EU, 2015) a declaration on 'Promoting citizenship and the common values of freedom, tolerance and non-discrimination through education' was agreed; in this they affirmed:

support of fundamental values that lie at the heart of the European Union: respect for human dignity, freedom (including freedom of expression), democracy, equality, the rule of law and respect for human rights. These

David Blundell and Peter Cunningham

values are common to the Member States in a European society in which pluralism, non-discrimination, tolerance, justice, solidarity and equality between women and men prevail.

These 'fundamental values', and the subsequent monitoring of progress of educational policy in response to these (EU, 2016), reflect Article 1 of the establishment of the Union in which 'The Member States confer competences on the Union to attain objectives they have in common, and the Union coordinates the policies by which the Member States aim to achieve these objectives' and Article 2 in which it is stated that 'The Union is founded on the values of respect for human dignity, liberty, democracy, equality, the rule of law and respect for human rights, including the rights of persons belonging to minorities' (EU, 1992). With respect to educational policy it is important to recognise that while nation states maintain autonomy over educational systems and structures, the curriculum also reflects objectives and values held in common. However, it should be noted that these values are often expressed in the curriculum as national values or as democratic values set alongside articles referencing national culture and history. For example, Article 1 of the constitution of the Danish Public School states that primary schools must make students familiar with Danish culture and history, and Article 3 states that schools must prepare students for participation, joint responsibility, rights and duties in a society based on freedom and democracy. In the UK, the Department for Education instructed schools in 2014 to include the promotion of 'British values' which Ofsted defined as: democracy; the rule of law; individual liberty; and mutual respect for and tolerance of those with different faiths and beliefs and for those without faith (Ofsted, 2015).

In detail, the declaration outlines a number of challenges to reinforce the teaching and acceptance of these common fundamental values and in doing so utilises the language of establishment, for example 'ensuring that the humanistic and civic values *we* share are safeguarded' (our emphasis). This risks falling into what Agnew (1994, p. 173) terms a 'territorial trap' with an assumption that boundaries of the state define boundaries of society and that the latter is straightforwardly 'contained' by the former, with the implication that challenges to these values come from those who are outside 'the container'.

10.5 The curriculum, rites of passage and European values

In order to understand the way in which the curriculum serves to promote and reproduce the sort of societal values found in the above declarations we use the concept of the rite of passage that is found in the work of geographer Elizabeth Kenworthy Teather. We argue that Teather's understanding of the rite of passage as a spatialised process can serve to illustrate how in seeking to reproduce a European consciousness through the curriculum there is a risk of opening up a harmful gulf between what the policy intends and its realisation; we suggest that this is because *what* is learned is intimately bound up not just with *where* and *how* it is learned but also how the learners place their identities in relation to what they are learning. This follows from what she says:

> rites of passage, transitional stages in life, are part of a learning and socialisation process . . . that the individual has to undergo in the course of the development of the self. This is necessary in the course of a life which inevitably involves 'an orderly change from one reference group to another' . . . again and again in the course of new experiences. This learning process comprises the acquisition of new knowledge and practices, many of them spatial. Place and identity are, therefore, a linked part of the learning process involved in the experience of a rite of passage from one life stage to another.
>
> (Teather, 1999, p. 20)

Teather draws on the concept of the rite of passage as identified in the early twentieth century by the anthropologist Arnold van Gennep who proposed that life could be understood as a series of thresholds to cross and changes to navigate: 'For groups, as well as for individuals, life itself means to separate and to be reunited . . . there are always new thresholds to cross: . . . the thresholds of birth, adolescence, maturity, and old age' (van Gennep, 1909 and 1960, pp. 189–90 in Teather, 1999, p. 13). He goes on to propose that these threshold crossings can be understood as structured by a three-stage schema marked by liminal processes of 1. *separation*, 2. *transition* and 3. *incorporation*. Van Gennep's rites of passage were derived from the study of societies very different from those of Western Europe and might be seen as rooted in a typically essentialist and Eurocentric approach to the search for universal structures and rational orderings underpinning human social worlds. However, Teather proposes that the language of the rite of passage and van Gennep's schema has utility when trying to understand the life-course in modern industrialised societies and in this context the experience of navigating the material and ideological threshold crossings that schooling requires. From Teather's work, the concept of rites of passage can be used to identify when children and young people cross thresholds – whether daily, weekly, termly or over an extended period of years – as their experience of schooling separates them from familiar social networks, directs their transition through the curriculum and seeks to re-incorporate them into normative social worlds that may differ significantly from the worlds of home and community.

Understanding children and young people's experience of schooling through the idea of a rite of passage where thresholds are encountered and crossed, can represent an unremarkable and commonplace description. This is especially the case under conditions where the change from one reference group to another is 'orderly' and does not require a disruptive *separation* from one social world to another, where the process of *transition* is accepted (even welcomed) and where *incorporation* is a straightforward *re*-incorporation into familiar social worlds. However, for other children and young people the processing of identity demanded by the curriculum understood in this way as a rite of passage

David Blundell and Peter Cunningham

exacts a high price and can be challenging even to the point of being experienced as a form of personal and moral violence when ties to family, community and other social networks are experienced as uninteresting, unwelcome or even harmful in meeting institutional targets. This was clearly articulated in what has become a familiar, if anachronistic in certain respects, passage from The Bullock Report of 1975 that examined reading, language development and its teaching in English schools:

> No child should be expected to cast off the language and culture of the home as he crosses the school threshold, nor to live and act as though school and home represent two totally separate and different cultures which have to be kept firmly apart. The curriculum should reflect many elements of that part of his life which a child lives outside school.
>
> (DES, 1975, para. 20.5)

Sacramento (2015), in reviewing good educational practice across Europe, echoes this sentiment and highlights the importance of policy and practice that aims to understand identity formation and achievement in the context of diverse local cultures, backgrounds and worldviews. More negatively, he argues that failure to do so risks generating personal, familial and community conflict that may translate into lower educational outcomes. Related to this, Blundell (2016, p. 180) cites evidence to suggest that many children and young people continue to practice self-censorship where the temporal and spatial separation required by school renders their cultural and linguistic identities unwelcome (ibid. p. 180).

Similarly, Thea Renda El-Haj (2007) presents the case of Khalida and not just the direct challenges to her identity in making a daily separation from home and entry into school but also the problems that a daily act of transition and incorporation into the community of the school and its norms presents for her. Khalida was born in the USA and spent her early childhood in the Palestinian West Bank, then returned as a teenager to America. At the heart of her conflicts and the daily tensions and disputes that follow from them is the normative curricular expectation that she salute the US flag at the beginning of every school day. Khalida does not identify with the flag as hers and baldly declares 'I was born here, but my home, it's not here'. Her unwillingness to submit to the required daily liminal transition from home to the school community that saluting the flag represents is compounded by Khalida's difficulties with the language surrounding her identity and, thus, incorporation into a recognisable and acceptable location within this community:

> I only think of myself as Arab – a Palestinian, actually. Most people ask me, 'You're a Palestinian American?' I told them, 'No, just Palestinian.' Then they start getting stupid about it: 'And then how do you know English?' I'm like, 'No, I'm American Palestinian. I just want to be a Palestinian.'
>
> (El-Haj, 2007)

These 'failures' to conform to the demands of institutional rites of passage and ascriptive language games found in formal and informal curricula places Khalida outside the container with very limited scope or invitation to negotiate her position, so that many young people like Khalida will be forever positioned in a liminal space, neither able to feel a sense of belongingness nor to have a forum within which to voice dissent and negotiate a meaningful sense of self. In the context of this chapter, without this commitment to understanding the pluralities found in the lived spaces and life-worlds of children and young people, the declaration of European values risks becoming an imposed checklist by which to assess and pigeon-hole degrees of difference, thereby evaluating whether or not they belong. An undergraduate student of the authors notes:

> My own family fled from crisis and civil warfare in Somalia in the 1990s, and we sought refuge in London, via Holland. London and Europe is now my home. I am very proud to be a European citizen and very grateful of the opportunities and freedoms that European society has given me and my family/community . . . It is very difficult to be a Muslim in the current context: I am now a victim of negative stares and I can sense the hostility from others on a routine basis as I walk the streets of London. I am scared and also frustrated that others think of me as a threat because of the mindless actions of a criminal minority.

The complexity of the local and global knowledges and affiliations this student holds, as well as the conflicts she experiences, finds an echo in research by Hörschelmann and El-Refaie (2014) with young people expressing diverse ethnic identities in the UK. For many of these young people local phenomena and global international events were readily and indivisibly linked, often because they were able to imbue them with immediate meaning through personal connections. By examination of these young people's lived spaces, El-Haj and Hörschelmann and El-Refaie challenge the slip-shod assertion that they are apathetic to politics or political concerns; rather, they suggest that for many of them a tribal-like affiliation to parties at the ballot-box has been replaced by a more complex political consciousness concerned with navigating the challenges of identity and belonging thrown up by everyday life and the plural social networks within which they live. Hörschelmann and El-Refaie found that, like Khalida in the USA, far from accepting the political institutions that have been given to them, many of the British young people they worked with wrestled with acutely felt dilemmas, challenges and difficulties often because these tensions were experienced and understood through highly personalised encounters and transnational social networks that transcended the more domestic purview and narrowly contained interests of the UK. The researchers found that theirs is a politics that leads them to question many taken-for-granted tenets rather than simply to accept them as constitutional 'givens'; in consequence the authors assert that: 'if "democracy" is to have any meaning and (young) people are to feel that their participation matters, then belonging through, not despite dissent, is essential for exercising citizenship.' (ibid.).

David Blundell and Peter Cunningham

10.6 Conclusion

From the outset we have suggested that much of our thinking about Europe, nations, curricula and schooling has been structured around a way of seeing their respective spaces as containers; moreover, that these containers are conceived as having some degree of structural congruency. However, Hörschelmann and El-Refaie's work (*inter alia*) suggests that the container with its fixed, impervious boundaries and implicit differentiation between internal and external space may at best be unhelpful in conceptualising emerging social realities and at worst may actively exclude by constructing young people like Khalida as 'the Other'. This does not mean that we should abandon a spatialised approach to understanding this aspect of the social world, but draw on fresh insights about space, place and spatiality drawn from the work of human geographers and other social scientists. Research on schools by Pike and Colquhoun (2012) may be instructive because it contrasts the school understood as territorial real estate with its spatiality as a social world. Taking a recent case where a school sought to impose healthy eating rules without having sought the consent of pupils, parents or the communities from which they were drawn, the researchers demonstrate that despite attempts to control their curricular, pedagogic and (even) moral footprint within the curtilage of their gates and walls, the school was enmeshed in numerous diverse and extensive social networks. These networks extended well beyond the territorial estate of the school buildings and into the homes and lives of the pupils – past, present and future. Moreover, like the young people in Hörschelmann and El-Refaie's research the social *reach* of these networks could not be understood by simple Matryoshka or Russian doll-like scalar nesting – Khalida's lived space of affiliations seems to be more immediately about places and people thousands of miles away as those with whom she lives cheek-by-jowl (Blundell, 2016) – this is the 'distanceless space' to which Heidegger alluded. In order to accommodate the experience of all young people it would seem vital to understand their lives and we argue that a spatialised approach to their experience can hold the key to opening up fresh insights.

In addressing this we propose that it is helpful to look at the work of Doreen Massey and her attempts to re-imagine space and spatiality. Drawing on the work of Manuel Castells and Henri Lefebvre, Massey proposes that we see space as having a social phenomenology whose fabric comprises human meanings and social value woven together in dynamic networked flows of information, encounter and change. In the following passage Massey suggests that far from being fixed and container-like, space is more helpfully understood as 'stories-so-far' or as a narrative work in progress, and so, far from a final accomplishment. We argue that Massey's work is helpful because it offers a better fit in considering the lived experience of many young people and has important implications for their relationship to institutions like school. Signally, she proposes:

> that we recognise space as always under construction. Precisely because space on this reading is a product of relations-between, relations which are necessarily embedded in material practices, it is always in the process of

being made. It is never finished; never closed. Perhaps we could imagine space as a simultaneity of stories-so-far.

(Massey, 2005, p. 9)

Almost by definition the rigidities of curricula conceived as impervious container-like spaces in which pupils are processed through one-dimensional rites of passage will severely curtail the wealth of stories-so-far and privilege dominant and dominating accounts. Furthermore, a verificationist 'tick-list' of European values would seem to be at odds with the demand for recognition of plural 'relations-between', where belonging can abide with dissent. This is perhaps because the very notion of stories-so-far implies not just a sense that space is unfinished but also that stories have story-tellers and that, in pursuit of better stories for us all, the stand-point of those story-tellers is vital in understanding the story they have to tell.

References

Adelman, C. (2000) 'Over two years, what did Froebel say to Pestalozzi?', *History of Education*, 29(2): 103–14.

Agnew, J. (1994) 'The territorial trap: The geographical assumptions of international relations theory', *Review of International Political Economy*, 1(1): 53–80.

Blacksell, M. (1981) *Post-War Europe: A Political Geography*, London: Hutchinson.

Blundell, D. (2012) *Education and Constructions of Childhood*, London: Continuum.

Blundell, D. (2016) *Rethinking Children's Spaces and Places: Attitudes in Contemporary Society*, London: Bloomsbury.

Bologna Group (2003) Communique of the Conference of Ministers responsible for Higher Education in Berlin 19 September 2003. www.ehea.info/pid34363/ministerial-declarations-and-communiques.html – last accessed 19.1.17.

Burr, V. (2003) *Social Constructionism*, London: Routledge.

Council of Europe (2010) *Recommendation CM/Rec(2010)7 of the Committee of Ministers to Member States on the Council of Europe Charter on Education for Democratic Citizenship and Human Rights Education (Adopted by the Committee of Ministers on 11 May 2010 at the 120th Session)*, Strasbourg: Council of Europe.

DES (1975) *A Language for Life (The Bullock Report)*, London: HMSO.

El-Haj, T. R. A. (2007) '"I was born here, but my home, it's not here": Educating for democratic citizenship in an era of transnational migration and global conflict', *eHarvard Educational Review*, 77(Fall): 285–316.

European Commission (2012) *Communication from the Commission to the European Parliament, the Council, the European Economic and Social Committee and the Committee of the Regions: Rethinking Education: Investing in Skills for Better Socio-economic Outcomes, 20.11.2012 COM (2012) 669 final*, Strasbourg: European Commission.

David Blundell and Peter Cunningham

European Union (1992) *Treaty on European Union Maastricht Official Journal C19*, 29 July 1992, Brussels: European Union.

European Union, (2000) *Lisbon European Council, 23 and 24 March 2000*, Lisbon: European Union.

European Union (2009) *Council Conclusions of 12 May 2009 on a Strategic Framework for European Cooperation in Education and Training ('ET 2020')*, 2009/C 119/02, Brussels: European Union.

European Union (2015) *Declaration on Promoting Citizenship and the Common Values of Freedom, Tolerance and Non-discrimination Through Education*, Informal Meeting of European Union Education Ministers, Paris, 17 March 2015, Brussels: European Union.

European Union (2016) *Education and Radicalisation – The Paris Declaration One Year On, 16 March 2016*, Brussels: European Union.

Eurydice (2012) *Citizenship Education in Europem*, Brussels: Education, Audio-visual and Culture Executive Agency.

Foley, P. (2001) 'The development of child health and welfare services in England (1900–1948)' in Foley, P., Roche, J. and Tucker, S. (eds), *Children in Society: Contemporary Theory, Policy and Practice*, Basingstoke: Palgrave pp. 6–20.

Foucault, M. (1972) *The Archaeology of Knowledge*, London: Tavistock.

Hahn, H.-J. (1998) *Education and Society in Germany*, Oxford: Berg.

Hörschelmann, K. and El-Refaie, E. (2014) 'Transnational citizenship, dissent and the political geographies of youth', *Transactions of the Institute of British Geographers*, 39(2014): 444f th.

Judd, D. and Surridge, K. (2002) *The Boer War*, London: John Murray.

Kjørholt, A. T. (2007) 'Childhood as a symbolic space: Searching for authentic voices in the era of globalisation', *Children's Geographies*, 5(1–2): 29–42.

Longstreet, W. S. and Shane, H. G. (1993) *Curriculum for a New Millennium*, Boston: Allyn and Bacon.

MacLure, S. (1986) *Educational Documents: England and Wales, 1816 to the Present Day*, London: Methuen.

Massey, D. (2005) *For Space*, London: Routledge.

Mayall, B. (2007) *Children's Lives Outside School and their Educational Impact*, Research Survey 8/1. http://cprtrust.org.uk/wp-content/uploads/2014/06/research-survey-8-1.pdf – last accessed 19.1.17.

OECD (2014) *PISA 2012 Results in Focus: What 15-Year-Olds Know and What They Can Do with What They Know*, Paris: OECD.

Ofsted (2015) *School Inspection Handbook from September 2015*, London: HMSO.

Pike, J. and Colquhoun, D. (2012) 'Lunchtime lock-in: Territorialisation and UK school meals policies' in Kraftl, P. and Horton, J. (eds), *Critical Geographies of Childhood and Youth: Contemporary Policy and Practice*, Bristol: Policy Press pp. 133–50.

Prout, A. and James, A. (1997, 2014) 'A new paradigm for the sociology of childhood? Provenance, promise and problems' in James, A. and Prout, A. (eds), *Constructing and Reconstructing Childhood: Contemporary Issues in the Sociological Study of Childhood*, London: Routledge pp. 7–32.

Qvortrup, J. (2001) 'School-work, paid work and the changing obligations of childhood' in Pullen, C. and Bolton, A. (eds), *Hidden Hands: International Perspectives on Children's Work and Labour*, London: Routledge Falmer.

Rose, N. (1997) *Governing the Soul: The Shaping of the Private Self*, London: Routledge.

Sacramento, R. B. (2015) *Migrant Education and Community Inclusion: Examples of Good Practice*, Brussels: Migrant policy Institute Europe and the Sirius Policy Network on the education of children and youngsters with a migrant background. www.sirius-migrationeducation.org/wp-content/uploads/2015/02/SIRIUS-CommunityInclusion-FINAL.pdf – last accessed 19.1.17.

Teather, E. (1999) *Embodied Geographies: Spaces, Bodies and Rites of Passage*, London: Routledge.

Van Gennep, A. (1909, 1960) *Rites of Passage*, London: Routledge and Kegan Paul.

Walford, R. (2001) *Geography in British Schools 1850–2000*, London: Woburn Press.

part IV

Social controversies

chapter 11

Riots and protest in Europe

Wendy Fitzgibbon

11.1 Introduction

Over recent years Europe has seen a number of direct action protest movements taking to the streets over diverse issues such as environmental concerns, perceptions of injustice in criminal justice, education changes and moves to criminalise squatters and travellers, to name but a few. These actions involve criminal trespass and violation of property, and engage young people drawn from the 'precariat': largely young people from deprived communities, either in and out of insecure, low wage, unskilled employment or facing the prospect of such a status when leaving secondary education. By examining recent examples across Europe, this chapter will critically apply the concept of the 'precariat' to understand the social problems posed by rioters engaged in protests.

Rioting in Europe has a history. Speaking of the eighteenth century, Eric Hobsbawm remarked that 'No other European country has so strong a tradition of rioting as Britain' (Hobsbawm 1968: 446). France, during the same period might be considered a close second (Rudé 1964). Space prevents a discussion of what lessons might be learned from riots at the beginning of industrial society for an understanding of those of the modern period except possibly the lesson that people are likely to resort to riot when peaceful methods of redressing grievances – largely relating to impoverishment and economic austerity – have, either in actuality or perception, failed (Ponticelli and Voth 2011a, 2011b).

The English riots of August 2011 involved an estimated 15,000 people, and spread to major cities in England (Bridges 2012; Reicher and Stott 2011; Singh 2012). These were the largest riots since the Second World War. They were the latest in a series of riots and disturbances which, according to Pitts (2011), amounted to 38 between 1958 and 2010 – the equivalent to approximately three events every four years. However, the main riots in the post-war period both in terms of size and political importance are considered to be the 1981 riots in Brixton (London) and Liverpool, the 2001 riots in West Yorkshire and the 2011 riots throughout the country.

Other European countries have similar histories. Notably, France has seen a number of riots in recent years, in 2005, 2007, 2009 and 2013. It is the 2005 events which have been seen as most rooted in social deprivation and marginalisation and thus stand comparison with those in England (Sutterlüty 2014; Canet *et al.* 2012). Other riots in France and also Sweden (e.g. Stockholm 2013) were more closely related to issues of immigration or ethnic conflict.

Riots in recent years in Greece and Spain which will also be briefly considered here have been of a more explicitly political nature and have arisen out of interaction between police and demonstrators in organised political events (Dalakoglou 2013; Navarréte-Moreno *et al.* 2012). Such political riots of course have a history in France (notably May 1968) but also in England with the well-known poll-tax riot of 1990 and the conflicts between police and mineworkers during the great strike of 1984–5 (Waddington 1992). Inevitably this discussion will be selective and will attempt to bring out the underlying common elements in some of the major cases.

11.2 What are riots?

All legal codes have a definition of riot; the most recent definition in England and Wales is the 1985 Public Order Act which creates riot as a statutory offence occurring when

> 12 or more persons who are present together use or threaten unlawful violence for a common purpose and the conduct of them (taken together) is such as would cause a person of reasonable firmness present at the scene to fear for his personal safety.

Anglo-Saxon jurisdictions tend to take this approach to riot as breach of the public peace, whereas in France riot is dealt with 'as a special case of resistance to public authority under the general heading of rebellion. Breach of the peace, which is central to the Anglo-American concept of riot, is not treated as an offence in French law' (Encyclopedia Britannica n.d.).

Such legal definitions focus on the disruptive effects of riot and say nothing about the motives or grievances or structure of riots. Nevertheless the reaction of the state, in terms of both criminal justice and social policy response, is an important part of the totality of the riot. Once a riot is underway, police reaction and behaviour becomes an important component of the dynamic – how long the riot continues, the extent of its spread and how it is ultimately resolved. Social policy responses usually come sometime later and may involve state intervention to address what are considered to be (often following a public or judicial inquiry) the underlying causes. Changes over time in the forms of state reaction are an important part of the changing nature of riots.

11.3 Precipitating riots, flashpoints and politics

It is never possible to explain the occurrence of riots purely in terms of the social discontent which underlies them. There must be some precipitating incident which actually brings people onto the streets. Riots are by nature episodic whereas the background social discontents they articulate may have considerable duration. How are those discontents mobilised into a riot? The precipitating factor in modern riots usually involves an encounter between angry – overwhelmingly young male – citizens and the police. One of the most developed schemes in social science for making this link is the 'flashpoints' approach associated with David Waddington (Waddington 1992, 2010; Waddington *et al.* 1989; King and Waddington, 2006) and more recently elaborated by Tim Newburn (Newburn 2015; see also Newburn *et al.* 2011).

Waddington's original flashpoint model was developed out of the understanding of the English riots of the 1980s (Brixton 1981 in particular) and the 1960s riots in the United States. The model identifies six 'integrated levels of analysis' (Waddington 1992: 13 et seq.) involving, in summary, structural conflicts derived from inequalities of power, the lack of access to legitimate peaceful forms of grievance articulation, cultural norms governing definitions of appropriate violence on the part both of rioters and police, the history of relations between disaffected groups and the police, situational factors governing the presence of 'legitimate' targets for the rioters and, finally, the immediate interaction between police and crowds in which norms of expected behaviour are violated (by both sides) and violence erupts. This model has been criticised on a number of levels. For example, P.A.J. Waddington sees it as too rigid and contrasts the idea of a single 'flashpoint' to a more fluid account of disorder as a developing process (Waddington 1994; see also Waddington 2012; Newburn 2015). Perhaps more important from the comparative viewpoint is the application of the model to other contexts, in particular the French riots of 2005 (Body-Gendrot 2013).

Before moving to comparative issues it is important to emphasise the distinct character of overtly political riots which may well be suppressed in the attempt to impose a single framework, such as the flashpoints model, on a diversity of events. The model simply refers (correctly) to the perceived lack of alternative legitimate channels for the expression of grievances. But if we compare the English 2011 and French 2005 riots with, say, those occurring in Greece and Spain during the same period (see p. 192) we can see that in the latter cases the 'rioters' were already politically mobilised and in the process of developing new forms of political expression when the riots occurred. A riot emerging out of a political demonstration – or a strike – is different from a riot emerging out of the mobilisation of otherwise passive bystanders to an incident involving the police and inciting anger on the part of citizens. There are of course examples of political riots in both England and France as noted already. In both varieties of riots the context, as flashpoint theory would indicate, is an interaction between citizens and the police but the dynamics are distinct.

11.4 The mobilisation of bystanders

The flashpoint model is at its strongest in dealing with the type of riot in which a single incident involving the police, such as a violent arrest, or raid on premises, provokes a crowd to gather, more police are deployed to the scene and a riot ensues. This was the precipitant in most of the major riots in the United States from the 1960s onwards (Kerner 1968; Feagin and Hahn 1973; Bergesen 1982), and was, as Waddington acknowledges (1992: 13), the inspiration for the flashpoints approach. The approach also incorporates the long history of racist policing of the Afro-American communities. It was this that enabled bystanders to identify immediately with those arrested as the fellow victims of police racism and to connect police racism to a spectrum of forms of discrimination to which the communities had long been subject.

The flashpoint sequence can be easily translated to most of the English and the French riots under consideration. The 1981 riots in the South London suburb of Brixton began with an incident in the midst of a massive police stop and search operation which largely targeted young black males (Scarman 1981; Lea and Young 1982, 1984). The 2011 English riots began in Tottenham with events following the police shooting of a young black man, Mark Duggan. Likewise the 2005 French riots began with two teenagers in Clichy-sous-Bois in the Seine-Saint-Denis suburb of Paris being electrocuted after entering an electric power facility believing they were being pursued by police who 'made unacceptable or at least disproportionate use of the state monopoly on the use of force' (Sutterlüty, 2014: 39; see also Canet *et al.* 2012; Body-Gendrot 2013: 13).

These types of incidents, involving initially relatively small numbers of individuals responding to actions by small numbers of police officers, then galvanise wider layers of individuals to gather and, if the circumstances are not conducive to a peaceful resolution, violence may erupt which then spirals out of control and, again depending on the circumstances, may spread to other regions of the city and other cities. This process involves two elements. First, there is a mobilisation of bystanders whereby a wider circle of initially passive onlookers come to identify with the victims of the particular incident on the basis that 'this could have been me'. Additionally, repressive action by police may be seen as 'yet another example' not only of oppressive police behaviour but of a generalised repression by state agencies in general. The second element is the actual 'flashpoint' in which neither the police nor the gathered crowd are prepared to accommodate or compromise. Thus in the Tottenham 2011 case police failed to respond to the demands of demonstrators gathered outside the local police station for an account of the circumstances of Mark Duggan's death from a suitably senior officer. The police then compounded matters by attempting to disperse the demonstrators and in the ensuing confrontation a young woman

Wendy Fitzgibbon

was pushed to the ground and hit by police. This acted as a second 'precipitating incident' sufficient to trigger widespread rioting (Waddington 2012; Reicher and Stott 2011; Platts-Fowler 2013).

Communication, transparency and accountability are all important factors in preventing disorder occurring. The failure of the authorities to respond to the demands of the demonstrators for clarification of the circumstances of Duggan's shooting by police in any way except defensively ignoring requests and then dealing with the crowd with force created a situation in which violent reaction was inevitable. The disorder exposed a legitimacy crisis, a crisis of authority and the inability of both police and government authority figures to command trust and respect (see Platts-Fowler, 2013). In the French (2005) case the original precipitating incident turned into a flashpoint with less of a delay. The deaths of the two young men were followed by demonstrations at the Clichy-sous-Bois police station from which the violence spread (Sutterlüty 2014: 39). Less evident here is either expectation by the crowd of police action which might have diffused the situation or, indeed, any habit on the part of a more militarised French police to make such gestures. Whatever the case, the rioting spread rapidly. Nevertheless, Sutterlüty underlines the parallels between the riots, including police incursion as precipitating event, a history of riots in both countries stretching back to the 1980s, the initial development of the riots in the most deprived urban areas, the rioting populations as suffering media stigmatisation as a dangerous underclass and, finally, a history of repressive and racially discriminatory policing – in particular the heavy policing inflicted on 'sensitive urban zones' by French governments – and revenge on the police was a predominant motive by rioters (ibid.: 47).

The mobilisation of bystanders process makes little sense without reference to a general reservoir of antagonism and anger on the part of those drawn into rioting, a feeling that normal political channels for the expression of grievances are effectively closed down and, in particular, a recent history of antagonistic relations between the riot-prone population and the police. These are all acknowledged in the flashpoints model.

The source of such antagonism among growing numbers of young people throughout Europe lies in the gradual displacement of welfare states and full employment by a regime of unemployment or insecure or *precarious* employment (Standing 2011), declining social mobility, increasing social inequality and marginalisation from channels of legitimate political representation (Wacquant 2007, 2010; Winlow and Hall 2013). These processes are reinforced by an increasing geographical exclusion from city centres throughout Europe (Doherty *et al.* 2008; Hardiman and Lapeyre 2004; Minton 2009; Hatherley 2012) and a deteriorating relationship with police and state agencies. These forms of social exclusion are frequently overlaid and reinforced by racial discrimination which tends to produce rioter populations disproportionately drawn from ethnic minority youth. A strong historical correlation between such social and economic austerity and riot should come as no surprise (see Ponticelli and Voth, 2011a, 2011b).

11.5 The political demonstration

The mobilisation of hitherto passive bystanders is not the only way in which riot may be precipitated. The political marginalisation from existing forms of grievance articulation may itself lay the foundation for the development of new social movements. Initially these may take the form of large, highly politicised public demonstrations and riot may be the outcome in various ways. A politically themed demonstration may become a riot in the absence of clear political leadership on the ground. This was Waddington's analysis of the 1990 anti-poll-tax riot in London. Noting that the demonstration mobilised many poor and homeless youth convinced of the injustice of the Thatcher government's new tax, Waddington quotes a participant to the effect that 'people realised that they weren't on their own and discovered how fragmented, and angry, and disaffected they were. And these feelings manifested themselves in brute force' (Waddington 1992: 21). The violence shown by the police is an additional factor due possibly to policy habituation to violent confrontation with demonstrators during the miners' strike of 1984–5 a few years previously (Jones 2009).

The Greek riots of 2010–12 had a clear political orientation – the government's austerity programme – and began as politically organised demonstrations in cities across Greece. As in the Spanish protests of 2011 and indeed the English riots of that year, social media played an important organising role. The precipitant incident in the worst riots, in Syntagma Square in Athens outside the Greek Parliament in June 2011 (the culmination of several months of demonstrations and street confrontations with police), was entirely political: the decision of the parliament to agree to the demands of the EU austerity programme. This was coupled with overtly aggressive policing. In 2009 the police shooting of a teenager provoked massive riots in major cities (Becatoros and Gatopoulos 2011). The demonstrations of 2011 had been organised by an incipient political movement organised by the Direct Democracy Now! or Indignant Citizens Movement but the reservoir of grievance of alienated marginalised youth was similar to Spain, France and England (Dalakoglou 2013). However, a crucial difference was the presence of the Trade Unions and many working class adults and families. These 'riots' were incidents in a continuum of highly politically organised peaceful demonstrations which in turn were linked to important political cleavages in the country.

Similarly, in Spain the riots of May 2011 were episodes in a longer, more organised political protest organised by new social movements, such as the 15-M movement (also more popularly known as the *Indignados*), embedded largely in marginalised youth and based on an alienation both from the government's post-2008 austerity programme and the perceived failure of the major political parties to combat the infliction of the consequences of the crisis on the poor and young people (Navarréte-Moreno *et al.* 2012). As in Greece and in riots more generally the actual riot took place in the context of large-scale peaceful demonstrations and sit-ins. Thus in May 2011 police beating of protestors at the end of a large demonstration in Madrid precipitated riots in the usual way. Subsequent anti-austerity marches to date have on occasion flared into clashes with police. In this

Wendy Fitzgibbon

case the riot can be seen as a variant of the political riot – as the breakdown of a balance between police and protestors in the context of on-going political demonstration.

11.6 'Shopping with violence': the role of looting in the English riots of 2011

It would be easy to draw a strong contrast between the highly politicised riots in Greece and Spain and the politically undirected riots of England 2011 and (perhaps) France 2005 rather than seeing them all, as have many radical commentators, as different aspects or moments of a general uprising of a precariatised *multitude* (Revel and Negri 2011; see also Klein 2013). A key factor in this discussion is the role of looting in the English case, more extensive than in France 2005, which otherwise has many similarities to the English example as noted above (Body-Gendrot 2013).

There is a school of thought which crosses the political spectrum but agrees on the nature of the English riots as nihilistic rampage. On the right of the political spectrum the British prime minister characterised the riots as 'not political protest . . . [but rather] . . . common or garden thieving, robbing and looting. And we don't need an enquiry to tell us that' (Newburn *et al.* 2011). Cameron did not initially want any form of public inquiry into the riots: the significance of this will be noted presently.

Several commentators from the political left came to very similar conclusions, characterising the riots as more to do with consumption than any form of rebellion against social marginalisation. The philosopher Slavoj Žižek (2011) famously characterised the riots as 'zero-degree protest, a violent action demanding nothing' while Zigmunt Bauman characterised them as 'not a rebellion or an uprising of famished and impoverished people . . . but a mutiny of defective and disqualified consumers, people offended and humiliated by the display of riches to which they had been denied access' (Bauman 2011: 11). The characterisation of rioters as apolitical consumers taking the opportunity to get 'free stuff' extended to academic criminology. Thus Treadwell *et al.* noted that apart from the immediate environs of Tottenham, where Mark Duggan had been shot, 'the majority of the people we interviewed had never heard of Mark Duggan . . . but they certainly knew about Prada and Rolex' (Treadwell *et al.* 2013:11). The authors conclude that the prevalence of consumerism, as reflected in looting, undermined the possibility of any political content to the riots and made it 'almost impossible for a potential collective of marginalised subjects to construct a universal political narrative that makes causal and contextual sense of their own shared suffering and offers a feasible solution to it' (ibid.: 3).

It is true that a unique feature of the 2011 English riots, as they spread beyond Tottenham to other areas and cities, was the extensive role of looting, often as the originating incident rather than an opportunist taking advantage of the general chaos. This is a contrast with the 2005 French events (Canet *et al.* 2012: 2).

Nevertheless a number of qualifications are necessary. First, looting was by no means the only activity during the riots. Platts-Fowler argues that the role of looting may have been exaggerated due to the value of property stolen and, interrogating *The Guardian* newspaper database of riot incidents, concludes 'the data indicates that two-thirds of riot incidents had little or nothing to do with looting' (2013: 21).

This perspective makes way for a more detailed account of the diversity of themes present – including, but not only, consumerism. In many areas the primary action was anger at the police (Reicher and Stott 2011). In surveys of rioters, hostility to the police was widespread. Of those brought before the courts for riot related offences 78 per cent of males and 43 per cent of females had been stopped and searched by police during the previous twelve months (Topping and Diski 2011; Waterton and Sesay 2012). Alongside this a theme of at least equal importance to the acquisition of consumer goods was the real or symbolic re-occupation of public space from which marginalised youth have been systematically excluded over preceding decades by a battery of measures such as Anti-Social Behaviour Orders, CCTV, dispersal zones, etc. A young rioter told Ben Little (2014) 'the real reason for the riots was taking back the spaces we've been pushed out of by the cops and society.'

Underlying all this were profound issues of power: the feeling of power-lessness experienced by young people excluded from large parts of society and economy and many felt an exhilaration by the fact that 'we rioted just to show the police we could . . . they couldn't stop us'. From this standpoint looting itself is not necessarily *only* a reflexion of desire for consumption. 'Shopping with violence' violates the norms of the marketplace – if you don't have the money you can't buy – and is therefore indicative of the presence of other elements in looting: as 'a spontaneous form of social organization' (McDonald 2012: 19; see also Collins 2009) which serves to give the riot structure, continuity and pur-pose. Young people tend to gather in symbolic locations such as shopping centres where lootable goods are readily available and looting is unsurprising. Imogen Tyler sums up the 2011 riots as marginalised youth involved in 'a collective insurgency against authority in its myriad forms, the police, the government, "the rich", all those whom they blamed for their inaudibility, their powerlessness' (Tyler 2013: 204).

11.7 Politics in the face of the decline of politics

The key difference, then, between the English riots of 2011 and those in Greece and Spain was not the lack of politics but the lack of leadership and organisation. Commentators on the 2005 French riots also stress similarities both regarding the rapid spread of the riots to cities far beyond the original conflict with the police and regarding the fact that, unlike the Spanish or Greek events, they took very much the form of 'proto-political revolt' (Canet *et al.* 2012: 12) and remained alienated from the more articulate student-based protest movement (Lagrange 2012: 32).

When Treadwell *et al.* comment that the rioters lacked 'a universal political narrative' they are simply identifying the lack of a cadre of 'organic intellectuals' capable of giving a precise form to the 'diffuse and generalised rage' (Lea and Hallsworth 2012: 31) evident on the streets. But this does not mean that the rioters were only interested in consumption and 'shopping'. Unlike in France, as discussed by Lagrange, for example, there may well have been some overlap between participants in the more politicised student demonstrations of the previous November (2010) and the riots of August 2011 (see, for example, Little 2014). Nevertheless the absence of political leadership among marginalised youth is probably the most important issue arising out of the English riots of 2011 but this has been unfortunately crowded out by the non-debate about the meaning of looting.

A comparison of the riots of the 1980s both in France and Britain shows the direction of movement towards increased marginalisation and disconnection of youth in deprived communities from political networks and linkages. After the riots in Les Minguettes (Lyon) in 1981, mainly by youth of North African heritage, various forms of political organisation developed which '*gradually drew closer to the traditional political parties, particularly those on the left . . . Nothing like that happened in 2005*' (Canet *et al.* 2012: 13). At the same time the government responded with a policy of neighbourhood interventions known under the umbrella of *Politique de la Ville* with funding initiatives for social housing, education, crime prevention, employment and social integration. Despite the seriousness of these initiatives it remains 'questionable whether policies against social exclusion produce a significant improvement in the concerned areas' (Stouten and Rosenboom 2013: 115). By the end of the 1990s, which had seen further rioting, these initiatives had become diluted and the emphasis had shifted to policing (Body-Gendrot 2013: 8; see also Waddington *et al.* 2009: 235–6). In response to the 2005 riots the government of Nicolas Sarkozy announced new funding for urban renewal (see Chrisafis 2008). But such initiatives were effectively interrupted by the global economic crash of 2008 from which Europe as a whole has yet to recover.

Meanwhile the left political parties had become seriously weakened, further marginalising the poor and especially the North African immigrant communities such that 'the enormous gap separating the political sphere from the lives of these people is undoubtedly a fundamental reason for the riots taking only a merely destructive form and failing to translate into political demands' (Sutterlüty 2014: 49). Thus:

> Left to themselves and held responsible for their own situation, deprived of organic intellectuals – as theorized by Gramsci – capable of giving meaning to their actions and merging them in a real social movement, the youths from the suburbs have violently expressed their rage.
>
> (Canet *et al.* 2012: 15; see also Lagrange 2012: 32)

Developments in England between the Brixton riots of 1981 and the riots of 2011 are broadly similar. In the aftermath of the 1981 riots both the socialist left and black radical groups did attempt to construct a political voice for the rioters (see Bateman 2012), though the linkages with mainstream politics were weaker than in France. But the immigrant working class, in particular the black communities who bore the brunt of repressive policing and rioted in 1981, were not absorbed fully into the political and organisational structures of the working class (Rex and Tomlinson 1979; Rex 1982). At the level of government response the well-known report by senior judge Lord Scarman (1981) attempted to remedy some of the worst effects of police racism and aggressive stop and search policies of the type that had precipitated the riots. He also called for institutional arrangements for liaison between police and the black communities in London. He understood the riots as a demand for social inclusion by those who had become marginalised through a combination of racial discrimination and economic decay.

Even at the beginning of the 1980s Scarman's liberal paternalism was out of sync with the gathering neoliberalism of the first Thatcher government (Hall 1982). Over the succeeding 30 years government attitudes to marginalised youth in deprived communities underwent a fundamental change. As Lea (2004) has traced, the old welfare paternalism exhibited by Scarman ('How has government failed to integrate these communities?') was displaced by the more neoliberal theme, notable in the response to riots in Yorkshire in 2001, of self responsibilisation ('How can these communities learn to take responsibility for themselves?'). Under the Blair governments various types of intervention such as the *New Deal for Communities* programmes aimed at *community cohesion* were initiated and these could perhaps be compared with the French measures noted above (see, for example, Potts 2007). But by the time of the 2011 riots Prime Minister Cameron's outburst to the effect that no inquiry was needed into the actions of 'common or garden' criminals echoed French President Sarkozy who, in response to the 2005 riots, had denounced the participants as 'scum' and 'riff-raff'.

The English riots of 2011 followed in the wake of the economic crisis of 2008 and the subsequent austerity programme of the Coalition government which emerged from the 2010 election, which was not an environment in which major urban renewal initiatives were likely. The official report on the riots which eventually emerged (Singh 2012) was a model of neoliberal self responsibilisation strategy and placed a major emphasis on schools and other educational institutions taking steps to increase 'resilience' and 'strength of character' among young people in deprived communities. Furthermore, the recommendations of the report, timid as they were, have been largely ignored by central government (Lammy 2013). There have been local funding initiatives. The mayor of London, for example, allocated £70 million for urban renewal. But the influence of neoliberalism has been evident in the emphasis given to commercial property developers focused on shopping precincts and high cost housing while the voices of community groups and the poor are marginalised. Indeed some post-riot urban renewal projects have been criticised as a variety of *social cleansing* (Lees 2013; Lea 2014). Riot, it is clear, is no longer functioning, as it did in the eighteenth century (Hobsbawm 1968), as a form of 'collective bargaining' in which the otherwise disenfranchised masses create a situation

Wendy Fitzgibbon

and the government, however reluctantly, makes concessions. Twenty-first-century rioters are *political orphans* (Younge 2011).

The more politicised events in Greece and Spain provide a contrast. However, the distinction between the European political riots and the English riots of 2011 can be artificially maximised both by exaggerating the degree of political coherence underlying the former and by exaggerating the element of 'mindless criminality' in the latter. But the two types of riot considered here (there are others) cannot be considered in isolation. Thus in England the highly politicised 1990 poll-tax riots came after a decade of riots beginning with the Brixton riots of 1981. Many participants in these political riots in 1990 would remember the miners pickets but also the 1981 riots. The poll-tax riots were followed by riots the following year in Cardiff and Oxford. Likewise in 2011 many rioters remembered the more politically organised student demonstrations of the previous November, which involved a good deal of disorder. Indeed some had also participated in these protests and had been on the receiving end of heavy policing and may well have articulated the frustrations of many who saw the former events as having got nowhere. Attitudes (e.g. to the legitimacy of street action including confrontations with the police or damage to property) have to be seen as conditioned by the period as a whole rather than understandable purely in terms of hermetically sealed separate events.

Riots can be an aspect of the painful birth of new types of social movements among young people who, as a 'multitude' destined for precarious labour or even surplus to the requirements of neoliberal capitalism are indeed orphaned from many of the older working-class political traditions now in deep crisis. Such movements develop unevenly and may encounter frequent demoralising setbacks. They may for a time find themselves entering the political mainstream only to be followed by setbacks and demoralisation. In Greece, for example, after the recent wave of demonstrations and street violence a degree of passivity has set in (Lapavitsas and Politaki 2014). Yet with the announcement of elections in 2015 in which the left party *Syriza* may possibly become the largest, a strong linkage with established political structures may become a possibility. Likewise in Spain the *Indignados* movement naturally ran out of steam in the short term but in the 2014 European elections the radical party *Podemos* secured five seats in the European Parliament (Kassam 2014). In both these countries new movements are currently linking marginalised youth to mainstream politics. But this may produce problems in the future and a subsequent defeat or impasse for either of these radical forces would drive marginalised youth back into the type of pessimism and alienation in which politics *takes the form of* looting and street violence, as in the UK, as *pre-political rage* (Hallsworth and Lea 2011). This latter may in the near future become the basis of new radical movements.

11.8 Conclusion

One should conclude on a note of caution. New social movements that are rooted in marginalised youth are not by virtue of that fact necessarily radical. The emergence of the far right in Europe also attempts to build itself among the same strata. Many precariously employed public sector workers may well be forced to join this strata and become seduced by rhetoric which blames 'others' for their situation (Fitzgibbon 2013). Guy Standing's study of the *precariat* (Standing 2011) subtitled 'the new dangerous class' argued that 'the ugly part of the precariat was seen in the fires of London and the riots across England in August, 2011' (Standing 2012: 1). Standing provides a fitting conclusion to the discussion,

> Politicians should beware. [The precariat] is a new dangerous class, not yet what Marxists would describe as a class-for-itself, but a class-in-the-making, divided into frustrated and bitter factions, but united in insecurity and fear . . . Part could turn to the extreme right, and is doing so; part could drift into anarchic behaviour, as we have seen in London, or political disengagement; part is looking for green social democracy, but cannot find it. The challenge is to forge an agenda and language that draws a majority into an edifying progressive consensus.
>
> (ibid.: 1–2)

References

Bateman T (2012) With the benefit of hindsight: the disturbances of August 2011 in historical context. 1st ed. In: Briggs, Daniel (ed.), *The English Riots of 2011: A Summer of Discontent*, Hook, UK: Waterside Press, pp. 91–110.

Bauman Z (2011) Fuels, sparks and fires: On taking to the streets. *Thesis Eleven*, 109(1), 11–16.

Becatoros E and Gatopoulos D (2011) Massive riots cripple Greece's main cities. *Huffington Post*, 25th May. Available from: www.huffingtonpost.com/2008/12/08/police-shooting-sparks-ri_n_149059.html (accessed 3rd January 2015).

Bergesen, Albert (1982) Race riots of 1967: an analysis of police violence in Detroit and Newark. *Journal of Black Studies*, 12(3), 261–74.

Body-Gendrot S (2013) Urban violence in France and England: comparing Paris (2005) and London (2011). *Policing and Society*, 23(1), 6–25.

Bridges L (2012) Four days in August: the UK riots. *Race and Class*, 54(1), 1–12.

Canet R, Pech L and Stewart M (2012) France's burning issue: understanding the urban riots of November 2005. In: Bowden B and Davis MT (eds), *Disturbing the Peace: Riots, Resistance and Rebellion in Britain and France, 1381 to the Present*, Basingstoke: Palgrave Macmillan, pp. 1–17.

Chrisafis A (2008) Sarkozy unveils 1bn plan to stop repeat of 2005 riots. *The Guardian*, 23rd January.

Collins R (2009) *Violence: A Micro-sociological Theory*. Princeton, NJ: Princeton University Press.

Dalakoglou D (2013) The movement and the 'movement' of Syntagma Square. *Cultural Anthropology Online*, 14th February. Available from: www.culanth.org/fieldsights/70-the-movement-and-the-movement-of-syntagma-square (accessed 15th January 2015).

Wendy Fitzgibbon

Doherty J, Busch-Geertsema V, Karpuskiene V, Korhonen J, O'Sullivan E, Sahlin I, Petrillo A and Wygnanska J (2008) Homelessness and exclusion: regulating public space in European cities. *Surveillance & Society*, 5(3), 290–314

Encyclopedia Britannica (n.d.) *Riot*. Available from: www.britannica.com/EBchecked/topic/504311/riot (accessed 13th December 2014).

Feagin, Joe and Hahn, Harlan (1973) *Ghetto Revolts: The Politics of Violence in American Cities*. New York: Macmillan.

Fitzgibbon W (2013) Riots and probation: governing the precariat. *Criminal Justice Matters*, 93(1), 18–19.

Hall S (1982) The lessons of Lord Scarman. *Critical Social Policy*, 2(2), 66–72.

Hallsworth S and Lea J (2011) Reconstructing Leviathan: emerging contours of the security state. *Theoretical Criminology*, 15(2), 141–57 [ISSN 1362-4806].

Hardiman PS and Lapeyre F (2004) *Youth and Exclusion in Disadvantaged Urban Areas: Policy Approaches in Six European Cities*. Trends in social cohesion No. 9, Strasbourg: Council of Europe.

Hatherley O (2012) *A New Kind of Bleak: Journeys Through Urban Britain*. London; New York: Verso.

Hobsbawm E (1968) *Labouring Men: Studies in the History of Labour*. London: Weidenfeld and Nicolson.

Jones R (2009) From Orgreave to the city. *Red Pepper*, June. Available from: www.redpepper.org.uk/From-Orgreave-to-the-City/ (accessed 6th January 2015).

Kassam A (2014) Podemos hopes to cement rise of citizen politics in Spain after election success. *The Guardian*, 27th May.

Kerner O (1968) *Report of the National Advisory Committee on Civil Disorders*. Washington, DC: US Government Printing Office.

King M and Waddington D (2006) Flashpoints revisited: a critical application to the policing of anti-globalization protest. *Policing & Society*, 15(3), 255–82.

Klein A (2013) More police, less safety? Policing as a causal factor in the outbreak of riots and public disturbance. In: Briggs D (ed.), *The English Riots of 2011: A Summer of Discontent*, Hook: Waterside Press, pp. 127–46.

Lagrange H (2012) Youth unrest and riots in France and the UK. *Criminal Justice Matters*, 87(1), 32–3.

Lammy D (2013) Eric Pickles has treated riot victims as if they do not exist. *The Guardian*, 5th August.

Lapavitsas C and Politaki A (2014) Why aren't Europe's young people rioting any more? *The Guardian*, 1st April.

Lea J (2004) From Brixton to Bradford: ideology and discourse on race and urban violence in the United Kingdom. In: Gilligan G and Pratt J (eds), *Crime, Truth and Justice*, Cullompton: Willan Publishing.

Lea J (2014) The 2011 riots: still talking? *The Chartist* (September/October), 22(3).

Lea J and Hallsworth S (2012) Understanding the riots. *Criminal Justice Matters*, 87(1), 30–1.

Lea J and Young J (1982) The riots in Britain 1981: urban violence and political marginalisation. In: Cowell D, Jones T and Young J (eds), *Policing The Riots*. London: Junction Books, pp. 5–21.

Lea J and Young J (1984) *What Is To Be Done About Law and Order?: Crisis in the Eighties*. Harmondsworth: Penguin.

Lees L (2013) Regeneration in London has pushed poor families out. *The Guardian*, 29th August.

Little B (2014) A growing discontent: class and generation under neoliberalism. *Soundings: A Journal of Politics and Culture*, 56, 27–40.

McDonald K (2012) They can't do nothin' to us today. *Thesis Eleven*, 109(1), 17–23.

Minton A (2009) *Ground Control: Fear and Happiness in the Twenty-First-Century City*. London: Penguin Books.

Navarréte-Moreno L, Díaz-Catalán C and Zúñiga R (2012) If you won't let us dream, then we won't let you sleep: demarcation of spaces and the rise of the Spanish 15-M. In: Briggs D (ed.), *The English Riots of 2011 A Summer of Discontent*, Hook: Waterside Press, pp. 247–360.

Newburn T (2015) The 2011 England riots in recent historical perspective. *British Journal of Criminology*, 55(1), 39–64.

Newburn T, Lewis P and Metcalf J (2011) A new kind of riot? From Brixton 1981 to Tottenham 2011. *The Guardian*, 9th December. Available from: www.theguardian.com/uk/2011/dec/09/riots-1981-2011-differences (accessed 22nd November 2014).

Pitts J (2011) Riotous assemblies. *Youth and Policy*, 107(November), 82–97.

Platts-Fowler D (2013) Beyond the loot. Available from: http://britsoccrim. org/new/volume13/pbcc_2013_Platts-Fowler.pdf (accessed 17th November 2014).

Ponticelli J and Voth H-J (2011a) Fact. There is a link between cuts and riots. *The Guardian*, 16th August. Available from: www.theguardian.com/ commentisfree/2011/aug/16/austerity-programmes-cause-riots (accessed 22nd November 2014).

Ponticelli J and Voth H-J (2011b) *Austerity and Anarchy: Budget Cuts and Social Unrest in Europe 1919–2008*. Discussion Paper. London: Centre for Economic Policy Research.

Potts G (2007) *French Lessons? A Cross-Channel Look at Regeneration, Cohesion and Integration*. London: Commission on Integration & Cohesion.

Reicher S and Stott C (2011) *Mad Mobs and Englishmen?: Myths and Realities of the 2011 Riots*. London: Constable & Robinson.

Revel J and Negri T (2011) The common in revolt. *UniNomade*. Available from: www.uninomade.org/commoninrevolt/ (accessed 6th January 2015).

Rex J (1982) The 1981 urban riots in Britain. *International Journal of Urban and Regional Research*, 6(1), 99–113.

Rex J and Tomlinson S (1979) *Colonial Immigrants in a British City: A Class Analysis*. London: Routledge & Kegan Paul.

Rudé G (1964) *The Crowd in History: A Study of Popular Disturbances in France and England, 1730–1848*. New York: John Wiley.

Scarman, Lord Justice (1981) *The Scarman Report: The Brixton Disorders 10–12 April 1981*. London: HMSO.

Wendy Fitzgibbon

Singh D (2012) *After the Riots: The Final Report of the Riots Communities and Victims Panel*. London: The Riots Communities and Victims Panel.

Standing G (2011) *The Precariat: The New Dangerous Class*. London: Bloomsbury Academic.

Standing G (2012) The precariat: the social democratic challenge. Available at www.guystanding.com/files/documents/Precariat_as_dangerous_class_for_Brazil_June_2012.pdf (accessed 5th January 2015).

Stouten P and Rosenboom H (2013) Urban regeneration in Lyon: connectivity and social exclusion. *European Spatial Research and Policy*, 20(1), 97–117.

Sutterlüty F (2014) The hidden morale of the 2005 French and 2011 English riots. *Thesis Eleven*, 121(1), 38–56.

Topping A and Diski R (2011) The women who rioted. *The Guardian*, 9th December. Available from: www.theguardian.com/uk/2011/dec/09/women-who-rioted-english-riots (accessed 23rd November 2014).

Treadwell J, Briggs D, Winlow S and Hall S (2013) Shopocalypse now: consumer culture and the English riots of 2011. *British Journal of Criminology*, 53(1), 1–17.

Tyler I. (2013) *Revolting Subjects: Social Abjection and Resistance in Neoliberal Britain*. London: Zed Books.

Wacquant L (2007) *Urban Outcasts: A Comparative Sociology of Advanced Marginality*. Cambridge: Polity.

Wacquant L (2010) Crafting the neoliberal state: workfare, prisonfare, and social insecurity. *Sociological Forum*, 25(2), 197–220.

Waddington D (1992) *Contemporary Issues in Public Disorder: A Comparative and Historical Approach*. London: Routledge.

Waddington D (2010) Applying the flashpoints model of public disorder to the 2001 Bradford riot. *British Journal of Criminology*, 50(2), 342–59.

Waddington D, Jones K and Critcher C. (1989) *Flashpoints: Studies in Public Disorder*. London: Routledge.

Waddington D, Jobard F and King M (eds) (2009) *Rioting in the UK and France*. Cullompton, Devon; Portland, OR: Willan.

Waddington PAJ (1994), *Liberty and Order: Public Order Policing in a Capital City*. London: UCl Press.

Waddington PAJ (2012) Explaining the riots. *Criminal Justice Matters*, 87(1), 10–11.

Waterton S and Sesay K (2012) Out of touch: a youth perspective. *Criminal Justice Matters*, 87(1), 28–9.

Winlow S and Hall S (2013) *Rethinking Social Exclusion: The End of the Social?* London: SAGE Publications.

Younge G (2011) These riots were political. They were looting, not shoplifting. *The Guardian*, 14th August.

Žižek S (2011) Shoplifters of the world unite. *London Review of Books*, 19th August.

chapter 12

Illegal drugs as a social problem

James Morgan and Daniel Silverstone

12.1 Introduction

Illegal drugs still present as a perennial but mutating social problem throughout the European Union. Over the last five years, the arrival of novel psychoactive substances (NPS) across Europe has added more variety to the longstanding basket of established illegal drugs. Yet, more striking is the divergent paths which European countries tread in their strategies of regulation, with one group of countries such as England and Sweden holding stoically to a prohibitionist and punitive social policy whilst others, most obviously the Netherlands and Portugal, pursuing policies of decriminalisation and diversion.

It is a comparison of England and the Netherlands which is explored here. Arguably, historically, the two countries' approaches to intoxication were always different, as is reflected in the portraits of the doughy red-faced burghers on the walls of Rijks' Museum. They contrast to the more pinched and austere portraits of the gentry hung in the National Portrait Gallery. Today, as outlined in the data below, the differences are definitely stark and, certainly, anyone who has visited the two capital cities will be acutely aware of them. In Amsterdam's entertainment area, neon lights warn tourists that white heroin is being sold as cocaine and the pungent smell of cannabis is common, whereas London's night time hotspots are characterised by an assiduously enforced smoking ban and warnings of a 'zero tolerance' approach to illegal drugs.

Underlying these differences is a broad similarity in the segmentation of drug taking which is shared across Europe, that is, the existence of two distinct types of illegal drug user – 'recreational' and 'problematic'. Recreational drug use refers to the episodic use of cannabis, ecstasy, LSD, amphetamines, cocaine and NPS, whilst problem drug use usually refers to the persistent use of heroin and crack cocaine, or injection of any drug (EMCDDA 2012; Bean 2002; Stevens 2011; Wincup 2013). Of course, these categories are crude and not hermetically sealed; recreational drug users become problem drug users, and vice versa. The recreational use of drugs, such as cannabis and ecstasy, can be problematic and indeed fatal, and there are numerous studies which illustrate that heroin use can be maintained alongside a productive life (Shewan and Dalgarno 2005; Warburton et al. 2005; Zinberg 1984). Nevertheless, scholars argue that recreational drug use is generally an attempt to create temporary intoxication, which takes the drug taker momentarily out of their controlled and regulated order. The physical high of the drug is complemented by a deeper mental pleasure, a 'controlled loss of control', a temporary escape from the stress and anxiety of modern European life (Measham 2004).

As pioneering sociologists pointed out, these recreational drug forays are made much more alluring and enduring by participants' indulgence in the rituals of drug taking and the creation of complex sub-cultures, replete with complicated argot and symbols (Becker 1953; Zinberg 1984). One of the most obvious is a cannabis sub-culture, which is now complex and hybrid. It is not just an alternative to a mainstream lifestyle but also consists of connoisseurs devoted to enhancing its quality and potency, as well as being incorporated into the more precarious but also somewhat ironically more consumerist social worlds of marginalised European urban youth (Sandberg 2012). Another obvious example is an illegal 'rave culture' which exploded in the UK in the late 1980s based on a seductive mixture of 'repetitive' beats and a then new drug, ecstasy. Although the original music is now consigned across Europe to the label 'old school', having been repressed, regulated and commodified, 'rave' has survived, splintered and prospered. For example, in the UK, whilst established dance clubs are closing, the popularity of dance music festivals has grown and their number has increased by around 500 per cent over the past 15 years, with established dance holiday destinations such as Ibiza retaining their popularity while new alternatives such as Croatia emerge as cheaper rivals (Ticketmaster 2015).

Meanwhile, some recreational drug users will develop into chronic and problem users, joining an ageing population of heroin users, increasingly mixed with episodic crack cocaine users and crack cocaine only users (Briggs 2013). The label 'problematic' can be taken to apply to the background of these users. Study after study suggests people who end up as chronic users of these drugs originate from backgrounds marked by social exclusion and personal victimisation (Bean 2002; Briggs 2013). Whilst recent authors shy away from any causative relationship between problematic drug use and crime, there are plenty of studies which explore how heavy users utilise criminality to part-fund their addiction (Pearson 1987; Parker et al. 1988; Taylor 1993; Bennett and Holloway 2007; Bean 2002; Morgan 2014; Moyle and Coomber 2015). Indeed in both the UK and the Netherlands problematic drug users are over-represented in prisons, amongst low level drug dealers and within the sex-worker profession (Prison Reform Trust 2014; Sanders et al., 2009). It is worth noting that users of both sexes often self-medicate to assist with mental health problems which both pre-date and can be brought on and worsened by excessive drug consumption

illegal drugs as a social problem

(Harocopos *et al.* 2003). Whilst the sub-cultures of recreational users remain on the whole socially acceptable, problem drug users also still suffer the stigma of rejection and opprobrium from both recreational drug users and the population at large.

Returning to the comparison, comparisons are now relatively easily made as there is a well-established architecture of monitoring which the European Union provides. The data published by the European Monitoring Centre for Drugs and Drug Addiction (EMCDDA) and Europol in relation to the trafficking and distribution of drugs is published on an annual basis and is supplemented by specific reports which document emerging trends, all of which is testament to the way preventing illegal drug use and the treatment of drug users is a key part of the European political agenda. This chapter seeks to compare the incidence of use, and highlight the emerging trends and key criminal justice responses in England and Wales and the Netherlands.

12.2 Drug use in England and Wales

The picture of drug use in England and Wales shows overall decline in the use of established illegal drugs since high water marks at the beginning of the millennium, despite some drugs seeming to regain popularity in the last few years. Meanwhile NPS, which mimic the effects of more established drugs, are still not as popular as the more traditional illicit recreational repertoire, but a phenomenon worth examining. Against this backdrop was a worrying jump in deaths attributed to drug use in the years 2014–15 (ONS 2016).

Evidence for a decline in use of illicit drugs comes from the most recent Crime Survey for England and Wales (CSEW) (Lader 2015). Of the adults between the ages of 16 and 59 who took part in this survey, 8.6 per cent took an illegal drug in the previous 12 months; this is compared to 11.2 per cent in 2004–5. When only looking at young adults, from 16 to 24 years of age, prevalence of last year drug use fell from 24.5 per cent to 19.4 per cent. Many argue that last year use points to a very wide range of behaviours (e.g. Stevens 2011), but last month use has also fallen in this time period: from 6.7 per cent to 4.7 per cent. This drop is not present in all types of drugs use in the United Kingdom; some variation can be seen between different drug types.

Misuse of opiates and crack cocaine has been placed together for analysis because, according to Wincup (2013), a dominant theme of drug policy in the United Kingdom is to equate their use with problem drug use. Hay *et al.* (2014) estimate there are 293,879 opiate or crack users in England alone, or alternatively 8.4 adults aged 16–64 per 1,000 in the population at large. The authors estimated 7.32 opiate users and 4.76 crack users per 1,000, with much overlap between these populations. Interestingly, Kilmer *et al.* (2013) show that the figure for 2006/7 was lower, despite other indicators suggesting declining drug use of this sort. Trautmann and McSweeney (2013) have noted that whereas treatment presentations for heroin use amongst the young, aged 16–24, have declined, presentations for those over 40 years of age have increased. The same authors also noted that first time treatment presentations for opiate use have been declining since 2006, with most of those in treatment being repeat visitors. This suggests an ageing and lingering population of opiate users, with comparatively few new young recruits.

Cannabis is still the most popular illegal drug in the UK, despite what looks like declining use. From 1998 until 2004 around 10 per cent of those surveyed by CSEW had used the drug in the last year; since the survey of 2009/10 the figure has been around 6.5 per cent. Looking more precisely at frequency of use, van Laar *et al.* (2013), for the *European Commission*, looked at different types of cannabis users which they classified into the following typology: chippers; occasional users; regular users; and intensive users. Through their responses to a web survey, cannabis users in the United Kingdom fit fairly evenly into these boxes, with 27 per cent chippers, 20 per cent occasional users, 27 per cent regular users and 26 per cent intensive users, which is close to the average for European states surveyed by van Laar *et al.* (2013).

The breakdown into types of cannabis user shows us that England and Wales is home to some highly prolific cannabis users. The mean annual consumption of intensive users who answered this survey was 489.4 grams per year, the highest that van Laar *et al.* (2013) found in Europe. That the median for intensive users is lower, at 286.4 grams per annum, points to some incredibly heavy cannabis users dragging the mean upwards. Although chippers use at the European average – mean 1 gram per year, median 0.6 per year – occasional and regular cannabis users both self-report above the European average. Either there is a tendency for respondents from England and Wales to overestimate their use, compared to other Europeans, or else a lot of cannabis is consumed. On top of that van Laar *et al.* (2013) report more of a preference for herbal cannabis, which tends to be stronger, rather than cannabis resin (hash). So by any measure it seems as though people in England and Wales, comparatively, like to get very stoned.

Frijns and van Laar (2013) see stimulants as being amphetamine, ecstasy (MDMA) and powder cocaine. Although not always the case, the EMCDDA and most commentators now see powder cocaine as a recreational drug (unless it is injected) and the use of crack cocaine as problem drug use. For ecstasy and cocaine, England and Wales top the group of European nations surveyed in terms of both last month and last year use (Frijns and van Laar 2013). For amphetamine only the Czech Republic saw a higher prevalence, both in terms of last year and last month usage. Using data from *CSEW* (Lader 2015), we see that ecstasy use has been rising since 2012/13, but this is still lower than the high point in 2001/2. Use of powder cocaine has also been on an upward trajectory since 2012/13, with a previous high water mark recorded in 2008/09. The *CSEW* does not give much detail about the use of amphetamine, as it has very much fallen out of favour since the 1990s, compared to other drugs. It is notable that drug use considered below the threshold of interest for the *CSEW* still appears high compared to other European nations. It should also be noted here that because of widespread abuse of methamphetamine in both the United States of America and Australia similar phenomena were expected in the United Kingdom. However, despite this and perhaps due to the cheap and plentiful amphetamines already available here, an epidemic of methamphetamine has not yet come to fruition. Ayres and Jewkes (2012) have discussed the portrayal of crystal meth (as methamphetamine is commonly known) and how this created an exaggerated hyper reality now associated with use of the drug; maybe this discourse dissuaded potential users.

Despite increases in use seen amongst these more traditional illicit stimulants, there is increasing concern around NPS. These are new drugs that mimic the effects of more established drugs. Use of these drugs took off around 2010 when both ecstasy and cocaine saw a drop in usage, perhaps due to problems surrounding supply, quality and price (Measham *et al.* 2010). As well as measuring the use of mephedrone, the first NPS to gain prominence, the CSEW (Lader 2015) also asked respondents about their general use of NPS for the first time. Whereas 2.8 per cent of those aged 16–24 reported having used one of these drugs, only 0.9 per cent of the more general adult population did so. Out of these drugs herbal smoking mixtures similar to cannabis were more popular than powders, salts and tablets. Nitrous oxide, more often known as laughing gas, is thought to be popular, but was not asked about in the CSEW covering 2014/15 (Lader 2015).

Mephedrone was only reported to have been used in the last year by 0.5 per cent of the general adult population and 1.9 per cent of the young adult population (Lader 2015), lower than a high of 4.4 per cent in 2010/11. Putting this into context, we saw above that adults are ten times more likely to have used cannabis in the last year. According to the EMCDDA (2015a) numbers seeking treatment for their mephedrone use in the United Kingdom rose sharply between 2010/11 and 2012/13, but seemingly levelled off in 2013/14, with 1,641 requesting treatment. Data on what harms are caused by this drug are hard to find; however, such numbers seeking treatment suggest they are not altogether absent.

According to the figures quoted above most drug use in England and Wales appears to be experiencing long term decline, albeit with a more recent upturn in the use of some substances. Despite this, figures released in 2016 covering deaths registered in England and Wales in 2015 show the highest number attributed to drug use since records began in 1993. Out of 3,674, 67 per cent (2,479) of these were related to illegal drugs rather than medicines, with 1,201 (48 per cent of those attributable to illicit drug use) deaths said to concern heroin or morphine (ONS 2016). It is suggested in the report from the ONS (2016) that this is probably an underestimate. The authors point to several reasons for this rise. The high purities of heroin being recorded from street seizures in the United Kingdom have been used to explain the increased mortality, as well as an ageing population of problem drug users and ecstasy tarnished with a dangerous compound known as PMZ being sold.

12.3 The Netherlands

The Dutch situation bears some resemblance to the trends in illicit drug use outlined above in terms of consumption in England and Wales. Whereas CSEW provided contemporary estimates of many forms of drug use, referring to drug

James Morgan and Daniel Silverstone

use occurring in 2014, Dutch data mostly comes from reports published by the *European Commission* (Trautmann *et al.* 2013) and the EMCDDA (2015a, 2015b, 2015c, 2015d). The chapters of the report edited by Trautmann *et al.* (2013) mainly make use of data covering Dutch drug use from 2008; the paper by the EMCDDA covers trends identified in 2014. As, unlike with the CSEW (Lader 2015), aggregates for drug use trends were not reported we shall go straight into assessing use of different types of drugs, starting with opioids and crack cocaine. In the main, data concerning the Netherlands also refers to adults between the ages of 16 and 64, making it comparable to much of the data reported on England and Wales.

Heroin is still the major opioid in the Netherlands; however, use seems comparatively rare compared to the United Kingdom. The EMCDDA (2015a, 2015b, 2015c, 2015d) estimate between 1.1 and 1.5 opiate users per 1,000 in the adult population; the prevalence was around seven times higher in the United Kingdom. As well as a comparatively small population of users, there is also a smaller proportion of those entering treatment in the Netherlands, at only 10.2 per cent of the total, far lower than in the United Kingdom where around half of those presenting for treatment are primary heroin users (EMCDDA 2015a). An even lower share of first time treatment entrants, 5.1 per cent, are heroin users, so like the situation in England and Wales new recruits seem to be declining.

It is also interesting to note that only 10 per cent of Dutch heroin users inject the drug, far lower than the 24 per cent of heroin users who inject in the United Kingdom. It is perhaps relevant here to cite the finding of Trautmann and Frijns (2013) that only 3 per cent of Dutch heroin users interviewed thought their heroin was 'very weak', where in the United Kingdom 43 per cent thought so. Using data collected from police seizures of street drugs in 2008, Kilmer *et al.* (2013) found the mean purity in the Netherlands to be 44.5 per cent, higher than the 34.9 per cent pure heroin found in the United Kingdom. Many more ethnographic or semi-structured interview studies have shown that heroin smokers often begin to inject when tolerance to the drug means they no longer get the desired effect from smoking. Plenty of harm reduction services dissuading heroin users away from injecting could also be posited as an explanation; however, perhaps paradoxically strong heroin might be keeping Dutch heroin users away from the dangers of heroin injection. The Netherlands is something of a European distribution hub for illicit drugs, with many of these ending up in England and Wales, where they may be diluted further before reaching the consumer (van Duyne and Levi 2005).

As crack use is seen as a problem drug, but not focused on as much as heroin, estimates of the prevalence of use tend to be uncertain or unreliable. Regarding the Netherlands this is also the case, as Frijns and van Laar (2013) used opiate use as a proxy for crack use. Their data showed 17,700 problem opiate users, where Frijns and van Laar (2013) assumed 75 per cent of these would also be crack users, whereas 60 per cent of crack users should also use heroin, leading to a figure of 22,125 crack users. They do not report this in terms of a proportion of the adult population so comparisons are tricky.

We move on to cannabis, which due to the well-known permissive regulation is emblematic of Dutch drug use. Close examination of usage trends shows this not to be the case. A report by the EMCDDA (2015a) shows higher lifetime prevalence amongst adults in England and Wales compared to the Netherlands, despite showing a slightly higher proportion of those in the 16–34 age bracket in Netherlands reporting last year use. The study by van Laar *et al.* (2013) shows that a greater share of Dutch cannabis smokers are 'chippers'. Using the same typology, England and Wales see a greater proportion of their cannabis users as being regular or intensive users than the Netherlands. Cannabis does not appear to be more popular or more frequently used in the Netherlands, despite their liberal policy.

With regard to stimulant use, whereas 1.1 per cent of those from England and Wales used amphetamine in the last year, only 0.4 per cent did so in the Netherlands (Frijns and van Laar 2013). By the same measure Frijns and van Laar (2013) show parity between the two areas with regard to ecstasy consumption; concerning cocaine they show that 2.2 per cent used the drug in the past 12 months in England and Wales, and only 1.2 per cent did so in the Netherlands. Concerning the main recreational stimulants, then, their use appears less popular in the Netherlands. When looking at drug markets this finding is confusing. Van Duyne and Levi (2005) report on how the Netherlands is a European distribution hub for many illicit drugs. Much cocaine arrives into the port of Rotterdam and also into Amsterdam Schiphol airport. Ecstasy and amphetamine are also produced in the Netherlands; van Laar *et al.* (2013) show that all of these drugs are cheaper in the Netherlands. These drugs being cheaper and purer should make them more popular there; however, this is not the case (EMCDDA 2015b).

Finally, NPS also do not appear to have been taken up by as many drug users in the Netherlands as they have in England and Wales. Honenbrink *et al.* (2015) report on the Global Drugs Survey (2014) which saw only 7 per cent of Dutch drug users reporting use of any NPS, compared to 39 per cent of British drug users. Perhaps low prices for more established drugs in the Netherlands have meant that there has been no need to switch; Trautmann (2013) suggests that searching for a cheaper high is a motivation for NPS use. However, Honenbrink *et al.* (2015) cite the Global Drugs Survey (2014) again to show Belgian drug users are less likely to use NPS than Dutch, so this may not be the case. Others might point to a harm reduction apparatus that include 'pill testing', water distribution to clubbers and emergency response organised around nightlife settings (EMCDDA 2015d). This could be set against a British situation where such measures are absent, or at least not part of the harm reduction infrastructure. Could this harm reduction apparatus make stimulant users less likely to switch away from more established drugs? Due to the novelty of this phenomenon, ready-made explanations are hard to come by.

Together with lower levels of drug use, people of the Netherlands do not appear to experience as much harm due to their drug use. Drug related mortality amongst Dutch people aged 16–64 is 7.0 per million (EMCDDA 2015c); this is dwarfed by the most recent figure calculated for England and

James Morgan and Daniel Silverstone

Wales – 44.6 cases per million of the population (EMCDDA 2015b). Indicators for HIV published on the same two sources also point towards bigger problems in the United Kingdom. Concerning these harms, the EMCDDA (2015a, b) do not sit on the fence. They see clear evidence that strong harm reduction policies in the Netherlands have reduced harm caused by drug use. The same explanations may not work for explaining lower levels of drug *use* found in the Netherlands; however, at the very least policy does appear capable of making the use of drugs less dangerous. The differing policy approaches are explored below.

12.4 Drug policy in the United Kingdom

The story of contemporary drug policy in the United Kingdom starts in 1971 with the passing of the Misuse of Drugs Act. Before this, what is now illicit drug use was normalised in Victorian times and then controlled under the 'British System' for decades after. This system gave precedence to the medical profession in managing drug issues, but this is not to say that prohibition of a number of substances was not in place also (van Duyne and Levi 2005). Across the Atlantic, American commentators lauded this approach, claiming it explained why the United Kingdom did not have widespread heroin use in deprived neighbourhoods, while the United States did (Stimpson and Oppenheimer 1982). This characterisation is not accurate, however, as due to the forces of globalisation and post-war wealth, drug use began to grow, even with the British System in place (Stimpson and Oppenheimer 1982). The reaction to these increased concerns about drug use, mostly taking place amongst bohemian sub-cultures, was to remove the capacity for physicians to prescribe maintenance doses of heroin and other opiates, while categorising illegal drugs in terms of their supposed harms, in classes: a; b; and c.

This approach has drawn its fair share of criticism. This is partly due to a perceived lack of rigour in deciding which drugs should be placed in which class (e.g. Nutt *et al.* 2007), and also because legislation failed to halt rising prevalence of drug use. Most stark was an increase in heroin use, replicating the American experience where unemployed young men, and some women, lived criminal lifestyles as users of this drug. The United Kingdom's own version of this phenomenon was born in the 1980s, and when there was evidence of heroin injectors spreading HIV the scare gained another powerful dimension (Parker *et al.* 1988). Government was concerned about this new heroin use and for the first time published a strategy (Home Office 1985). The first policy carried a pitiful tone, talking of the ruin suffered by addicts and those around without pouring scorn on the drug users themselves. The solution was better enforcement, as if heroin could be kept off our streets by the long arm of the law. Within a year an update to this first strategy was published, and the link with HIV was made (Home Office 1986). Soon needle exchanges opened up so that heroin injectors would not use contaminated injecting equipment. Methadone also began to be prescribed. If heroin users drank this opiate syrup every day they would not need heroin, so they would inject less, and spread less disease.

International comparisons show the needle exchange policy to have been a success, as rates of HIV infection amongst injection drug users are less than in countries such as Sweden, Russia, Thailand and the United States who brought in needle exchange later, although higher than the Netherlands which brought in such measures earlier (Reuter and Stevens 2007). Throughout the 1990s though, fears moved from spreading disease to driving crime. With the New Labour government, quickly came a new type of policy (Stevens 2011). Offenders caught committing certain trigger offences were prescribed methadone, in the hope that this would reduce offending. In fact from the mid to late 1990s crack cocaine was also seen as a problem drug, as seen in the drugs strategies published in 1998 and 2002 especially (Home Office 1998, 2002). However, as no substitute exists, crack use has been subject to less drug treatment (Reuter and Stevens 2007).

Trying to solve drug problems through substitute prescription continues to spark debate as authors such as McKeganey (2010) and Yates and Malloch (2010) view this as undermining the idea that drug use must be reduced and recovery pursued. Stevens (2011) thinks such substitute therapies may be helpful but questions the evidence base, while Caulkins and Kleiman (2011) see the policy as wise. This debate has also been played out in public with Will Self and Russell Brand arguing against methadone maintenance (Hayes 2015). Politically, the former coalition government agreed in their 2010 published strategy (Home Office 2010) that treatment must aim towards abstinence, with quite some bombast. However, substantively, little has changed in drug treatment service provision (Wincup 2013). Substitution therapies, such as methadone maintenance, continue to dominate; money has not been made available for extra abstinence based treatment.

So far we have mainly heard about efforts to control so called problem drug use, mainly use of heroin and crack cocaine. However, other aspects of policy have been of note. Media campaigns such as the iconic *Heroin screws you up, just say no*, and, *Talk to Frank* have seen a lot of money spent on them, with the government noticeably cagey about showing what purpose they have served. This also applies to the *Blueprint* initiative for drugs education in schools, which according to Bennett and Holloway (2010) was brought into existence based on a selective reading of evidence. Goldacre (2009) reviewed the government's own evaluation study, finding poor methods of analysis and, if anything, evidence that the programme caused further drug use amongst young people.

Finally, it is worth reviewing the current efforts of policy makers trying to deal with emerging concerns regarding NPS, often referred to as legal highs. When these burst onto the scene, as described earlier in the chapter, government did not know what to do. Mephedrone was hastily added to the misuse of drugs act as a Class B drug (Home Office 2010), with this based on limited evidence (Nutt 2010). Next came temporary banning orders. Under this law new drugs would be made illegal for 12 months whilst research into their dangerousness was carried out (Home Office 2011). Since then, during the election year of 2015, something far more radical and out of step with most European policy has been suggested and now brought into law. This is the

James Morgan and Daniel Silverstone

general ban on NPS (Barber 2015), where anything not specifically legislated for that has a psychoactive effect on humans is de facto illegal to possess or trade in. Writing in 2015, Sumnall and Atkinson showed that in Europe only Poland and Ireland have adopted this draconian policy. Sumnall and Atkinson (2015) also showed that the more common strategies for controlling NPS have stopped short of prohibiting them alongside already illegal drugs. A variety of EU nations, including Italy, Ireland, Poland, Portugal, Romania and Sweden have used consumer protection laws to control new drugs, for example by prosecuting those whose sale of NPS involves mislabelling or flouts existing licensing laws. Others, including Austria, Finland, Germany, Hungary, the Netherlands, Norway and Spain have charged vendors for selling unlicensed medicines. The United Kingdom has so far been using some of these protections; however, it is currently voting to usurp them with the general ban.

Writing after this was proposed, but before it was voted in, Sumnall and Atkinson (2015) stated their objections. Despite availability of these drugs likely being curtailed somewhat as shops and websites close in fear of legal consequences, the prognosis does not appear rosy. For Sumnall and Atkinson (2015) the experience in Ireland and Poland should serve as a caution. Following initial drops in usage of NPS, after little more than a year things picked up again and currently Irish youth use more NPS than anyone else in Europe. To date, whenever panic ensues over some novel forms of drug taking the Academic Committee on the Misuse of Drugs (ACMD), of which Sumnall is a member, will review the evidence and stake a case to the Home Secretary. Successive Home Secretaries have tended to ignore scientific advice on drugs when it does not fit with their political agenda, but at least they have publicly had to do so. Now drugs are made illegal without consultation. Then there is also the danger of 'organised' crime networks seizing the market for banned drugs, as has already reportedly happened with mephedrone in the United Kingdom (Sumnall and Atkinson 2015).

The ban, accompanied by punitive sanctions including prison for those who sell NPS, would be in keeping with the overall approach taken to those involved in the consumption, distribution and importation of illegal drugs. As the prison population of England and Wales has grown the numbers of people imprisoned for drug offences has grown with it. It is estimated by the Prison Reform Trust (2014) that 'at the end of March 2014, 15 per cent of men and 13 per cent of women in prison were serving sentences for drug offences'. Although the figures vary from year to year this amounts to approximately 10,000–11,000 people Within this group are a growing (until last year) number of foreign national prisoners who number approximately 10,000–12,000 of the prison population. Around 30 per cent of their number are convicted of drug offences, often with high tariffs (over five years) with women in particular over-represented (approximately 50 per cent; Banks 2011). This is despite the repeated research evidence which shows women are most likely to be the most vulnerable and exploited parts of drug trafficking organisations; their imprisonment is unlikely to disrupt them (Bean 2002; Green, 1996).

Finally, critics allege that the impact of the UK's drug policy falls disproportionately on ethnic minorities. Whilst the scale of disproportionality is not of the same scale as that outlined by critics of the US (Wacquant 2009), it is worth mentioning here. For example, a study reviewing police stop and searches published in 2009 revealed that 'black people were, in other words, 6.3 times more likely to be stopped and searched for drugs than white people', with lesser but still significantly more searches occurring for other ethnicities (Asian people were 2.5 times more likely to be stopped; Release 2011: 1). The issues of sentencing are picked up in annual reports published by the Ministry of Justice. Although the figures are not as stark as those outlined above, it is the case that in the sentencing of both Class A and Class B drugs, a higher proportion of white offenders received conditional discharges compared to other ethnic groups. The proportional difference is less stark than the police stop and search figures but still ranges from between 5 and 9 per cent. Finally, although the figures are small, caution is advised, it is the case that Black and Asian offenders had higher custody rates for production, supply and intent to supply offences (Ministry of Justice 2015: 92).

12.5 Drug policy in the Netherlands

The story of contemporary drug policy in the Netherlands starts with the passing of the 1976 Opium Act. This amendment confirmed the distinction between 'hard' and 'soft' drugs, suggested in a 1972 report by a government 'Working Group on Narcotic Drugs'. This fundamental split continues today and the Dutch government maintains there are two types of illegal drugs. Schedule 1 lists the substances classified as hard drugs, for example: heroin; cocaine; amphetamine; ecstasy; and GHB. Schedule II specifies the substances classified as soft drugs: cannabis products (hash and marijuana); and sleeping pills and sedatives such as Valium and Seresta (Government of the Netherlands 2016). It is the Dutch approach to soft drugs, described currently as 'toleration', which has attracted the most critical attention and will be explored first.

The toleration of soft drugs, in particular cannabis, was the product of a public health approach to drug use which attempted to regulate the market in illegal drugs which first, in the late 1960s, saw a surge in middle class cannabis use, whilst later, in the late 1980s, a rapid increase in heroin use. The government, mindful of EU and UN stipulations which meant legalisation was out of the question, wanted to separate the drug markets and regulate them as much as possible (Pakes and Silverstone 2012). The advantages of regulation are threefold. Customers ought to be able to buy the product from a legal supplier, reducing the strain on the criminal justice system. Second, the quality of the product can be regulated. Third, the regulation of the market can lead to greater transparency and monitoring by the government (Spapens, 2012; Spapens et al. 2014). The policy, although not legalising the use, sale or cultivation of cannabis, means that in small quantities the use, growth or sale of the drug is only a misdemeanour and not one which is enforced by the police or courts. In practice, one of the most significant innovations that has followed from this

James Morgan and Daniel Silverstone

decision is the licensing of coffee shops, where although alcohol is not sold, cannabis is. These have numbered in their thousands, although are now in their hundreds, and are tolerated as safe places where cannabis can be bought away from the predations of unlicensed multi-commodity drug dealers.

In the context of prohibitionist policies throughout Europe, it is remarkable that they still exist, but they do, with growing restrictions over time. Although opinion polls show sustained support for coffee shops from the Dutch public, their relative success has led to issues relating to both supply and demand (McDonald-Gibson 2014). First, in relation to supply, a sizeable and lucrative market for cannabis could not be met by small growers tolerated by the Dutch government. Instead, established criminals started to operate with the concurrent violent disputes expected in illegal markets. As a result, there have been several resource intensive proactive attempts by the police to target the large scale cultivators of cannabis. Second, the demand for cannabis has not been limited to Dutch citizens. Their European neighbours, including the British, gravitated in large numbers to Dutch cities, especially those close to the Belgian and French border. Consequently, areas in the vicinity of coffee shops were subject to large numbers of international drug 'tourists' and drug importers which in turn led to more types of drugs being traded and issues of social nuisance (Spapens 2012).

The response has been to impose restrictions on the numbers of coffee shops, most straightforwardly by implementing standard licensing criteria, background checks on owners, by raising the age of entry and by ensuring that they are not located close to schools. More controversial are the attempts to restrict membership to only Dutch citizens. These efforts have resulted in multiple iterations, including a *wiedpass* (a Dutch only membership card) proposed for those allowed to use a coffee shop but subsequently abandoned. This has now been replaced by a ban on non-Dutch buyers,[1] although in Amsterdam, the city with still the most coffee shops, this policy is not enforced and coffee shops continue as before (Pakes and Silverstone 2012; Rolles 2014).

Other notable Dutch policy initiatives relate to Schedule 1 drugs such as heroin and ecstasy. Here the Dutch have implemented harm reduction policies, both before other European countries and in greater numbers than other countries. For example, there are more supervised drug consumption rooms in the Netherlands than anywhere else in Europe (EMCDDA 2015b: 2). These spaces not only provide safe places to consume drugs but also offer other health and social care services. The Dutch also offer recalcitrant and ageing addicts the possibility not just of methadone treatments but also the prescription of pure heroin (Roes 2014).

In relation to ecstasy, which historically and currently is produced in the Netherlands or near its borders, the Dutch approach is complex. As for its supply, there have been determined multi-agency efforts to tackle ecstasy producing groups and restrict precursors; yet there is also a harm reduction approach to its consumption. For example, there are widely available testing facilities for consumers to check the purity of their pills in clinics as well as in night-clubs and dance festivals (EMCDDA 2016; Spapens 2012).

Given the above, it is unsurprising that the Netherlands imprisons fewer people per capita than England, but its drug policy is not without issues of discrimination. In response to persistent drug importation from Latin America, incoming flights from the Netherlands Antilles, Aruba, Venezuela and Suriname arriving at Schiphol airport were subject to '100 per cent controls' with all passengers, their luggage and aircraft being checked (Kleemans, Soudijn and Weenink 2012: 24). This has also led to episodic allegations of discriminatory searches of black passengers at Schiphol airport (Fukushima and Kaplan 2006). It is therefore unsurprising that, although the figures are not as readily available, it seems as if ethnic minorities are more overly represented in Dutch prisons, and foreign nationals even more so, than in the UK (Boone and Swaaningen 2013).

12.6 Conclusion

To conclude, although the UK and the Netherlands have experienced similar illegal drug problems in the course of the last 30 years, their responses have diverged considerably. Ironically, although the UK had a global reputation for a pioneering non-prohibitionist approach to illegal drug control, it is in fact the Netherlands which ought to have this mantel. Today, the two countries, despite their similar issues of financial austerity, experience their drug problems very differently. It seems that the Dutch system still maintains a safe place for recreational hedonism while, as far as possible, the secondary impact of problematic drug use has been contained. In contrast, the UK remains a dangerous place to be taking all types of illegal drugs, whether for pleasure or to contain pain, and drug users need to be wary of the state as well as of the drugs themselves. Unfortunately, with the arrival of NPS, rather than swapping good practice, it looks as if the paths of the UK and the Netherlands are set to diverge even further.

Note

1 This ban was challenged as discriminatory but was upheld by the Dutch courts, who based their arguments on a European Court of Justice ruling in 2010 in which judges said the ban was justified by the objective of combating drug tourism and reducing public nuisance.

Bibliography

Ayres, T. and Jewkes, Y. (2012) The haunting spectacle of crystal meth: A media-created mythology? *Crime Media Culture*, 8(3): 315–32.
Banks, J. (2011) Foreign national prisoners in the UK: explanations and implications. *The Howard Journal of Criminal Justice*, 50(2): 184–98. Available at http://shura.shu.ac.uk/6803/1/Banks_Foreign_National_Prisoners.pdf, accessed 1.2.2016.
Barber, S. (2015) *The Psychoactive Substances Bill 2015*. London: House of Commons Library. Available at http://researchbriefings.parliament.uk/ResearchBriefing/Summary/CBP-7334, accessed 10.2.2016.

James Morgan and Daniel Silverstone

Bean, P. (2002) *Drugs and Crime*. Cullompton: Willan.

Becker, H. (1953) Becoming a marijuana user. *American Journal of Sociology*, 59(3): 235–43.

Bennett, T. and Holloway, K. (2007) *Drug–Crime Connections. Cambridge Studies in Criminology*. Cambridge: Cambridge University Press.

Bennett, T. and Holloway, K. (2010) Is UK drug policy evidence based? *International Journal of Drug Policy*, 21(5): 411–17.

Bennett. T. H. and Holloway, K. (2012) The impact of take-home naloxone distribution and training on opiate overdose knowledge and response: An evaluation of the THN project in Wales. *Drugs: Education, Prevention & Policy*, 19(4): 320–8.

Boone, M. and Swaaningen, R. (2013) Regression to the mean: Punishment in the Netherlands. In V. Ruggiero and M. Ryan (eds) *Punishment in Europe: A Critical Anatomy of Penal Systems*. London: Palgrave, pp. 9–32.

Briggs, D. (2013) *Crack Cocaine Users. High Society and Low Life in South London*. London: Routledge.

Caulkins, J. P. and Kleiman, M. A. R. (2011) Drugs and crime. In Michael Tonry (ed.) *Oxford Handbook of Crime and Criminal Justice*. Oxford: Oxford University Press, pp. 275–320.

CPS (2016) Victims and witnesses: Going to court: Sentencing. Available at www.cps.gov.uk/victims_witnesses/going_to_court/sentencing.html, accessed 19.2.2016.

Economist (2014) Hoffman's habit: How to make heroin less deadly. Available at www.economist.com/news/united-states/21595963-how-make-heroin-less-deadly-hoffmans-habit, accessed 1.2.2016.

EMCDDA (2012) Methods and definitions. Available at www.emcdda.europa.eu/stats07/PDU/methods, accessed 19.2.16.

EMCDDA (2015a) *European Drug Report: Trends and Developments*. Available at www.emcdda.europa.eu/system/files/publications/974/TDAT15001ENN.pdf, accessed 19.2.2016.

EMCDDA (2015b) *Perspectives on Drugs: Drug Consumption Rooms: An Overview of Provision and Evidence*. Available at www.emcdda.europa.eu/topics/pods/drug-consumption-rooms, accessed 21.1.17.

EMCDDA (2015c) Prevalence of drug use > Cannabis > Lifetime prevalence (%) > All adults (15-64). Available at www.emcdda.europa.eu/data/stats2015, accessed 10.2.2016.

EMCDDA (2015d) Harm reduction overview for the Netherlands. Available at www.emcdda.europa.eu/country-data/harm-reduction/Netherlands, accessed 1.2.2016.

EMCDDA (2016) Recent changes in Europe's MDMA/ecstasy market: Results from an EMCDDA trendspotter study, April 2016.

Frijns, T. and van Laar, M. (2013) Amphetamine, ecstasy and cocaine: Typology of users, availability and consumption estimates. In F. Trautmann, B. Kilmer and P. Turnbull (eds) *Further Insights into Aspects of the EU Illicit Drugs Market*. Luxembourg: Publications Office of the European Union.

Available at http://ec.europa.eu/justice/anti-drugs/files/eu_market_full.pdf, accessed 21.1.2017.

Fukushima, A. and Kaplan, D. (2006) Guilty until proven innocent: Racial profiling at Schiphol Airport. Available at www.humanityinaction.org/knowledgebase/146-guilty-until-proven-innocent-racial-profiling-at-schiphol-airport, accessed 10.2.2016.

Global Drug Survey (GDS) (2014) Available at www.globaldrugsurvey.com/facts-figures/theglobal-drug-survey-2014-findings/, accessed 18.7.2014.

Goldacre, B. (2009) Bad science: A blueprint for how not to do research. *The Guardian* 13 June 2009. Available at www.theguardian.com/science/2009/sep/19/bad-science-blueprint-school-drugs, accessed 10.2.2016.

Government of the Netherlands (2016) Toleration policy regarding soft drugs and coffee shops. Available at www.government.nl/topics/drugs/contents/toleration-policy-regarding-soft-drugs-and-coffee-shops, accessed 1.2.2016.

Green, P. (1996) *Drug Couriers: A New Perspective.* London: The Howard League.

Harocopos, A., Dennis, D., Turnbull, P., Parsons, J. and Hough, M. (2003) *On the Rocks: A Follow-up Study of Crack Users in London.* London: Criminal Policy Research Unit.

Hay, G., dos Santos, A. R. and Worsley, R. (2014) *Estimates of the Prevalence of Opiate Use and/or Crack Cocaine Use, 2011/12: Sweep 8 Report.* Liverpool: John Moores University, Centre for Public Health. Available at www.nta.nhs.uk/uploads/estimates-of-the-prevalence-of-opiate-use-and-or-crack-cocaine-use-2011-12.pdf, accessed 19.2.2016.

Hayes, P. (2015) Elitism is what unites Russell Brand and Iain Duncan Smith on drug policy. Available at http://theconversation.com/elitism-is-what-unites-russell-brand-and-iain-duncan-smith-on-drug-policy-36813, accessed 10.2.2016.

Home Office (1985) *Tackling Drug Misuse: A Summary of the Government's Strategy.* London: Home Office.

Home Office (1986) *Tackling Drug Misuse: A Summary of the Government's Strategy 2nd edition.* London: Home Office.

Home Office (1998) *Tackling Drugs to Build a Better Britain: The Government's 10-Year Strategy for Tackling Drug Misuse.* London: The Stationery Office. Available at www.archive.official-documents.co.uk/document/cm39/3945/3945.htm, accessed 10.2.2016.

Home Office (2002) *Updated Drug Strategy 2002.* London: Home Office. Available at www.erpho.org.uk/Download/Public/8342/1/updated-drug-strategy-2002.pdf, accessed 10.2.2016.

Home Office (2010) *A Change To The Misuse Of Drugs Act 1971: Control of Mephedrone and Other Cathinone Derivatives.* London: Home Office. Available at www.gov.uk/government/publications/a-change-to-the-misuse-of-drugs-act-1971-control-of-mephedrone-and-other-cathinone-derivatives, accessed 10.2.2016.

Home Office (2011) Temporary banning powers factsheets. London: Home Office. Available at www.gov.uk/government/publications/temporary-banning-powers-factsheets, accessed 10.2.2016.

James Morgan and Daniel Silverstone

Honenbrink, L., Nugteren-van Lonkhuyzen, J., Van Der Gouwe, D. and Brunt, T. M. (2015) Monitoring new psychoactive substances (NPS) in The Netherlands: Data from the drug market and the Poisons Information Centre. *Drug and Alcohol Dependence*, 147: 109–15.

Kilmer, B., Taylor, J., Hunt, P. and McGhee, P. (2013) Sizing national heroin markets in the EU: Insights from self–reported expenditures in the Czech Republic and England. In F. Trautmann, B. Kilmer and P. Turnbull (eds) *Further Insights into Aspects of the EU Illicit Drugs Market*. Luxumbourg: European Commission. Available at http://ec.europa.eu/justice/anti-drugs/files/eu_market_full.pdf, accessed 19.2.2016.

Kleemans, E., Soudijn, M. and Weenink, A. (2012) Situational crime prevention and cross-border crime. In K. Bullock, R. Clarke and N. Tilley (eds) *Situational Prevention of Organised Crimes*. London: Routledge, pp. 17–35.

Lader, D. (2015) *Drug Misuse: Findings from the 2014/15 Crime Survey for England and Wales 2nd Edition*. London: Home Office. Available at www.gov.uk/government/uploads/system/uploads/attachment_data/file/462885/drug-misuse-1415.pdf, accessed 19.2.2016.

McDonald-Gibson, C. (2014) Why Dutch mayors want to cultivate cannabis. *The Independent* 3 February. Available at www.independent.co.uk/news/world/europe/why-dutch-mayors-want-to-cultivate-cannabis-9102858.html, accessed 10.2.2016.

McKeganey, N. (2010) *Controversies in Drug Policy*. New York: Palgrave MacMillan.

Measham, F. (2004) Play space: Historical and socio-cultural reflections on drugs, licensed leisure locations, commercialisation and control. *International Journal of Drug Policy*, 15(5): 337–45.

Measham, F., Moore, K., Newcombe, R. and Welch, Z. (2010). Tweaking, bombing, dabbing and stockpiling: The emergence of mephedrone and the perversity of prohibition. *Drugs and Alcohol Today*, 10(1): 14–21.

Ministry of Justice (2015) Statistics on Race and the Criminal Justice System 2014. A Ministry of Justice publication under Section 95 of the Criminal Justice Act 1991. Available at www.gov.uk/government/uploads/system/uploads/attachment_data/file/480250/bulletin.pdf, accessed 1.2.2016.

Morgan, N. (2014) The heroin epidemic of the 1980s and 1990s and its effect on crime trends - then and now. Research Report 79. Available at www.gov.uk/government/uploads/system/uploads/attachment_data/file/332952/horr79.pdf, accessed 10.2.2015.

Moyle, L. and Coomber, R. (2015) Earning a score: An exploration of the nature and roles of heroin and crack cocaine user-dealers. *British Journal of Criminology*, 55(3): 534–55.

Nutt, D. (2010) Lessons from the mephedrone ban. *The Guardian* 28 May. Available at: www.theguardian.com/commentisfree/2010/may/28/mephedrone-ban-drug-classification, accessed 21.1.2017.

Nutt, D., King, L. A. and Blakemore, C. (2007) Development of a rational scale to assess the harm of drugs of potential misuse. *The Lancet*, 24; 369 (9566): 1047–53.

ONS (Office for National Statistics) (2016) Deaths related to drug poisoning in England and Wales, 2015 registrations. Available at www.ons.gov.uk/peoplepopulationandcommunity/birthsdeathsandmarriages/deaths/bulletins/deathsrelatedtodrugpoisoninginenglandandwales/previousReleases, accessed 20.10.2016.

Pakes, F. and Silverstone, D. (2012) Cannabis in the global market: A comparison between the UK and the Netherlands. *International Journal of Law, Crime and Justice*, 40(1): 20–30.

Parker, H., Bakx, K. and Newcombe, R. (1988) *Living With Heroin*. Milton Keynes: Open University Books.

Pearson, G. (1987) Social deprivation, unemployment and patterns of heroin use. In N. Dorn and N. South (eds) *A Land Fit for Heroin*. Basingstoke: MacMillan Educational, pp. 62–83.

Prison Reform Trust (2014) Prison: the facts. Bromley Briefings Summer 2014. Available at www.prisonreformtrust.org.uk/Portals/0/Documents/Prison%20the%20facts%20May%202014.pdf, accessed 21.1.17.

Release (2011) The numbers in black and white: Ethnic disparities in the policing and prosecution of drug offences in England and Wales. Available at www.release.org.uk/publications/numbers-black-and-white-ethnic-disparities-policing-and-prosecution-drug-offences, accessed 1.2.2016.

Reuter, P. and Stevens, A. (2007) *An Analysis of UK Drug Policy*. London: UK Drug Policy Commission. Available at http://kar.kent.ac.uk/13332/1/analysis_of_UK_drug_policy.pdf, accessed 19.2.16.

Roes, T. (2014) Only in the Netherlands do addicts complain about free government heroin. Available at https://news.vice.com/article/only-in-the-netherlands-do-addicts-complain-about-free-government-heroin, accessed 21.1.2017.

Rolles, S. (2014) Cannabis policy in the Netherlands: Moving forwards not backwards. *Transform: Getting Drugs Under Control*. Available at www.tdpf.org.uk/blog/cannabis-policy-netherlands-moving-forwards-not-backwards, accessed 1.2.2016.

Sandberg, S. (2012) Cannabis culture : A stable subculture in a changing world. *Criminology and Criminal Justice*, 13(1): 63–79.

Sanders, T., O'Neill, M. and Picher, J. (2009) *Prostitution: Sex Work, Policy and Politics*. London: Sage.

Shewan, D. and Dalgarno, P. (2005) Evidence for controlled heroin use? Low levels of negative health and social outcomes among non-treatment heroin users in Glasgow. *British Journal Health Psychology*, 10(1): 33–48.

Spapens, T. (2011) Interaction between criminal groups and law enforcement: The case of ecstasy in the Netherlands. *Global Crime*, 12(1): 19–40.

Spapens, T. (2012) The question of regulating illegal markets: The gambling and cannabis markets in the Netherlands. *Journal of Law and Social Sciences*, 2(1): 30–7.

Spapens, T., Muller, T. and Bunt, H. (2014) The Dutch drug policy from a regulatory perspective. *European Journal of Criminal Research*, 21(1): 191–205.

Stevens, A. (2011) *Drugs, Crime and Public Health: The Political Economy of Drug Policy*. Abingdon: Routledge.

Stimpson, G. V. and Oppenheimer, E. (1982) *Heroin Addiction: Treatment and Control in Britain.* London: Tavistock.

Sumnall, H. R. and Atkinson, A. (2015) The new Psychoactive Substances Bill: A quick introduction. Available at www.cph.org.uk/blog/the-new-psychoactive-substances-bill-a-quick-introduction/, accessed 19.2.2016.

Taylor, A. (1993) *Women Drug Users: An Ethnography of a Female Injecting Community.* Oxford: Oxford University Press.

Ticketmaster (2015) Ticketmaster unveils state of play: Dance music report. Available at http://blog.ticketmaster.co.uk/music/ticketmaster-unveils-state-of-play-dance-music-report-19650, accessed 1.2.2016.

Trautmann, F. (2013) Exploring trends in the illicit drugs market and drug policy responses in the EU. In F. Trautmann, B. Kilmer and P. Turnbull (eds) *Further Insights into Aspects of the EU Illicit Drugs Market.* Luxembourg: European Commission. Available at http://ec.europa.eu/justice/anti-drugs/files/eu_market_full.pdf, accessed 19.2.2016.

Trautmann, F. and Frijns T. (2013) Exploring heroin consumption. In F. Trautmann, B. Kilmer and P. Turnbull (eds) *Further Insights into Aspects of the EU Illicit Drugs Market.* Luxembourg: European Commission. Available at http://ec.europa.eu/justice/anti-drugs/files/eu_market_full.pdf, accessed 19.2.2016.

Trautmann, F. and McSweeney T. (2013) Heroin market: Use characteristics, size of the market and impact of OST on the heroin market. In F. Trautmann, B. Kilmer and P. Turnbull (eds) *Further Insights into Aspects of the EU Illicit Drugs Market.* Luxembourg: European Commission. Available at http://ec.europa.eu/justice/anti-drugs/files/eu_market_full.pdf, accessed 19.2.2016.

Trautmann, F., Kilmer, B. and Turnbull, P. (2013): *Further Insights into Aspects of the EU Illicit Drugs Market.* Luxembourg: European Commission. Available at http://ec.europa.eu/justice/anti-drugs/files/eu_market_full.pdf, accessed 19.2.2016.

van Duyne, P. C. and Levi, M. (2005) *Drugs and Money: Managing the Drug Trade and Crime-Money in Europe.* London: Routledge.

van Laar, M., Frijns, T., Trautmann, F. and Lombi, L. (2013) Cannabis market: User types, availability and consumption estimates. In F. Trautmann, B. Kilmer and P. Turnbull (eds) *Further Insights into Aspects of the EU Illicit Drugs Market.* Luxembourg: European Commission.

Wacquant, L. (2009) *Punishing the Poor.* Durham, NC: Duke University Press.

Warburton, H., Turnbull, P. and Hough, M. (2005) Occasional and controlled heroin use. Not a problem? York: Joseph Rowntree Foundation. Available at www.jrf.org.uk/sites/default/files/jrf/migrated/files/1859354254.pdf, accessed 1.2.2016.

Wincup, E. (2013) *Understanding Crime and Social Policy.* Bristol: Policy Press.

Yates, R. and Malloch, M. (eds) (2010) *Tackling Addiction: Pathways to Recovery.* London: Kingsley.

Zinberg, N. (1984) *Drug, Set and Setting: The Basis for Controlled Intoxicant Use.* New Haven, CT: Yale University Press.

chapter 13

Homosexuality and homophobia in Europe

María E. López

13.1 Introduction

It is illegal to be homosexual in almost 80 countries around the world. In total, more than 2.7 billion people still live under regimes that condemn homosexuality with imprisonment and lashes. In Iran, Mauritania, Nigeria, Saudi Arabia, Somalia (South), Sudan and Yemen, homosexuality is punishable by death (ILGA, 2014). The situation is the opposite in volatile Europe, resulting from endless discussions about gender and sexual equality and about the governments' rights to interfere in the private lives of citizens. Anti-homophobic legal measures and guidelines reflect the institutional commitment in Europe to end homophobia as a social problem and to preserve sexual freedom and free speech.

Although it is not possible to cover in detail here the legal situations of sexual minorities in all European countries, this study shows evidence that the ways in which sexual symbols and meanings are generated and transformed change across nations in Europe. Throughout Europe, culture, power and ethics play decisive roles in the battle for a definition and organisation of negotiated meanings, which connect closely with emotions, bodies and identities. Hence, there is a link between social behaviour and the law. Homosexuality and/or homophobia, depending on the country you look at, are still considered social problems in Europe by conservative ideologies, which collide with those who advocate progressive changes in the debate about sexual rights. The political ambiguity often forces the homosexual community to justify the way in which they live their lives, mainly in regard to the ongoing debate about the legal boundaries to same-sex marriage and child adoption. For example, the UK referendum to leave the European Union materialises the crisis of global identity and insecurity in the country, as well as the scepticism of an extensive part of the British population regarding the politics in favour of social integration. Although migration is a central topic of discussion, politicians, mainly at the core of the Conservative Party, are re-opening the debate on a variety of social topics only a few weeks after the referendum. Such is the case with the legal boundaries to homosexual marriage in the UK, as shown in the press interviews with Theresa May and Andrea Leadsom in their attempts to lead the Conservative Party in July 2016. Precisely the ambiguity on the situation of homosexuals in the UK, as compared to that in Poland, is the object of study in this chapter.

This chapter examines the ideologies behind the construction of homophobia and homosexuality as social problems in two European countries with opposite historical and cultural backgrounds and 'sexual scripts': the UK and Poland. This is because in a collective/global world, sexuality never forms on its own but depends upon collective/international conduct. I use here John Gagnon and William Simon's definition of a 'sexual script' from their hugely influential book *Sexual Conduct: The Social Sources of Human Sexuality* (1973). The book understands sexuality as a combination of fluid meanings organised loosely into scripts that provide guidance of the 'right' sexual identity and who people 'must' feel attracted to versus 'deviant' sexual conduct, where and when people can engage in such conduct, and why they can do so. Scripts are presented as wide open to variations of societies, groups, people and even in the same person. Scripts needs to be examined at the interpersonal level (what people do to each other), psychically (how people come to inhabit their own emotional and symbolic sexual worlds and sexual scripts) and at a wide social level (historical and cultural). This provides the key arguments to distinguish among the interpersonal homophobia (happening at the personal level and in the private sphere of family), institutional homophobia (dictated by the law) and cultural homophobia (dictated by the social environment and related to social construction and common sense) happening in the UK and Poland. Comparing the legal situation for LGBT people in both countries provides a revealing picture of the ways in which ideologies influence the sense of 'sexual others' and of self-defining the body at the national level. For example, institutional homophobia in Poland provokes the social exclusion of a social group and breaks the social cohesion. In the UK, however, there is detailed legislation to fight hidden homophobia rather than homosexuality in school and work. In both places, the existing legislation and public debate prove the need to regulate sexual behaviour and social attitudes towards non-heterosexual identities.

This chapter looks at the devastating impact of homophobic conduct on individuals in the social contexts of work, school and family and to what extent institutionalised homophobia affects individuals to the point of contributing to the development of internalised homophobia. In order to survive institutionalised invisibility, the homosexual is invited to hide their sexual tendency and to pretend to adapt to the norm. In this context, the physical appearance of the individual is the stigma associated with the homosexual. Here, Goffman's theories on spoiled identity and stigma are essential to understand that, in order to gain acceptance (rather than tolerance), homosexuals are driven to hide their 'imperfection' from public view (Goffman, 1963). Extreme cases of homophobia may result in deep isolation for fear of being discovered, causing a devastating effect for the individual regarding their pride and identity. Some people decide to remain hidden (or rather imprisoned) in order to avoid negative experiences. They suffer so-called 'interior exile' at being criminalised and their existence is reduced to invisibility. To discuss the issue of homophobia as a social problem is to discuss visibility in the public sphere as related to the concept of physical appearance. In order to break with it, the excluded individual is entitled to engage in the struggle to be present (and represented) in a society driven by the heteronormative model. Associations acting in defence of sexual equality, for example ILGA and Stonewall, aim to give visibility to sexual discrimination, for instance through the organisation of gay parades, which still entails a problem in some European countries.

I use the terms 'sexual minorities' and 'LGBT people' interchangeably, with the latter being an umbrella term covering a very heterogeneous group of lesbian, gay, bisexual and transgender people, who often feature together as a group in efforts in the local and international political arenas to get better social representation and more political support. I believe that symbolic interactionism provides a grounded understanding of the social life of citizens and of the construction of homosexuality and homophobia as social problems in the European context. The symbolic nature of social life is therefore central to understanding ideologies and attitudes – both homophobic and tolerant – towards sexual freedom in the European context. At the heart of social life lie the processes of language and communication and the ability to identify and thus reject the 'others' at the interpersonal and institutional levels. All human beings dwell in what we call 'otherness' by developing a role-taking ability, acquiring sympathy and empathising with fellow humans. The development of language helps us to define our identities, our bodies and others. This indicates the importance of the role of institutions in the construction of definitions and symbols via, for example, the law.

13.2 Mapping homophobia in Europe

Both the UK and Poland have followed the EU legislation since they became members: the UK in 1973 and Poland in 2004. Things are meant to change in the UK after the referendum to leave the EU. As it stands today, the UK has not modified the legislation on this, although the issue of homosexual marriage is already a topic of discussion among politicians in their competition to lead the Conservative Party. Nevertheless, the implications that the UK exit will have for sexual minorities will be visible after the period of two years required to complete the separation process from the EU. With all that, it is worth noting that the

María E. López

UK will leave the EU but will remain in Europe. Therefore, the current situations of sexual minorities in the UK and Poland need to be analysed in the light of the EU legislation.

The Treaty of Lisbon (2000) expanded the legal basis of the Charter of Fundamental Rights so that the protection of fundamental rights is one of the basic tenets of EU law today. The launch of the Treaty of Lisbon forced the European institutions and treaties to list the fundamental human rights and freedoms for citizens and to refer to those fundamental rights as general principles of community law. The EU Court of Justice has contributed greatly over time to the development of and respect for those fundamental rights. Today, EU scholars and politicians acknowledge social exclusion as the segregation of people from multiple spheres of life and the inability to participate fully in societal life.

Despite the principle of equality and non-discrimination being fundamental in the protection of human rights in the European context, national laws are still ambiguous and inefficient in regard to the protection of the fundamental rights of gays and lesbians across Europe. The laws affecting LGBT people vary by country. In Ukraine, Romania, Bulgaria, Poland and Greece, for instance, same-sex civil unions scarcely confer the rights associated with marriage. In Germany and Austria, civil unions are equal to marriage, but the law is ambiguous in relation to same-sex-couple adoption and there are no protectionist laws against gay hate crime. The situation is worse in Switzerland, where same-sex marriage recognition is made through registered partnership only, adoption for same-sex couples is illegal and there is no protection against hate crime. Spain, the UK, France, Sweden and Norway, among others, recognise same-sex marriage and adoption, although in Sweden the law against gay hate crime is still unclear. In Holland, the situation for LGBT people is quite good, except for the absence of legislation against gay hate crime. In Italy, institutionalised homophobia is incorporated into religious education. In Portugal, there are only some rights against discrimination in the workplace, and adoption by same-sex couples is illegal.

Public authorities and/or counter-demonstrators have often obstructed the fundamental right to freedom of assembly (e.g. gay parades) in a number of EU Member States. Incidents have been reported in Bulgaria, Estonia, Latvia, Poland and Romania. Calls for improving the rights of LGBT people have invariably met with negative responses from some politicians and representatives of religious groups in the Czech Republic, Cyprus, Hungary, Italy and Malta, too. In other Member States, however, LGBT organisations celebrate pride events with the support of government ministers, political parties and even religious organisations. Such is the case with the Netherlands. In 2008, three government ministers and the mayor of Amsterdam participated in the Canal Gay Pride event in Amsterdam. In Sweden, the Minister for EU Affairs opened the 2008 Stockholm Euro Pride event, which attracted more than 80,000 participants. In Spain, the Equality Minister participated in the 2008 Madrid Pride event, together with hundreds of thousands of participants from all over Europe. In France, more than half a million people joined the Paris Gay Pride event in 2008, including the mayor of Paris (ILGA Europe, 2008).

Tendentious laws or simply legal gaps determine the grade of institutional homophobia still happening across Europe. The 2012 European Commission Special Eurobarometer showed that the acceptance of gay, lesbian and bisexual people is higher in Northern and Western Europe, as compared to that in Eastern European countries. The Eurobarometer showed different levels of tolerability among Europeans regarding a LGBT person being appointed to the highest elected political position in their country. Comfort levels were low in Eastern European countries such as Latvia (3.2), Slovakia (3.4), Romania (3.6) and Bulgaria (3.7). On the other side, Denmark (6.4) and Sweden (8.8) scored the highest (European Commission, 2012). The 2014 ILGA Annual Review also denounced new forms of criminalisation of LGBT people through the spread of anti-propaganda laws in Armenia, Belarus, Georgia, Latvia and Ukraine, which are adopting restrictive laws and policies against the human rights of LGBT people (ILGA, 2014).

Most homophobic people in Europe, national surveys report, act out their phobias of gay people in non-violent ways. Relatives may avoid their lesbian and gay family members, co-workers may be distant to homosexual employees or people simply may never ask about homosexual acquaintances' lives. Hidden homophobia spreads across European countries' social environments, including in those countries that often present themselves as leaders in the economic and social fields. A 2007 study in the UK showed that half the respondents would be unhappy about a relative forming a long-term relationship with a transsexual person (Bromley et al., 2007). In Denmark, 53 per cent of respondents, who were men aged between 15 and 24, said that they did not accept (nor tolerate) homosexuality (Sundhedsstyrelsen [The National Board of Health], 2006). A 2006 study showed that 32 per cent of Germans still believed that the sight of two homosexuals kissing was disgusting (Institut für interdisziplinäre Konflikt und Gewaltforschung [IKG], 2006). In Lithuania, 47 per cent of the respondents considered homosexuality an illness that should be treated, 69 per cent did not want homosexuals to work in schools and 50 per cent objected to homosexuals working in the police force (The Market and Opinion Research Centre, 'Vilmorus Ltd', 2006). In Bulgaria, 42 per cent of respondents would not like to have a homosexual as a friend or colleague, and 47 per cent would not accept that their child was homosexual (Sociological Agency Skala, 2007).

These figures provide evidence that the positive politics on social inclusion and against gay hate crime and speech violence are not fully effective in eradicating homophobia in Europe. In the words of Renato Sabbadini, executive director of the ILGA, 'the fact that a country adopts progressive legislation is not necessarily a guarantee of the fact that the lives of LGBT people living in it will improve or cease to experience discrimination and violence' (Ball, 2014). Sabbadini is referring here to the open debate about the effectiveness of anti-homophobia laws in Europe, where heterosexual normativity still works as a stabilising tool that supports the subtle, non-violent but systematic violation of sexual minorities' fundamental rights. It is a matter of concern that this is also happening in the European states with protective and egalitarian legislation in place. Ironically, 'coming out of the closet' in repressive environments makes

María E. López

the stigma of homosexuality visible and throws individuals into suffering invisibility. In this context, to suffer invisibility is to suffer double invisibility. Once an individual has been labelled, the invisibility also becomes physical, as the person is isolated and ignored by former colleagues who deny the individual's existence. The latter has high consequences for the individual, too, who resents society, is isolated and is likely to suffer mental health problems relating to substance abuse, eating disorders, homelessness, depression and suicide.

Like members of other minorities, homosexuals subject to stigmatisation suffer from chronic and acute stress. The mental health problems that may appear among LGBT adults tend to be explained in social or socio-political terms rather than in psychological terms, as they arise largely from the social context. The concepts of 'minority stress' and 'gay-related stress' are often used to tackle the impact of institutional homophobia on the LGBT individual, who is often driven to suffer internalised homophobia, including suicidal thoughts. The mental health services can present additional difficulties for LGBT people, bearing in mind the fact that, until quite recently, psychiatry saw homosexuality as a psychopathology; some doctors and therapists still subscribe to this vision.

13.3 Hidden homophobia in Britain

Being gay in Britain (as in most of the Western world) is to live a gender, sexuality and identity within cultural borders. Culture, power and ethics in the UK help in the construction of emotions, bodies and selves. Until roughly 30 years ago, the meanings of gayness were a major concern in the construction of British culture, as the norms regulating gender and sexuality were sealed into heterosexuality and family only. Indeed, to 'come out' in Britain in most parts of the twentieth century was to recognise a crime, sickness and pathology. Homosexuals had no place and no visibility in the cultural world, and gay culture was a taboo pushed to the extreme borders of society (Weeks, 1977). By the start of the twenty-first century, 'gayness' had come out from this underground position and blossomed into new lifestyles and cultures. Plummer refers to the shift as follows:

> cabinet ministers became openly gay, television mainstreamed gay, and Elton John, superstar, could arrive openly at Princess Diana's funeral with his boyfriend. For those who would wish to look, gay culture is now everywhere to be seen. From being 'the love that dared not speak its name', it has now become a veritable Tower of Babel! It is part of British culture!
> (Plummer, 2000)

Today, UK legislation presents homophobia (rather than homosexuality) as a social problem. Legal advances regarding sexual equality have provided LGBT people with rights regarding marriage, adoption and protection from hate crime and violent speech. The figures show that British society seems to be sensitive towards sexual equality and tolerant towards non-heterosexual scripts. British society demands legal action to reduce public prejudice and hidden homophobia against sexual minorities in the country, including that inflicted against migrants escaping from sexual harassment in their homelands. Charities like the UK Lesbian & Gay Immigration Group (UKLGIG) promote equality and dignity for LGBT people who seek asylum in the UK or who wish to immigrate to join their same-sex partner.

A 'YouGov' 2012 report showed, for instance, that two in five people believed that none of the main political parties – the Conservatives, Labour and the Liberal Democrats – are truly gay-friendly (Stonewall, 2012a). More than half of the respondents demanded more in this regard. Seven in ten people believed that Great Britain must lead the struggle against homophobia abroad, too. The report shows that, regardless of the legislation in place, 6 per cent of British people of working age (2.4 million people of working age) have witnessed verbal homophobic bullying at work in the last five years, and 2 per cent (800,000 people of working age) have seen physical homophobic bullying at work. These may not seem high numbers in terms of percentages, but the real figures are worrying. In December 2014, London Metropolitan Police reported that hate crimes targeting the LGBT community rose to as many as 100 cases a month, with a monthly increase of 21.5 per cent since March 2014. In June of the same year, 175 cases of homophobic crime were reported, and hate crime aimed at transgender people had risen to 86.2 per cent (Gander, 2014).

Likewise, LGBT British people claim that they are victims of what I will refer to as hidden homophobia in the labour environment when they are not promoted, are dismissed, feel ostracised, feel isolated or are subject to unwanted and moralising advice. This manifests in several social environments in the UK. Given the legislation in place, these events occur in a subtle way and within a legal framework so that they cannot be reported. More than one in three people believe that employers are responsible for tackling it (Stonewall, 2012a).

Britons perceive religion as one area where LGBT people are most likely to hide their sexual orientation and suffer hidden homophobia. For most of history, religions have laid out codes, commandments and ways of living for societies to observe. Humanitarian as they often are in providing a code of values on how to live a proper life, religious views are also indications of hate in marking out the despised sexual other. In most of these early codes, same-sex relations were strongly condemned. In the UK, over the past two decades, the leaders of the Anglican Church, the Roman Catholic Church, the Evangelical Alliance and other Christian organisations have opposed at every stage the comprehensive equality legislation on sexual orientation and gender identity brought in by governments. Cardinal Keith O'Brien, president of the Bishops' Conference of Scotland and Britain's most senior Catholic, made deeply offensive comments on all attempts to redefine marriage for the whole of society at the 'behests of a small minority of activists'. He labelled gay marriage a 'grotesque subversion of a universally accepted human right' (O'Brien, 2012). Stonewall (2012b) shows, however, that the mentality of people of faith in Britain is quite different from that of their leaders. Three in five respondents supported the government's

María E. López

decision to extend civil marriage to same-sex couples, and four in five believed that LGBT people should be able to express their sexual orientations in all circumstances.

Hidden homophobia happens in UK schools, too. According to the Stonewall Education Guide (Stonewall, 2012b), almost nine in ten secondary school teachers and half of primary school teachers said that pupils in their schools had experienced homophobic bullying. The report also shows that nine in ten secondary school teachers and seven in ten primary schools had heard pupils use expressions like 'that's so gay' and 'you're so gay' in a derogatory manner and terms like 'poof', 'faggot', 'dyke' and 'queer'. Regarding the curriculum, a third of secondary school teachers said that they do not address issues of sexual orientation in the classroom. The fact that the school curriculum omits LGBT issues can be taken as a means of discrimination in itself. Fewer than one in five secondary school teachers said that their school stocks library books and information about homosexuality. In the same vein, very few teachers said that they had received specific training on tackling homophobic bullying (Stonewall, 2012a). The lack of visibility of the issue of homosexuality in schools in the UK is striking if you take into account the fact that they have the duty to prevent and tackle all forms of bullying, including homophobia.

Overall, the data above provides evidence that homosexuals live in a relatively good situation in the UK, especially if we compare it with other European countries. It also shows, however, that despite the preventive legal measures against homophobia, social exclusion and homophobia still constitute social problems and a source of concern for the UK government. Action has been taken in this regard. For example, in January 2015, it was announced that the first specialist state school in Britain for lesbian, gay, bisexual and transgender young people would open its doors within the next three years in the centre of Manchester. The school plans to take 40 full-time students from across the area and will offer up to 20 part-time places for young people who want to continue attending a mainstream school. 'This is about saving lives', said Amelia Lee, strategic director for LGBT Youth North West.

> Despite the laws that claim to protect gay people from homophobic bullying, the truth is that in schools especially, bullying is still incredibly common and causes young people to feel isolated and alienated, which often leads to truanting and, in the worst-case scenarios, to suicide.
>
> (Hill, 2015)

These sorts of legal actions against homophobia result from a long process of reflection and dialogue on the social meanings and borders of sexual rights in the UK – especially those that focus on women's rights, transgender movements and homophile/queer movements – as well as on the way sexuality is presented to society. The gay movement had its antecedents in the Stonewall riots against the New York police in 1969 and the Gay Liberation Front (GLF) that took place in London in 1970. Without such movements, no rights could be claimed. However, like all social movements, it did not arrive overnight. One cannot leave aside the enormous (although slightly belated) contribution from the sociology of sexuality to the process of legalising and accepting homosexuals in the social portrait of the country.

Symbolic interactionists – such as Mead and Goffman – have referred to the process of 'being attuned to the other' as being encompassed by role taking. Hence, understanding the other's situation and needs demands effective communication and 'a moral imagination': the capacity to empathise with others and to see the possibilities for ethical actions. I argue that UK anti-homophobic politics result from the existence of 'a moral imagination', understood as the dialogue between LGBT people and 'the others' (i.e. non-queer people and institutions, which are also representative of more-conservative and hetero-sexual social sectors). Growing out from the 1990s politics of gender and sexual equalities, the UK law developed ideas like intimate citizenship, which makes reference to the citizen's right to choose their partner, their sexual orientation or to have a child or not (Plummer, 2003). The law in the UK provides the right shelter for a citizen to make choices in this regard in their personal life without fear of breaking the moral norms of society. Hence, the limits between the private and the public sphere are far apart. The private sphere, the UK law implies, is not the jurisdiction of the justice system. The idea of intimate citizenship also raises the issue as to whether society can ever allow for radical, transgressive, dissident or queer citizens and invites reflection on the meaning of being radical, transgressive or queer. It also challenges the social construction of stigma and 'the normal' as a whole set of negative stereotypes associated with homosexuality (Goffman, 1963; Herek, 1998).

In spite of the rise in homophobic attacks in London in 2014, the work to do in schools and, above all, the uncertainty in regard to policies to preserve social justice for the homosexual community, we can conclude that the UK is one of the most advanced European countries in the fight against homophobia. In other areas of the continent, LGBT people must survive high levels of social prejudice and legal mechanisms that encourage the social exclusion of the so-called 'bad gays'. Such is the case with Poland, as we shall see next.

13.4 Heteronormativity and 'the other' in Poland

Life is not easy for homosexuals in Poland, where 96 per cent of the population identify as Catholics and where ethnic and racial minorities only represent 2 per cent of society. The Catholic Church became a source of influence in Polish politics after the fall of socialism in 1989. Poland became an EU Member State in May 2004, five years after joining NATO and 15 years after the end of communist rule. Like in the UK, the lack of visibility is key to tackling the construction of homosexuality (rather than homophobia) as a social problem in Poland. In spite of the minor advances made in recent years, the Polish Constitution, passed in 1997, clearly defines marriage as a union between a man and a woman and ignores all evidence on the existence of homophobic conduct. The open dialogue on the Holocaust has made it unacceptable to make anti-Semitic comments in public. Unfortunately, no such taboo exists when it comes to homosexuality, which is seen as a social problem, a stigma, a dysfunction, a deviation from the norm and a threat against the 'appropriate' moral values of the country, which are very much sustained in a traditional heterosexual family model. The social norms surrounding family in Poland strongly encourage heterosexual marital cohesion as a stable union that ensures stability and pro-creation (Aleksandra *et al.*, 2007). Like in the UK, the lack of sexual education in Polish schools leads to misunderstandings about the fundamental nature of sexual orientation. The idea of granting LGBT people specific civic rights is relatively new in Poland and is often perceived as a form of privilege.

In the late 1990s, homosexuals in Poland began to fight invisibility in a more active way by engaging in unauthorised parades and marches. Participants faced physical and verbal harassment from both counter-demonstrators and police. The milestone was set by the 2001 Equality Parade, the first in the history of Poland, where LGBT people demanded recognition and legal equality for a community labelled as a social problem. The situation escalated in 2005, when the president of Warsaw, Lech Kaczynski, made the parade illegal. People gathered, though, and the police (at the order of Ryszard Kalisz, the then Minister of Interior Affairs in the Democratic Left Alliance government) pro-tected the demonstration. From 2005 to 2007, harsh anti-homosexual resent-ment entered the political sphere through conservative/nationalistic/populist coalition governments. In 2007, one of the ministers from the League of Polish Families accused homosexual activists of pederasty, and the ex-president Lech Kaczynski attacked what he called 'the homosexual culture' and suggested that widespread homosexuality would mean the end of human life as we know it. In March 2011, the ruling Civic Platform Party had to suspend one MP, Robert Wegrzyn, for saying he opposed gay marriage 'but wouldn't mind watching lesbians' (Pidd, 2011).

Paradoxically, Krystian Legierski, a lawyer, social activist and proprietor of gay clubs in Poland, believes that the rhetoric of hate and discrimination has been so extravagant and ridiculous that it has uncovered the absurdity of homophobia: 'It doesn't mean we shouldn't care about them, because they're well organised. But for now, they lose' (Gray, 2011). Indeed, something has changed in Poland in the last few years. Since the time when gay rights marches were banned in Warsaw, a growing acceptance of LGBT people has arrived hand in hand with a flourishing economy. The visibility of homosexuals has increased in Poland. The Polish media has played an important role in supporting the LGBT movement by, for example, producing articles and opinion pieces that condemn the homophobic rhetoric used by politicians. In 2011, Robert Biedron made history in Poland for being the country's first publicly gay parliamentarian. In December 2014, he became the first homosexual mayor in the country. The 38-year-old's political successes are a marker of how quickly this deeply con-servative and Catholic country has changed in the decade since it joined the EU. Following what the Polish media calls 'the Biedron effect', a record number of candidates came out publicly before the 2014 local elections (Associated Press in Warsaw, 2014). None won seats, but gay rights activists were hugely encouraged by the willingness of more and more public figures to 'come out'. Whether this was a result of growing understanding and acceptance of LGBT issues in Poland or simply a reaction against the current government is unclear at this point. In all cases, the situation for LGBT people in Poland has a long way to go before it catches up with the rest of Europe.

Poles consider homosexuality a private matter: a view possibly inherited from a recent communist past. Unlike in the UK, the limits between the public and private spheres in Poland are blurred, so the government enjoys the right to interfere in the most-intimate questions of citizenship, like the borders of the 'right' sexual orientation and identity. This explains the big impact caused by a coalition government that supports the idea of a strong heterosexual citizen with a strong sense of national identity: the perceived best defence tool against the external, destabilising influence. In this view, the ideal Polish citizen is an active and 'normal' heterosexual who obeys the 'correct' option. This is why homosexuality (rather than homophobia, like in the UK) is presented as a social problem in Poland, resulting in a cul-de-sac for sexual minorities, who have to survive the ongoing risks of social exclusion, isolation and (in extreme cases) mental health problems.

Kinga Dunin, a renowned feminist and columnist for the *Gazeta Wyborcza*, agrees that the roots of homophobia rely on the morals associated with the heteronormative model widely enhanced by communism for decades. However, what is specific to Poland, in her view, is the way in which right-wing populist parties use homophobia as a political tool. Homosexuals seem to be considered a new common enemy against whom society might unite (Baranowska, 2008). The issue of sexual rights is used to exemplify the negative consequences that challenging the social norms can have in Poland. This explains the significantly paradoxical situation for homosexuals in Poland. Derrida's (1976) binary logic of the supplementary explains it well. He suggests that the evaluation of social minorities is established across difference so that what appears to be outside the norm is well inside it. Considering this in the context of Poland, the definition of homosexuality (i.e. the 'incorrect' option) validates the definition of heterosexuality (i.e. the 'correct' choice). A heterosexual Pole male is mainly defined in opposition to what he is not: that is to say, an effeminate homosexual.

The implications of this concept are enormous at the social level. Polish institutions present sexual minorities as inexistent identities, and society pretends that they do not exist. As in other European countries, Poles act out their phobias of LGBT people by being distant to them or simply by never asking about their lives. Reflecting on the implications of the discursive construction of homosexuality in Victorian times, Foucault (1978) says that homosexuals did not exist before they were labelled as such (although homosexual practices did, of course). For him, the impact of jurisprudence and literature on defining the species and subspecies of homosexuality, pederasty and even 'psychic hermaphroditism' enhanced the opposite discourse. Hence, homosexuals began to speak in their own name, demanding their legitimacy and recognition by using the same terminology and categories that discredited them medically (Foucault, 1980). The Polish government presents homosexuals as having

María E. López

identities that threaten the stability of the country, hence causing the social problem label. At the same time, the government claims that homosexuality does not exist – as much as British people pretend homophobia does not exist. However, the attempt to silence and control sexual activists, with the excuse of acting in defence of the stability of the country, contains a contradiction in itself. The social resistance to suppressing homophobia ultimately proves that the notions of sexuality and homophobia constitute an issue of concern in European countries, as we will see next.

13.5 Social science, (homo)sexuality and visibility in Europe

Sexual rights have moved through certain phases, histories and stages in Europe towards what is called 'the globalisation of sexuality' (Plummer, 2003), which places the topics of sexuality at the centre of debate in the European political and social arenas in the twenty-first century. All evidence of clashing between traditional moralities and progressive changes causes commotion in the public opinion and the media in regard to the issue of sexual rights (Hunter, 1990). An example of this is the enormous controversy caused in the international press by an ex-football player from Aston Villa (Premier League), Thomas Hitzlsperger, revealing his homosexuality in a journal article in January 2014 (Honigstein, 2014). Hitzlsperger's case brought into light the fact that homosexuals hide their sexual orientation among the football elite and keep silent about homophobic harassment for fear of losing their jobs. *Der Spiegel* went directly to the point in its article 'Hidden Homophobia: Is Germany Really as Liberal as It Seems?', revealing conservative and restrictive social attitudes in Germany regarding the acceptance of homosexuality (Kistner *et al.*, 2014). The 'coming out of the closet' of Hitzlsperger is only one example that sexuality and homophobia constitute an issue of concern for Western European society.

Other than small contributions, sociologists ignored the topic of human sexuality for most of the twentieth century. Max Weber devoted some time to writing about the rationalisation of love, the Chicago School made some small forays into the sexual underworld of that city, and Kingsley Davis looked at the meanings of prostitution. In 1952, the *Diagnostic and Statistical Manual of Mental Disorders* labelled homosexuality as a mental problem. Hence, until the 1970s, the term 'deviance' was profusely used as a means to define those stigmatised individuals who did not accommodate the heterosexual norm. Things reversed when the psychologist George Weinberg pointed at homophobia (rather than homosexuality), sexual offenders and hostile attitudes as problems worthy of scholarly analysis and political intervention in his book *Society and the Healthy Homosexual* (1972). 'I would never consider a patient healthy unless he has overcome the prejudice against homosexuality', Weinberg wrote (ibid.). These theories meant a dramatic shift in how the fields of medicine, mental health and behavioural science have looked at homosexuality since then. These were the first steps towards a new perspective on the construction of sexual minorities under the prevalence of the heterosexual norm.

In the 1970s and 1980s, ethnographers started documenting life in gay and lesbian communities. Political sociologists pulled lessons from gay and lesbian movements and started researching the impact of sexuality-based discrimination. Survey researchers proved the prevalence of both anti-gay sentiments and non-normative sexual practices. Throughout the 1990s, the sociology of sexuality aimed to show evidence that 'sexual meanings, identities, and categories were inter-subjectively negotiated social and historical products' (Epstein, 1996). By the mid-1990s, queer theorists like Judith Butler and Eve Sedgwick had invited scholars to contest traditional heteronormativity and to scrutinise sexuality as a discursively produced, unstable and arbitrary mean: the result of fluidity and betweenness (Butler, 1993, 2004; Sedgwick, 1990). They blamed society and history for the negative effects they caused on perceptions, interactions and outcomes regarding sexuality in the world. Queer theory resulted in a new sociology of gender and sexuality that helped to build awareness of the inequalities experienced by subordinate groups (e.g. women and homosexuals, among others). During the 1990s, theorists also moved towards the development of ideas around sexual and reproductive rights and their links to citizenship. David Evans' *Sexual Citizenship* (1993) pioneered the theoretical discussion of these ideas, whilst international campaigning started attempts to establish gender and sexual rights on world agendas through the work of the United Nations, the World Women's Movement, UNICEF and the International Lesbian and Gay Movement, among others (Weeks, 1998; Richardson, 2000; Plummer, 2003).

Today, the relationship between sexual identity and politics is undeniable, with the study of sexuality and homophobia (on the basis of Weinberg's approach) being fundamental areas in the study of emotions (Stets and Turner, 2007; Nardi and Schneider, 1998). The centrality of the concept of phobia provides a model for conceptualising (through legal discourse) a variety of reproving attitudes in relation to sexual discrimination, for example lesbophobia, biphobia, transphobia, effeminophobia, heterophobia and AIDS-phobia (early in the AIDS epidemic, to characterise the stigma attached to HIV).

During the last decade, the globalisation concept has imposed a liberal ideology on the legal and social construction of sexuality in Europe. Back in 1934, Mead determined the ways in which identity shifts towards a 'generalised other' whose existence fits in with the international twenty-first-century global model (i.e. global markets, global means, global governments, global cultures and global individuals):

> We are realising ourselves as members of a larger community. The vivid nationalism of the present should, in the end, call out for an international attitude of the large community . . . If we assert our rights, we are calling for a definite response just because they are rights that are universal – a response which everyone should, and perhaps will, give.

> (Mead, 1934)

The struggles over sexual rights nowadays take place not only in national arenas but also in global ones.

María E. López

13.6 Conclusion

Being part of Europe involves participating in universalising attitudes, emergent global flows and what has now become the European global standard of human rights. We see it embodied in the work of many NGOs, like ILGA and Stonewall, and in the work of the European Parliament. The long socialist/communist past (1945–89) makes things complicated for Poland, where gay rights were invisible and hardly articulated until quite recently and are now starting to 'find a voice'. Although there is work to do in the prevention of homophobia, the UK is today one of the most advanced countries regarding legal protection for sexual minorities. There is uncertainty on what will happen in the near future of the country away from the EU.

There is consensus that the European Parliament gets involved in the struggle against homophobia beyond the production of reports and the adoption of resolutions and amendments. The limitations for the European Parliament regarding interfering in the national politics of Member States are key here, as these limitations make the institution's tasks difficult. Despite the good will at the continental level, discrimination, harassment and hate crime against LGBT people still happen in most of Europe, often in countries that define themselves to be avant-garde when it comes to the LGBT social movement. A lot of work remains to be done in the establishment of legal and equalitarian coverage for LGBT people in the European context so that homosexuality is not perceived as a social problem. The process must take on a dialogue on the legitimacy of governments in regulating sexual identity, the borders between the public and private spheres, and, ultimately, the rights of all citizens to enjoy social inclusion.

Bibliography

Aleksandra, M., Downing, L. and Lieser, J., 2007. 'Hate in the headlines: Media reactions to homophobic rhetoric in Poland', *Humanity in Action*. www.humanityinaction.org/knowledgebase/164-hate-in-the-headlines-media-reactions-to-homophobic-rhetoric-in-poland, accessed July 2016.

Associated Press in Warsaw, 2014. 'Poland elects its first openly gay mayor', *The Guardian*, 1 December. www.theguardian.com/world/2014/dec/01/poland-elects-openly-gay-mayor-robert-biedron, accessed July 2016.

Ball, J., 2014. 'More than 2.7 billion people live in countries where being gay is a crime', *The Guardian*, 16 May. www.theguardian.com/world/2014/may/16/countries-where-being-gay-is-a-crime, accessed July 2016.

Baranowska, K., 2008. 'Polacy sa bardziej nietolerancyjni od innych', *Rzeczpospolita*. www.rp.pl/artykul/88470.html, accessed July 2016.

Bell, D. and Binnie, J., 2000. *The Sexual Citizen: Queer Politics and Beyond*. Oxford: Polity.

Bromley, C., Curtice, J. and Given, L., 2007. *Attitudes to Discrimination in Scotland: 2006*. Edinburgh: Scottish Government Social Research.

Butler, J., 1993. *Bodies that Matter: On the Discursive Limits of Sex*. New York: Routledge.

—— 2004. *Undoing Gender*. London: Routledge.

Derrida, J., 1976. *Of Grammatology*. Baltimore, MD: Johns Hopkins University Press.

DiPlacido, J. and Herek, G. M., 1998. 'Minority stress among lesbians, gay men, and bisexuals: A consequence of heterosexism, homophobia, and stigmatization', *Psychological Perspectives on Lesbian and Gay Issues*, 4, pp. 138–59.

Ellison, G. and Satara, T., 2014. 'Homophobic bullying in Britain's schools', April, YouGov. www.stonewall.org.uk/sites/default/files/teachers_report_2014.pdf, accessed January 2017.

Epstein, S., 1996. *Impure Science: AIDS, Activism, and the Politics of Knowledge (Medicine and Society)*. Berkeley and Los Angeles, CA: University of California Press.

European Commission, 2010. 'Employment, social affairs and inclusion'. http://ec.europa.eu/social/main.jsp?catId=751, accessed July 2016.

—— 2012. *Special Eurobarometer 393: Discrimination in the EU in 2012*. Co-ordinated by the Directorate-General Communication, Brussels. www.ec.europa.eu/public_opinion/archives/ebs/ebs_393_en.pdf/rights/, accessed March 2016.

European Union Agency for Fundamental Rights, 2009. 'Homophobia and discrimination on grounds of sexual orientation and gender identity in the EU Member States: Part II – the social situation'. http://fra.europa.eu/en/publication/2011/homophobia-and-discrimination-grounds-sexual-orientation-and-gender-identity-eu, accessed February 2017.

Evans, D., 1993. *Sexual Citizenship*. London: Routledge.

Foucault, J., 1978. *History of Sexuality. Volume I*. Trans from the French by Robert Hurley. New York: Pantheon Books.

—— 1980. Power/knowledge: selected interviews and other writings. Trans from the French by Colin Gordon. New York: Vintage.

Gagnon, J. and Simon, W., 1973. *Sexual Conduct: The Social Sources of Human Sexuality*. Chicago: Aldine Publishing.

Gander, K., 2014. 'Rise in racist, religious and homophobic hate crimes in London', *The Independent Sunday Journal*, 2 December. www.independent.co.uk/news/uk/crime/rise-in-racist-religious-and-homophobic-hate-crimes-in-london-9899009.html, accessed July 2016.

Goffman, E., 1963. *Stigma: Notes on the Management of Spoiled Identity*. London: Penguin Books.

Graff, A., 2006. 'We are (not all) homophobes: A report from Poland', *Feminist Studies*, 32(2, Summer), pp. 434–49.

Gray, J., 2011. 'Krystian Legierski: An interview with the Polish gay rights campaigner', *New Internationalist Magazine*, Issue 444. 1 July. http://newint.org/columns/makingwaves/2011/07/01/legierski-poland-gay-rights/, accessed July 2016.

Herek, G. M., 1998. *Stigma and Sexual Orientation: Understanding Prejudice against Lesbians, Gay Men and Bisexuals*. London: Sage Publications.

Hill, A., 2015. 'School for LGBT pupils planned for Manchester', *The Guardian*, 15 January. www.theguardian.com/education/2015/jan/16/school-for-lesbian-gay-bisexual-transgender-pupils-manchester, accessed July 2016.

Honigstein, R., 2014. 'Thomas Hitzlsperger: I finally figured out that I preferred living with a man', *The Guardian*, 8 January. www.theguardian.com/football/2014/jan/08/thomas-hitzlsperger-gay-footballer-interview, accessed July 2016.

Hunter, J. D., 1990. *Culture Wars*. New York: Basic Books.

ILGA Europe, 2008. 'Lesbian, gay, bisexual and transgender rights: Freedom of assembly. Diary of events by country'. www.ilga-europe.org, accessed January 2017.

—— 2014. Annual Review. www.ilga-europe.org, accessed January 2017.

Institut für interdisziplinäre Konflikt und Gewaltforschung [IKG], 2006. 'Indikatoren des Syndroms Gruppenbezogene Menschenfeindlichkeit im Vergleich'. www.uni-bielefeld.de/ikg/index.htm, accessed July 2016.

Kistner, A., Kurbjuweit, D., Müller, A.-K. and Salden, S., 2014. 'Hidden homophobia: Is Germany really as liberal as it seems?', *Spiegel Online*, 13 January. www.spiegel.de/international/germany/germany-debates-gay-rights-after-pro-footballer-hitzlsperger-comes-out-a-943216.html, accessed July 2016.

Mead, G. H., 1934. *Mind, Self and Society: From the Standpoint of a Social Behaviourist*. Chicago, IL: University of Chicago Press.

Nardi, P. M. and Schneider, B. E., 1998. *Social Perspectives in Lesbian and Gay Studies: A Reader*. London: Routledge.

O'Brien, K., 2012. 'We cannot afford to indulge this madness', *The Telegraph*, 3 March. www.telegraph.co.uk/comment/9121424/We-cannot-afford-to-indulge-this-madness.html, accessed July 2016.

Pidd, H., 2011. 'Debunking stereotypes: Poles are homophobic', *The Guardian*, 4 April. www.theguardian.com/world/2011/apr/04/debunking-stereotypes-poles-are-homophobic, accessed July 2016.

Plummer, K., 2000. 'Gay cultures/straight borders', in D. Morley and K. Robbins (eds), *British Cultural Studies* (pp. 387–98). Oxford: Oxford University Press.

—— 2003. *Intimate Citizenship: Personal Decisions and Public Dialogues*. Seattle, WA: University of Washington Press.

—— 2012. 'Critical sexuality studies', in G. Ritzer (ed.), *The Wiley-Blackwell Companion to Sociology* (pp. 243–68). Malden, MA: Wiley-Blackwell.

Richardson, D., 2000. *Rethinking Sexuality*. London: Sage.

Sedgwick, E., 1990. *Epistemology of the Closet*. Berkeley, CA: University of California Press.

Sociological Agency Skala, 2007. 'From antidiscrimination to equal opportunities: Innovative methods and effective practices of the Commission for Protection against Discrimination', Luxmbourg: European Commission.

Stets, J. E. and Turner, J. H. (eds), 2007. *Handbook of the Sociology of Emotions*. New York: Springer.

Stonewall, 2012a. 'Living together: British attitudes to lesbian, gay and bisexual people in 2012'. www.stonewall.org.uk/documents/living_together_2012. pdf, accessed July 2016.

—— 2012b. *Working with Faith Communities*. Stonewall Education Guide. www.stonewall.org.uk/sites/default/files/working_with_faith_communities. pdf, accessed January 2017.

Sundhedsstyrelsen [The National Board of Health], 2006. *Ung2006. De 15-24-åriges seksualitet*. Copenhagen: Sundhedsstyrelsen.

The Market and Opinion Research Centre 'Vilmorus Ltd', 2006. *Discrimination against Various Social Groups in Lithuania*. Vilnius: Vilmorus Ltd.

Weeks, J., 1977. *Coming Out: Homosexual Politics in Britain from the Nineteenth Century to the Present*. London: Quartet Books.

—— 1998. 'The sexual citizen', *Theory, Culture and Society*, 15(3–4), pp. 35–52.

Weinberg, 1972. *Society and the Healthy Homosexual*. New York: St Martin's Press.

Index